References for the Rest of Us

COMPUTER BOOK SERIES FROM IDG

Are you intimidated and confused by computers? Do you find that traditional manuals are overloaded with technical details you'll never use? Do your friends and family always call you to fix simple problems on their PCs? Then the ... *For Dummies®* computer book series from IDG is for you.

... *For Dummies* books are written for those frustrated computer users who know they aren't really dumb but find that PC hardware, software, and indeed the unique vocabulary of computing make them feel helpless. ... *For Dummies* books use a lighthearted approach, a down-to-earth style, and even cartoons and humorous icons to diffuse computer novices' fears and build their confidence. Lighthearted but not lightweight, these books are a perfect survival guide for anyone forced to use a computer.

> *"I like my copy so much I told friends; now they bought copies."*
>
> **Irene C., Orwell, Ohio**

> *"Quick, concise, nontechnical, and humorous."*
>
> **Jay A., Elburn, Illinois**

> *"Thanks, I needed this book. Now I can sleep at night."*
>
> **Robin F., British Columbia, Canada**

Already, hundreds of thousands of satisfied readers agree. They have made ... *For Dummies* books the #1 introductory level computer book series and have written asking for more. So, if you're looking for the most fun and easy way to learn about computers, look to ... *For Dummies* books to give you a helping hand.

IDG BOOKS WORLDWIDE

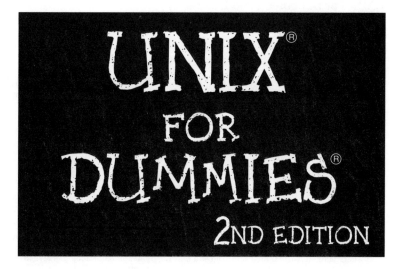

UNIX® FOR DUMMIES®
2ND EDITION

by John R. Levine and Margaret Levine Young

FIFTH
5
ANNIVERSARY
**IDG
BOOKS**
WORLDWIDE

IDG Books Worldwide, Inc.
An International Data Group Company

Foster City, CA ♦ Chicago, IL ♦ Indianapolis, IN ♦ Braintree, MA ♦ Dallas, TX

UNIX® For Dummies®, 2nd Edition

Published by
IDG Books Worldwide, Inc.
An International Data Group Company
919 E. Hillsdale Blvd., Suite 400
Foster City, CA 94404

Library of Congress Catalog Card No.: 95-76832

ISBN:1-56884-905-2

Printed in the United States of America

10 9 8 7 6 5 4 3 2 1

2A/RZ/QR/ZV

Distributed in the United States by IDG Books Worldwide, Inc.

Distributed by Macmillan Canada for Canada; by Computer and Technical Books for the Caribbean Basin; by Contemporanea de Ediciones for Venezuela; by Distribuidora Cuspide for Argentina; by CITEC for Brazil; by Ediciones ZETA S.C.R. Ltda. for Peru; by Editorial Limusa SA for Mexico; by Transworld Publishers Limited in the United Kingdom and Europe; by Al-Maiman Publishers & Distributors for Saudi Arabia; by Simron Pty. Ltd. for South Africa; by IDG Communications (HK) Ltd. for Hong Kong; by Toppan Company Ltd. for Japan; by Addison Wesley Publishing Company for Korea; by Longman Singapore Publishers Ltd. for Singapore, Malaysia, Thailand, and Indonesia; by Unalis Corporation for Taiwan; by WS Computer Publishing Company, Inc. for the Philippines; by WoodsLane Pty. Ltd. for Australia; by WoodsLane Enterprises Ltd. for New Zealand.

For general information on IDG Books Worldwide's books in the U.S., please call our Consumer Customer Service department at 800-762-2974. For reseller information, including discounts and premium sales, please call our Reseller Customer Service department at 800-434-3422.

For information on where to purchase IDG Books Worldwide's books outside the U.S., contact IDG Books Worldwide at 415-655-3021 or fax 415-655-3295.

For information on translations, contact Marc Jeffrey Mikulich, Director, Foreign & Subsidiary Rights, at IDG Books Worldwide, 415-655-3018 or fax 415-655-3295.

For sales inquiries and special prices for bulk quantities, write to the address above or call IDG Books Worldwide at 415-655-3200.

For information on using IDG Books Worldwide's books in the classroom, or ordering examination copies, contact Jim Kelly at 800-434-2086.

For authorization to photocopy items for corporate, personal, or educational use, please contact Copyright Clearance Center, 222 Rosewood Drive, Danvers, MA 01923, or fax 508-750-4470.

About the Authors

Margaret Levine Young and **John R. Levine** were members of a computer club in high school — before high school students, or even high schools, *had* computers. They came in contact with Theodor H. Nelson, author of *Computer Lib* and inventor of hypertext, who fostered the idea that computers should not be taken seriously and that everyone can and should understand and use computers.

Margy has been using small computers since the 1970s. She graduated from UNIX on a PDP/11 to Apple DOS on an Apple II to MS-DOS and UNIX on a variety of machines. She has done all kinds of jobs that involve explaining to people that computers aren't as mysterious as they might think, including managing the use of PCs at Columbia Pictures, teaching scientists and engineers what computers are good for, and writing and cowriting computer manuals and books, including *Understanding Javelin PLUS, The Complete Guide to PC-File, The Internet For Windows For Dummies Starter Kit, MORE Internet For Dummies, WordPerfect For Windows For Dummies* (with David C. Kay), and *The Internet For Dummies Quick Reference.* She has a degree in Computer Science from Yale University.

John wrote his first program on an IBM 1130 (a computer roughly as powerful as your typical modern digital wristwatch, only harder to use) in 1967. His first exposure to UNIX was while hanging out with friends in Princeton in 1974. He became an official system administrator of a networked computer at Yale in 1975. He started working part-time for Interactive Systems, the first commercial UNIX company, in 1977 and has been in and out of the computer and network biz ever since. He got his company put on Usenet (see Chapter 28) early enough that it appears in a 1982 *Byte* magazine article, which included a map of Usenet sites. He used to spend most of his time writing software, but now he mostly writes and cowrites books (including *Internet SECRETS* [with Carol Baroudi], *The Internet For Dummies* [also with Carol Baroudi], *The Internet For Dummies Quick Reference,* and *MORE Internet For Dummies,* all published by IDG Books Worldwide) because it's more fun. He also teaches some computer courses, publishes and edits an incredibly technoid magazine called *The Journal of C Language Translation,* and moderates a Usenet newsgroup. He holds a B.A. and a Ph.D. in Computer Science from Yale University, but please don't hold that against him.

Welcome to the world of IDG Books Worldwide.

IDG Books Worldwide, Inc., is a subsidiary of International Data Group, the world's largest publisher of computer-related information and the leading global provider of information services on information technology. IDG was founded more than 25 years ago and now employs more than 7,500 people worldwide. IDG publishes more than 235 computer publications in 67 countries (see listing below). More than 60 million people read one or more IDG publications each month.

Launched in 1990, IDG Books Worldwide is today the #1 publisher of best-selling computer books in the United States. We are proud to have received 8 awards from the Computer Press Association in recognition of editorial excellence, and our best-selling ...For Dummies™ series has more than 17 million copies in print with translations in 25 languages. IDG Books Worldwide, through a recent joint venture with IDG's Hi-Tech Beijing, became the first U.S. publisher to publish a computer book in the People's Republic of China. In record time, IDG Books Worldwide has become the first choice for millions of readers around the world who want to learn how to better manage their businesses.

Our mission is simple: Every one of our books is designed to bring extra value and skill-building instructions to the reader. Our books are written by experts who understand and care about our readers. The knowledge base of our editorial staff comes from years of experience in publishing, education, and journalism — experience which we use to produce books for the '90s. In short, we care about books, so we attract the best people. We devote special attention to details such as audience, interior design, use of icons, and illustrations. And because we use an efficient process of authoring, editing, and desktop publishing our books electronically, we can spend more time ensuring superior content and spend less time on the technicalities of making books.

You can count on our commitment to deliver high-quality books at competitive prices on topics consumers want to read about. At IDG Books Worldwide, we value quality, and we have been delivering quality for more than 25 years. You'll find no better book on a subject than an IDG book.

John J. Kilcullen

John Kilcullen
President and CEO
IDG Books Worldwide, Inc.

Acknowledgments

The authors thank Jordan Young, Antonia Saxon, Meg Young, and Zac Young for putting up with us while we updated this book. Margy also acknowledges the essential support of Lexington Playcare Center and Barbara Begonis.

Thanks also go to Steve Dyer, for help with our Internet connection and information about X Windows, to Ralph Sims of Northwest Nexus, for help with Linux, and to our other Internet providers, including TIAC (Bedford, Massachusetts), the World (Brookline, Massachusetts), ClarkNet (Ellicott City, Maryland), and Cornell University (Ithaca, New York).

Mike Kelly did a great job shepherding the text through the arduous process of morphing into a book, with help from all the other great folks at IDG Books. And thanks to Megg Bonar and Diane Steele, who refrained from laughing at us when we promised that we'd make our deadline.

(The publisher would like to give special thanks to Patrick J. McGovern, without whom this book would not have been possible.)

Credits

Executive Vice President,
Strategic Planning and Research
David Solomon

Senior Vice President and Publisher
Milissa L. Koloski

Editorial Director
Diane Graves Steele

Acquisitions Editor
Megg Bonar

Brand Manager
Judith A. Taylor

Editorial Manager
Kristin A. Cocks

Editorial Executive Assistant
Richard Graves

Editorial Assistants
Stacey Holden Prince
Kevin Spencer

Acquisitions Assistant
Suki Gear

Production Director
Beth Jenkins

Supervisor of Project Coordination
Cindy L. Phipps

Pre-Press Coordinator
Steve Peake

Associate Pre-Press Coordinator
Tony Augsburger

Media/Archive Coordination
Paul Belcastro

Project Editor
Michael Kelly

Editors
Tamara S. Castleman
Diane L. Giangrossi
Suzanne Packer

Technical Reviewer
Larry Barr

Project Coordinator
Valery Bourke

Production Staff
Gina Scott
Carla C. Radzikinas
Patricia R. Reynolds
Melissa D. Buddendeck
Dwight Ramsey
Robert Springer
Theresa Sánchez-Baker
Kathie S. Schnorr
Linda M. Boyer
Dominique DeFelice
Maridee V. Ennis
Angela Hunckler
Mark Owens
Chad A. Poore
Laura Puranen

Proofreader
Phil Worthington

Indexer
Steve Rath

Cover Design
Kavish + Kavish

Contents at a Glance

Cartoons at a Glance

By Rich Tennant

Table of Contents

Introduction

*W*elcome to *UNIX For Dummies,* 2nd Edition! There are lots of books about UNIX, but most of them assume that you have a degree in computer science, would love to learn every strange and useless command UNIX has to offer (and there are plenty), and enjoy memorizing unpronounceable commands and options. This book is different.

Instead, this book describes what you really do with UNIX — how to get started, what commands you really need, and when to give up and go for help. And we describe it all in plain, ordinary English.

About This Book

This book is designed to be used when you can't figure out what to do next. We don't flatter ourselves that you are interested enough in UNIX to sit down and read the whole thing. When you run into a problem using UNIX ("I thought I typed a command that would copy a file, but it didn't respond with any message. . ."), just dip into the book long enough to solve your problem.

We have included sections about these kinds of things:

- ✔ Typing commands
- ✔ Copying, renaming, or deleting files
- ✔ Printing files
- ✔ Finding where your file went
- ✔ UNIX commands for people who know DOS

In this edition, we've added information about Linux, a new, widely used version of UNIX, and about the Internet, to which many UNIX computers are connected.

How to Use This Book

Use this book as a reference. (Or use it as a decorative paperweight — whatever works for you.) Look up your topic or command in the table of contents or the index; they refer to the part of the book in which we describe what to do and perhaps define a few terms, if absolutely necessary.

In the back of the book are two information gold mines:

- An alphabetical list of UNIX commands (not all the commands — there are thousands — but the ones you're most likely to use) is in Chapter 29.
- A glossary of terms, so your office mate can't boggle you with comments about hardware and soft links.

When you have to type something, it appears in the book like this:

```
cryptic UNIX command to type
```

Type it just as it appears. Use the same capitalization we do — UNIX cares deeply about CAPITAL and small letters. Then press the Enter or Return key (we call it Enter throughout this book). The book tells you what should happen when you give each command and what your options are. Sometimes part of the command is in *italics;* the italicized stuff is a sample name, and you have to substitute the actual name of the file, computer, or person affected.

Chapter 25 lists error messages you might run into, and Chapter 26 lists common user mistakes. You might want to peruse the latter to avoid these mistakes before they happen.

Who Are You?

In writing this book, we have assumed these things about you:

- You have a UNIX computer or terminal.
- You want to get some work done on it.
- Someone has set it up so that, if you turn it on (in many cases, it's left on all the time), you are talking to UNIX.
- You are not interested in becoming the world's next great UNIX expert.

How This Book Is Organized

This book has seven parts. The parts stand on their own — you can begin reading wherever you want. This section lists the parts of the book and what they contain:

Part I: Before the Beginning

This part tells you how to get started with UNIX, including figuring out which kind of UNIX you are using. (You need to know this information later because commands can differ from one type of UNIX to another.) You learn how to log in, type UNIX commands, and ask for help. For Linux users, we include a short chapter on what it's all about, why Linux is cool, and how to get more information about Linux.

Part II: Some Basic Stuff

Like most computer systems, UNIX stores information in files. This part explains how to deal with files — creating, copying, and getting rid of them. It also talks about directories so that you can keep your files organized, finding files that have somehow gone astray, and printing files on paper. We also stuck in a chapter about the computer itself, in case you need to deal with or care for disks, tapes, or other hardware-ish items.

Part III: Of Mice and Computers

Many UNIX users must deal with a GUI — a graphical user interface. This part explains the purpose of GUIs and introduces the most common one: Motif.

Part IV: Getting Things Done

This part talks about getting some work done in UNIX. It also gives step-by-step instructions for using the four most common text editors to create and change text files, how to run several programs at the same time (to get confused several times as fast), and a Rosetta stone to help DOS users figure out how to use UNIX.

Part V: The World Outside the UNIX Biosphere

Most UNIX systems are connected to networks, and many are connected to the biggest network of them all: the Internet. This part prepares you for the world of communications, including instructions for sending and receiving electronic mail and for transferring files over the network.

Part VI: Help!

If disaster strikes, check this part of the book. It includes information about what to do if something bad happens, what to do about backups, and a list of common UNIX error messages.

Part VII: The Part of Tens

This part is a random assortment of other tidbits about UNIX, including common mistakes and how to get on-line help — all organized in convenient ten-item lists, sort of. This part also lists our favorite UNIX commands alphabetically. If you are smart, you will never try to read the UNIX reference manuals, which are written in a strange dialect of neo-Bulgarian. Use this part of *UNIX For Dummies* instead.

Icons Used in This Book

This symbol lets you know that some particularly nerdy, technoid information is coming up, giving you the opportunity to skip it.

This symbol indicates that a nifty little shortcut or time-saver is explained, or a piece of information you can't afford to be without.

Watch out below — time to duck and cover!

This symbol indicates information that applies only if your computer is on a network. If it is not, you can skip to the next section.

This symbol reminds you about something presented in an earlier section of the book, or something you need to remember to do.

This cute symbol tells you that there's information specifically about Linux (see Chapter 3 for what Linux is).

What Now?

That's all you need to know to get started. Whenever you hit a snag in UNIX, just look up the problem in the table of contents or index of this book. You will have the problem solved in a flash — or you will know to find some expert help.

Because UNIX was not designed to be particularly easy to use, don't feel bad if you have to look up a number of topics before you feel comfortable using the computer. Most computer users, after all, never have to face anything as daunting as UNIX. (Point this out to your DOS and Macintosh user friends!)

If you have comments about this book, and your computer can send electronic mail via the Internet, you can send them to us authors at unix@dummies.com. You'll get an automatic response from our friendly robot, and possibly a response from a human. We promise that we read all of our e-mail, although if we wrote personal answers to every message, we'd have no time to write any more books.

Part I
Before the Beginning

The 5th Wave — By Rich Tennant

"WHAT DO YOU MEAN THERE'S A UNIX OPERATING SYSTEM IN THE LOBBY?"

In this part...

OK, so now you're a UNIX user. This means that you have been inducted, kicking and screaming, into a fraternity of hard-bitten, humorless nerds with a religious dedication to a 20-year-old computer system written by the same people who came up with direct-distance dialing. What? You don't feel religious or dedicated? We can't blame you.

If you're like most new UNIX users, a zealot came by, connected your terminal or workstation, gave you five minutes of incomprehensible advice, demonstrated a few not very exciting games (I mean, since when can you play solitaire better with a $10,000 workstation than with a $1.29 deck of cards?) and disappeared. Now you're on your own.

Since you're here anyway, let's talk about the absolute minimum you need in order to get your UNIX system's attention, persuade it that you are allowed to use it, and maybe even accomplish something useful.

Chapter 1

Start 'Er Up, UNIX!

Turning Your Computer On and Off

If you think that turning your computer on and off is easy, you may be wrong. Because UNIX runs on so many almost-but-not-quite-compatible computers — all of which work somewhat differently — you first must figure out which kind of UNIX computer you have before you can turn it on.

A dumb terminal

The simplest way to hook up to a UNIX system is with what's known (sneeringly) as a *dumb terminal*. You can identify a dumb terminal by a complete absence of mice and floppy disks and all that other stuff that causes confusion in a more advanced computer. There's a lot to be said for dumb terminals: They're simple and reliable. With UNIX, you can do hundreds, if not thousands, of things wrong to totally scramble a more advanced machine; these same boo-boos make no difference to a dumb terminal.

Turning a dumb terminal on is easy. You find the power switch (probably on the back) and flip it on. Because there are no pesky disks and stuff, you can turn it on or off whenever you want and not break anything. People make long, sort of theological arguments about whether to leave the picture tube on all the time. Personally, we turn off our terminals overnight and don't worry about them at other times.

Once you turn on the terminal, you use it to communicate to the computer that is running UNIX. If it is directly wired to the computer, UNIX asks you to log in before you can do anything else (see "Hey, UNIX! I Want to Log In" later in this chapter). If not, you may have to do some additional steps to call the computer or otherwise connect to it.

If a train stops at a train station, what happens at a workstation?

A *workstation* is a computer with a big screen, a mouse, and a keyboard. You may say, "I have a PC with a big screen, a mouse, and a keyboard. Is it really a workstation?" Although UNIX zealots get into long arguments over this question, for our purposes, we'll say that it is.

What you were hoping we wouldn't tell you: the difference between a PC and a workstation

First, you have to understand that this isn't a technical question — it's a theological question. Back in olden days (like about 1980), telling the difference was easy. A workstation had a large graphical screen — at least large by the standards of those days — 1,000K of memory, a fast processor chip, and a network connection, and it cost about $10,000. A PC had a lousy little screen, 64K of memory, a slow processor chip, and a floppy or two, and it cost more like $4,000.

Well, these days your typical $1,000 PC has a nice screen (a lot nicer than what the workstation used to have) 4,000K of memory, a fast 486 processor, a big disk, and a network connection. That's a lot better than what people used to call a workstation. Does that make a PC a workstation? Oh, no. Modern workstations have even better screens, buckets of memory, a turbo-charged processor chip, you get the idea. What's the difference?

Maybe it's the software that people use: Most workstations are designed to run UNIX (or in a few cases, proprietary systems similar in power

to UNIX) while PCs run DOS or Windows or the Macintosh software. But wait, there are perfectly good versions of UNIX that run on PC hardware, and Windows NT runs on a lot of boxes that everyone agrees are workstations. Now what? You can get into esoteric arguments about the speed of the connection between the guts of the computer, on the one hand, and the disks, screens, and networks, on the other hand, and argue that workstations have faster connections than PCs, but there are examples that don't fit there, too.

As far as we can tell, if a computer is *designed* to run DOS or Windows or the Mac OS, then it's a PC, while if it's *designed* to run UNIX, then it's a workstation. If this sounds to you like a pretty feeble and arbitrary distinction, you understand perfectly. Here at UNIX For Dummies Central, we have a couple of large PCs running UNIX (which makes them look, to our eyes, just like workstations) and a couple of other smaller ones running Windows. Works fine for us.

Turning on a workstation is easy enough: You reach around the back and turn on the switch. Cryptic things that appear on the screen tell you that UNIX is going through the long and not-at-all-interesting process of starting up. Starting up can take anywhere from 10 seconds to 10 minutes, depending on the version of UNIX, number of disks, phase of the moon, and so on. Sooner or later, UNIX demands that you log in. To find out how, skip to the section, "Logging In: U(NIX) Can Call Me Al," later in this chapter.

Turning off a workstation is a more difficult problem. Workstations are jealous of their prerogatives and *will* punish you if you don't turn them off in exactly the right way. Their favorite punishment is to throw away all the files related to whatever you were just working on. The exact procedure varies from one model of workstation to another, so you have to ask a local guru for advice. Typically, you enter a command along these lines:

```
shutdown +3
```

or

```
halt
```

This command tells the workstation to shut down (in three minutes in the first example). With some versions of UNIX, that would be too easy. The version we use most often uses the `halt` command.

If you use Linux, type this command to shut the system down right away:

```
shutdown -r now
```

The workstation then spends a while putting a program to bed or whatever else it does to make it feel important because it knows that you're waiting there, tapping your feet. Eventually, it tells you that it's done; at that point, turn it off right away before it gets any more smart ideas.

An approved method for avoiding the hassle of remembering how to turn off your workstation is never to shut off your computer (although you can switch the screen off). That's what we do.

X marks the terminal

An *X terminal* is similar to an extremely stripped-down workstation that can run only one program — the one that makes X Windows work. See Chapter 11, "The Big GUIs (the Big Gooey Whats?)," to find out what X Windows are (or don't — it's all the same to us). Turning an X terminal on and off is pretty much like turning a regular dumb terminal on and off. Because the X terminal doesn't run programs, turning it off doesn't cause the horrible problems that turning off a workstation can cause.

The PC masquerade ball

Because PCs are so cheap these days, it is common to press a PC into duty as a terminal. You run a *terminal emulator* program on the PC, and suddenly your mild-mannered PC turns into a super UNIX terminal. (Truthfully, it's more the other way around: You make a perfectly good PC that can run Leisure Suit Larry and other business productivity-type applications act like a dumb terminal that can't do much of anything on its own.)

When you finish with UNIX, you leave the terminal emulator, usually by pressing Ctrl-X or some equally arcane combination of keys. (Consult your local guru: There's no standardization.) Like Cinderella at the stroke of midnight, the terminal-emulating PC turns back into a real PC. To turn it off, you wait for the PC's disks to stop running (carefully scrutinize the front panel until all the little red or green lights go out) and then reach around and turn off the big, red switch. If you don't wait for the lights to go out, you're liable to lose some files.

Hey, UNIX! I Want to Log In

Whether you use a terminal or a workstation, you have to get the attention of UNIX. You can tell when you have its attention because it demands that you identify yourself by logging in. If you use a workstation, when UNIX is done loading itself, it is immediately ready for you to log in. But you terminal users (X or otherwise) may not be so lucky.

If you're lucky, your terminal is attached directly to the main computer so that it immediately displays a friendly invitation to start work, something like this:

```
ttyS034 login:
```

Well, maybe the invitation isn't that friendly. By the way, the `ttyS034` is the name UNIX gives to your terminal. Why doesn't it use something easier to remember, like Fred or Muffy? Beats us!

This catchy phrase tells you that you have UNIX's attention and that it is all ears (metaphorically speaking) for you to log in. You can skip the next section and go directly to "Logging In: U(NIX) Can Call Me Al."

If your UNIX system displays a terminal name, make a note of it. You don't care what your terminal's name is, but, if something gets screwed up and you have to ask an expert for help, we can promise you that the first thing the guru will ask is, "What's your terminal name?" If you don't know, the guru may make a variety of nerd-type disparaging comments. But, if you can say, "A-OK, Roger. That's terminal `tty125`," your guru will assume that you are a with-it kind of user and maybe even try to help you.

Yo, UNIX!

If you're using a PC with a modem, you probably will have to tell the modem to call the UNIX system. All terminal emulators have a way to make the call with two or three keystrokes, but all these ways are different, of course. (Are you surprised?) You have to ask your local guru for info.

Once your terminal is attached to the computer, turned on, and otherwise completely ready to do some work, UNIX, as often as not, doesn't admit that you're there. It says nothing and appears to ignore you. In this way, UNIX resembles a recalcitrant child — firm but kind discipline is needed here.

The most common ways to get UNIX's attention are shown in this list:

- ✔ Press the Return or Enter key. (We'll call it the Enter key in this book, if you don't mind.) Try it two or three times if it doesn't work the first time. If you're feeling grouchy, try it 20 or 30 times and use a catchy cha-cha or conga rhythm. It doesn't hurt anything and is an excellent way to relieve stress.

- ✔ Try other attention-getting keystrokes. Ctrl-C (hold down the Ctrl key, sometimes labeled Control, and press C) is a good one. So is Ctrl-Z. Repeat to taste.

- ✔ If you're attached to UNIX through a modem, you may have to do some speed matching (described in a minute). You do this by pressing the Break key a few times. If you're using a terminal emulator, the Break key may be disguised as Alt-B or some other hard-to-find combination. Ask your guru.

Two modems can talk to each other in about 17,000 different ways, and they have easy-to-remember names, like B212, V.32, and V.22bis. (*Bis* is French for "and a half." Really.) After you call the UNIX system's modem with your modem, the two modems know perfectly well which way they're communicating, but UNIX sometimes doesn't know. Every modem made since about 1983 announces the method it's using when it makes the connection. Because the corresponding piece of UNIX code dates from about 1975, though, UNIX ignores the modem's announcement and guesses, probably incorrectly, at what's being used.

If you see something like ~xxx~~r.!" on-screen, you need to try *speed matching*. Every time you press Break (or the terminal emulator's version of Break), UNIX makes a different guess at the way its modem is working. If it guesses right, you see the login prompt; if it guesses wrong, you see another bunch of ~xxx~~~@(r)!" or you see nothing. If UNIX guessed wrong, press Break again. If you overshoot and keep Breaking past your matched speed, keep going and it'll come around again.

After a while, you will learn exactly how many Returns, Enters, Breaks, and whatnots your terminal needs in order to get UNIX's attention. It will become second nature to type them, and you won't even notice what a nerd you look like while you do it. There's no way around that last part, unfortunately.

Logging In: U (NIX) Can Call Me Al

Every UNIX user has a user name and a password. Your system administrator assigns you a user name and a password. You can and should change your password from time to time, but you're stuck with your user name.

Before you can start work, you must prove your bona fides by logging in, that is, by typing your user name and password. How hard can it be to type two words? Really, now. The problem is this: Because of a peculiarity of human brain wiring, you will find that you can't enter your user name and password without making a typing mistake. It doesn't matter whether your user name is *al* — you will type *Al, la, a;L,* and every other possible combination.

UNIX always considers upper- and lowercase letters to be different: If your user name (sometimes also called your login name) is *egbert,* you must type it exactly that way. Don't type *Egbert, EGBERT,* or anything else. Yes, we know that your name is *Egbert* and not *egbert,* but your computer doesn't know that. UNIX user names almost always are written entirely in lowercase. Pretend that you're a disciple of e. e. cummings.

When you type your user name and password and make a mistake, you may be tempted to backspace over your mistake. If only life were that easy. Guess how you backspace over typing errors when you type your user name and password? You use the # key, of course! (We're sure that it made sense in 1975.) Some — but not all — versions of UNIX have changed so that you can use Backspace or Delete; you may have to experiment. If you want UNIX to ignore everything you have typed, press @, unless your version of UNIX has changed the command key to Ctrl-U (for *untype,* presumably — doubleplusungood). So, Egbert (as you typed your user name), you may have typed something like this:

```
ttyS034 login: Eg#egberq#t
```

Finish entering your user name by pressing Enter or Return.

After you type your user name, UNIX asks you to enter your password, which you type the same way and end by pressing Enter (or Return, but we'll call it Enter). Because your password is secret, it doesn't appear on-screen as you type it. How can you tell whether you've typed it correctly? You can't! If UNIX agrees that you've typed your user name and password acceptably, it displays a variety of uninteresting legal notices and a message from your system administrator (usually `delete some files, the disk is full`) and passes you on to the shell, which you learn about in Chapter 2.

If UNIX did not like either your user name or your password, UNIX says `Login incorrect` and tells you to start over with your user name.

In the interest of security, UNIX asks you for a password even if you type your user name wrong. This arrangement confuses the bad guys but not nearly as much as it confuses regular users. So, if UNIX rejects your password even though you're sure that you typed it correctly, maybe you typed your user name wrong.

Password Smarts

Like every UNIX user, you should have a password. You can get along without a password only under these circumstances:

- ✔ You keep the computer in a locked room to which you have the only key, and it's not connected to any network.
- ✔ You don't mind whether unruly 14-year-olds borrow your account and randomly insert dirty knock-knock jokes in the report you're supposed to give to your boss tomorrow.

The choice of your password deserves some thought. You want something easy for you to remember but difficult for other people to guess. Here are some bad choices for passwords: single letters or digits, your name, the name of your spouse or significant other, your kid's name, your cat's name, or anything less than eight letters long. (Bad guys can try every possible seven-letter password in under a day.)

Good choices include something like your college roommate's name misspelled and backward. Throw in a digit or two, or some punctuation, and capitalize a few letters to add confusion so that you end up with something like *yeLLas12*. Another good idea is to use a pair of words, like *fat;Head*.

You can change your password whenever you're logged in, by using the passwd program. It asks you to enter your old password to prove that you're still who you were when you logged in (computers are notoriously skeptical). Then the passwd program asks you to enter your new password twice, to make sure that you type it, if not correctly, at least consistently. None of the three passwords you type appears on-screen, of course. We'll tell you how to run the passwd program in Chapter 2.

Some system administrators do something called *password aging;* this strategy makes you change your password every once in a while. Some administrators put rules in the passwd program that try to enforce which passwords are permissible, and some even assign passwords chosen randomly. This idea is terrible because the only way you can remember a password you didn't choose is to write it on a Post-It note and stick it on your terminal, which defeats the purpose of having passwords.

In any event, be sure that no one but you knows your password. Change your password whenever you think that someone else might know it. UNIX stores passwords in a scrambled form so that even the system administrator can't find out what yours is. If you forget your password, the administrator can give you a new one, but she can't tell you what your old one was.

If you really want to be paranoid about passwords, don't use a password that appears in any dictionary. Some system breakers may decide to use UNIX's password-encryption program to encrypt every last word in a dictionary, then compare each of the encrypted words to your password. Another thing to keep you awake at night.

Ciao, UNIX!

Logging out is easy — at least compared to logging in. You usually can type logout. Depending on which shell you're using (a wart we worry about in Chapter 2), you might have to type exit instead. In many cases, you can press Ctrl-D to log out.

You will know that you have logged out successfully because UNIX either invites the next sucker to log in or hangs up the phone.

Chapter 2
What Is UNIX, Anyway?

*T*his chapter tells you how to figure out which kind of UNIX system you have gotten involved with. If you *really* don't think that you care, skip this chapter. As you read the rest of this book and run into places where you need to know which kind of UNIX or shell you are using, you can always come back here.

Why Do We Ask Such Dumb Questions?

"What is UNIX?" UNIX is UNIX, right? Not entirely. UNIX has evolved feverishly for 25 years, sort of like bacteria in a cesspool — only not so attractively. As a result, there have been many varieties of UNIX along the way. They all share numerous characteristics, but (we bet this doesn't surprise you) differ just enough that even experienced users are tripped up by the differences between versions.

As Diverse as Bacteria in a Cesspool

Indulge us as we tell a historical parable. Imagine, for the moment, that UNIX is a kind of automobile rather than a computer system. In the early days, every UNIX system was distributed with a complete set of source code and development tools. If UNIX had been a car, this distribution method would have been the same as every car being supplied with a complete set of blueprints, wrenches, arc-welders, and other car-building tools. Now imagine that nearly all these cars were sold to engineering schools. You might expect that the students would get to work on their cars and, pretty soon, no two cars would be the same. That's pretty much what happened to UNIX.

Bell Labs released the earliest editions of UNIX only to colleges and universities (because Bell Labs was The Phone Company at that time, it wasn't supposed to be in the software business); a variety of more-or-less scruffy mutants sprang up, and different people modified and extended different versions of UNIX.

Although about 75 percent of the important stuff is the same on all UNIX systems, it helps to know which kind of UNIX you're using, for two reasons. You can tell which of several alternatives applies to you. You can impress your friends by saying things like "HP-UX is a pretty good implementation of BSD, although it's not as featureful as SunOS." It doesn't matter whether you know what it means — your friends will be amazed and speechless.

Throughout this book, we note when a command or feature being discussed differs among the major versions of UNIX. And when we talk about the popular new Linux system, you'll see our cute Linux icon in the margin. We won't waste your time with a family tree of UNIX systems. The following sections describe the most common kinds of UNIX systems.

The two main versions of UNIX are BSD UNIX and System V. Although they differ in lots of little ways, the easiest way to tell which one you're using is to see how you print something. If the printing command is lp, you have System V; if it's lpr, you have BSD. (If the command is print, you cannot be using UNIX; nothing in UNIX is that easy.)

Berkeley UNIX: the techno-UNIX

One school that received an early copy of UNIX was the University of California at Berkeley. With some government money (your tax dollars at play), it added every bell and whistle it could think of to its version of UNIX. No student's career was complete without adding a small feature to Berkeley UNIX; you can still see on BSD UNIX the greasy fingerprints of a generation of students, particularly a guy named Bill, about whom you will hear more later.

When word got out about all the swell stuff Berkeley had done, the Berkeley people made official Berkeley Software Distributions of their hacked-up UNIX code (code-named BSD UNIX). As Berkeley kept making changes, it gave numbers to its versions. (Most workstations run some version of BSD UNIX.) The most widely used versions of BSD UNIX are 4.3 and 4.4. Berkeley promises that 4.4 (known as 4.4BSD) will be the last version. We can only hope.

Berkeley graduates fanned out across the country, working for and even starting new computer companies. Most of these companies sell some descendant of BSD UNIX. Many of the founders of Sun Microsystems came from Berkeley; Sun markets SunOS and Solaris. Hewlett-Packard has HP-UX, Digital Equipment has Ultrix, and IBM has AIX (a mixture of BSD UNIX and too much other stuff to contemplate).

Free to be, BSD

Shortly before 4.4BSD came out, the folks at Berkeley realized they had made so many changes to BSD over the years that there was practically none of the original AT&T code left. Until that time, everyone who got a copy of BSD had to first get a license from AT&T (which was fairly expensive for non-academic customers) so that they could legally use the AT&T code in BSD. But Berkeley then made the 99 percent of BSD not derived from AT&T code available to the world for free. Lawsuits naturally ensued ("See? This code is the same in AT&T and in Berkeley UNIX!" "Yeah, but you guys at AT&T took it from us, not the other way around." "Oops.") but were settled pretty quickly, so suddenly there was 99 percent of a free version of BSD UNIX.

Several groups quickly rewrote the missing 1 percent, adapted the BSD code for 386 and newer PC-compatible machines, and made all the code available over the Internet. Two projects, called FreeBSD and NetBSD (which would be one project except that the people involved don't like each other), continue to improve and update the freely available BSD, while a company called Berkeley Software Design offers an inexpensive commercially supported version of BSD. BSD lovers around the world rejoiced, since now you can have a real BSD UNIX system for only the cost of a moderate sized PC, $1,500 or so.

The freely available BSDs would be the dominant version of UNIX, were it not for Linux, discussed in the section, "The Linux phenomenon," later in this chapter.

System V for victory

Meanwhile, back at The Phone Company, legions of programmers were making different changes to UNIX. They gave their versions of UNIX Roman numerals — which are classier than plain ol' digits. Their current version of UNIX is known as System V. There are many versions of System V; these subversions are known as System V Release 1 — or SVR1, and SVR2, SVR3, and SVR4. Most non-workstation versions of UNIX are based on System V or occasionally its predecessor, System III. (System IV? Not ready for prime time, we guess.)

After sniping for years, Sun Microsystems, from the BSD camp, and AT&T, of the System V camp, decided to bury the hatchet and combine all the features of BSD and System V into the latest version of System V, SVR4, which has so many goodies it's only slightly smaller than a blimp and is widely regarded as a godsend to makers of large disks needed to hold it all. If your system runs SVR4 or its descendants, pay attention to the hints about both BSD *and* System V. The last version of SVR4 was SVR4.2. (Where *do* they get these numbers?)

Around the time that SVR4 came out, a lot of vendors started to complain that Sun and AT&T were trying to corner the UNIX market with SVR4 and, in self-defense, created the "vendor neutral" OSF/1 (which we get to in the next section). To prove to the world that SVR4 was just as open as could be, AT&T spun off their UNIX department into an outfit called UNIX International. After a while, AT&T got tired of the whole business, and System V was sold to Novell (the NetWare people), who retitled it UNIXWare. After a lot more political shenanigans that we won't try to untangle here, the UNIX trademark ended up belonging to X/Open, a standardization group based in England, while the actual product descended from SVR4, UNIXWare, still belongs to Novell.

Helpful advice to Sun users: Although Sun changed the name of its software from SunOS to Solaris, it didn't change the way it worked (at least in Solaris 1.0, which is still a BSD-flavored UNIX). So, if you use Solaris 1.0, follow instructions for BSD UNIX. Solaris 2.0 is based on SVR4, however, so you have to worry about both BSD and System V. Is this clear? We're still confused about it.

To ensure mystification, we introduce OSF/1

When System V and BSD UNIX merged to form SVR4, many UNIX vendors were concerned that, with only one version of UNIX, there would be insufficient market confusion. They started the Open Software Foundation, which makes yet another kind of UNIX: OSF/1. OSF/1 is mostly BSD but is also a goulash of some System V, a lot of code from the MACH project at Carnegie Mellon University (hey, it was free), and a lot of other miscellaneous eyes of newts and toes of frogs. Although Digital Equipment Corporation is the primary company that ships OSF/1, IBM's AIX also is related to OSF/1.

If you use OSF/1, pay attention to the BSD advice and you should be OK.

The Linux phenomenon

Without a doubt the most surprising UNIX development in recent years has been the appearance, seemingly from nowhere (but actually from Finland) of Linux, a rather nice freely available version of UNIX. Linux is such a big deal that we devote an entire chapter to it (the next one, in fact) so read all about it there.

Linux resembles SVR4 as much as it resembles any other version of UNIX.

What's GNU?

No tour of UNIX versions is complete without a visit to the Free Software Foundation in Cambridge, Massachusetts. The FSF was founded by a brilliant but quirky programmer named Richard Stallman who came from MIT, where people wrote lots and lots of software and gave it all away. He firmly (some would say fanatically) believes that all software should be free and set up the

TECHNICAL STUFF

What, an actual standard?

Many of the versions of UNIX claim to be standard, in some sense or another. (One of the few versions that *doesn't* claim to be standard is Linux, which, of course, is one of the most widely used versions. Typical.)

A few years back, a group at the Institute of Electrical and Electronic Engineers (the IEEE), a large professional group of people with pocket protectors, decided that the huge variety of versions of UNIX was getting to be a pain, so they started to define a common version of UNIX, now known as POSIX. Unlike many of the putative standards declared by the various competing UNIX camps, POSIX is defining an actual standard, trying to come up with the largest possible common set of UNIX features that *all* UNIX systems either already support or could easily be modified to support. The POSIX effort is producing what will eventually be a huge set of standards for everything from shell commands to printer management to real-time instrument control, and will doubtless take until the end of time to complete.

Fortunately, the first two parts of POSIX completed are probably the most useful. POSIX 1003.1 (the 1003 presumably means that the IEEE already had 1002 standards before POSIX came along) defines features for C language programmers on POSIX systems, and 1003.2 defines the set of common user commands.

Most UNIX systems now support 1003.2 ("dot two" to UNIX aficionados), so you can count on seeing most if not all of the POSIX commands on any modern UNIX system you want. This has also somewhat lessened the divergence among UNIX systems, as some vendors throw away their quirky versions of commands in favor of standard POSIX-compatible ones. (There's still enough wiggle room in POSIX that it hasn't lessened the divergence as much as you might hope.)

Incidentally, POSIX stands for *P*ortable *O*perating *S*ystem *I*nterface, with an *X* thrown in to make it sound cooler. The name was invented by Richard Stallman of GNU fame. If you're wondering how to pronounce it, the "POS" in POSIX sounds the same as the "pos" in positive.

FSF to produce lots of high-quality free software, culminating in a complete free version of UNIX. Despite quite a lot of initial skepticism, the FSF has raised enough money and been given and lent enough equipment to do just that. The FSF's project GNU (for *G*NU's *N*ot *U*NIX) has so far produced versions of most of the UNIX user-level software. The best known and most widely used pieces are the text editor GNU Emacs, which we discuss in Chapter 13, most of the other basic UNIX utilities, and the GNU C compiler (GCC), which is now used on all of the free versions of UNIX including Linux, as well as on a few commercial ones.

The GNU crowd continues to work on new stuff, including their *pièce de résistance,* the GNU Hurd, a complete working version of the guts of the UNIX system. Early on, fans of free software awaited the GNU Hurd with great eagerness, but now that Linux and the freely available BSD versions have arrived, the eagerness has abated somewhat. But Hurd or no Hurd, GNU Emacs, GCC, and the GNU utilities are here to stay.

What the FSF means by "free" software is a little different from what you might expect: It means freely available, not necessarily available for free. That means that if you can find someone willing to pay you a million bucks for some GNU software, that's perfectly OK. But that person, and anyone else to whom you give or sell GNU software, has to be free to give or sell it, in turn, to other people without restriction. The intention is that people can make money by supporting and customizing software, not by hoarding it. Opinions vary on the long-term practicality of this plan, but for now, the FSF sure has written some popular software, and there is at least one company named Cygnus Support that makes a pretty good business supporting it.

XENIX and other antiques

A few older versions of UNIX just won't die. The most notable version is XENIX, originally from Microsoft Corporation and later sold by the Santa Cruz Organization (SCO), a Microsoft affiliate.

XENIX is considered to be hopelessly obsolete. On one hand, it occupies much less disk space than do more modern versions of UNIX, but on the other, it runs much faster. (To be fair, it's missing some of the more modern versions' zoomy features, but not many you'd likely notice.)

Because XENIX is based on one of the ancestors of System V, most System V advice applies to XENIX.

How Can You Tell?

When you log in to your UNIX system, a variety of copyright notices usually flash by, with an identification of the kind of UNIX you are accessing. Carefully scrutinize the information on the screen and you may be able to tell which version you have.

Another approach is to type the command `uname` and press Enter. Sometimes this command displays the name of your computer (like `aardvark` or `acctg3`), but sometimes it displays the version of UNIX you are running. On Linux systems, it says `Linux`.

If you can't tell which UNIX you have, break down, grovel, and ask your local UNIX expert. When you figure out which kind of UNIX you are running, write it down on the Cheat Sheet in the front of this book. You never know when you might need to know this stuff.

If you're using a dumb terminal or an X terminal (or a PC acting like a dumb terminal), the kind of UNIX you're using depends on the maker of the main computer you're attached to — not on the maker of the terminal. Generally, you see the identification of the main computer in a message it sends to the terminal just before or just after you log in.

Cracking the Shell

Now that you have figured out which general variety of UNIX you have, you must figure out one other vital consideration: which shell you're using. You might say, "I don't want to use *any* shell; I just want to get some work done," but the shell is the only way to get where you want to.

The guts of UNIX are buried deep in the bowels of a computer and don't deign to deal with such insignificant details as determining what users may want to do. That nasty business is delegated to a category of programs known as shells. A *shell* is a program that waits for you to type a command and then executes it. From the UNIX point of view, a shell is nothing special, just the first program UNIX runs after you log in. Because you can designate any program to run when you log in, any fool can write a shell — indeed, many have done so. About a dozen UNIX shells are floating around, all slightly incompatible with each other (you probably guessed that).

Fortunately, all the popular shells fall into two groups: the Bourne (or Korn or BASH) shell and the C shell. If you can figure out which of the two categories your shell is in, you can get some work done. (You're getting close!)

If you use a GUI (see Chapter 11), you see windows and icons after you log in, not a boring little UNIX prompt. But you still need to use a UNIX shell from time to time, usually to perform housekeeping tasks.

You can easily tell which kind of shell you're using. If UNIX displays a $ after you log in, you have a Bourne-style shell; if UNIX displays a %, you're using the C shell. Traditionally, System V systems use the Bourne shell, and BSD systems use the C shell. These days, however, because all versions of UNIX come with both shells, you get whichever one your system administrator likes better. Preferences in command languages are similar to preferences in underwear: People like what they like, so you get what you get.

Linux systems usually come with the BASH shell, a Bourne-style shell.

After you have determined whether you have a Bourne-style shell ($) or a C shell (%), note this fact on your Cheat Sheet in the front of this book.

The Bourne and Bourne Again shells

The most widely used UNIX shell is the Bourne shell, named after Steve Bourne, who originally wrote it. The Bourne shell is on all UNIX systems. It prompts you with $, after which you type a command and press Enter (or Return). Like all UNIX programs, the Bourne shell itself is a program, and its program name is sh. Clever, eh?

There are a few alternative versions of the original Bourne shell, most notably the Bourne Again shell (or BASH, whose program name is bash) from the GNU crowd. This version of the Bourne shell is used in many places because of its price — it's free. Some claim that it's still overpriced, but we won't get into that. BASH is enough like the original Bourne shell that anything we say about the Bourne shell applies also to BASH. The most notable advantage of BASH is that it has "command editing," a fancy way of saying that you can use the arrow keys on your keyboard to correct your commands as you're typing them.

The Korn-on-the-cob shell

After the Bourne shell was in common use for a couple of years, it became apparent to many people that it was so simple and coherent a single person could understand all its features and use them all effectively. Fortunately, this shameful situation was remedied by a guy named Dave Korn who added about a thousand new features to the Bourne shell and ended up with the Korn shell (called ksh). Mostly people who write *shell scripts* (sequences of shell commands saved in a file) are interested in most of the new features, so you can probably consider the Korn shell to be the same as the Bourne shell. Most versions of the Korn shell also have command editing.

She sells C shells

No, the C shell wasn't written by someone named C; it was written by Bill, the guy we mentioned earlier. (He sells C shells by the C shore? Probably.) We would discuss our opinion of the C shell at length, except that Bill is 6'4", in excellent physical shape, and knows where we live. The C shell's program name is csh.

The most notable difference between the C shell and other leading shell brands is that the C shell has many more magic characters (characters that do something special when you type them). Fortunately, unless you use a lot of commands with names like ed!3x, this isn't a problem.

There are many versions of the C shell; most differ in which bugs are fixed and which are still there. You may run into a program called tcsh, a slightly extended C shell with command editing.

TECHNICAL STUFF

Who says the C shell isn't user-friendly?

If you use the C shell, be aware that some punctuation characters do special and fairly useful things.

An exclamation point (!) tells the C shell to do a command again. Two of them (! !) means to repeat the last command you typed. One of them followed by the first few characters of a command means to repeat the last command that started with those characters. For example, type ! cp to repeat the last cp command you gave. This is great for lazy typists.

Use carets (^) to tell the C shell to repeat a command with some change. If you type this:

`^old^new`

the C shell repeats the last command, substituting "new" for "old" wherever it appears in what you typed. You can use slashes (/) in a similar way, but carets are easier. The C shell also uses colons (:) to perform truly confusing editing of previous commands, which we won't get into.

In Chapter 7, the "UNIX Is History!" section has more on reissuing shell commands.

Are There Any Good Programs On?

You may be wondering why we refer sometimes to commands and sometimes to programs. What's the difference?

A *command* is what you type to tell UNIX (or actually the shell) what to do. A *program* is a file that contains executable code. The confusion comes because in UNIX, to run a program, you just type its name. (In old-fashioned operating systems, you usually typed something like "RUN BUDGET_ANALYSIS" to run a program called BUDGET_ANALYSIS.)

When you type a command, such as ls or cp or emacs (a text editor we'll talk about in Chapter 13), the shell looks at it carefully. There are a few commands that the shell knows how to do all by itself, including cd and exit. If the command isn't one that the shell can do by itself, it looks around for a program stored in a file by the same name.

Finally! You're Ready to Work

We wrap up this chapter with a little advice about hand-to-hand combat with the shell. There are many commands you can give to your shell. Every shell has about a dozen built-in commands, most of which aren't very useful in day-today use. All the other commands are the names of other programs. The fact that every UNIX system has hundreds of programs lying around translates into hundreds of possible shell commands.

One nice thing about UNIX shells is that, within a given shell, the way you type commands is completely consistent. To edit a file called my-calendar, for example, and use an editor called e, you type this line:

```
$ e my-calendar
```

The shell runs the e editor, which does whatever it does. When you finish, you return to the shell, where you can issue another command.

Whenever you see a UNIX prompt (either $ or %), a shell is running, waiting to do your bidding. In this book, we usually refer to the entire package — UNIX plus shell — as UNIX so that we don't confuse things. We say, "Use the ls command to get UNIX to display a list of files" rather than "Use the ls command to get the shell to get UNIX to display a list of files." OK?

Now you know which kind of UNIX you are using, which shell you are using, and why you care. Let's look at a few UNIX (or shell) commands you can use to begin getting something done.

We could tell you the password, but then we'd have to kill you

When you logged in, you probably hated your password because someone else picked it. Hating your password is a good reason to change it. Another reason you might want to change it is that, to get this far, you enlisted the aid of some sort of expert and had to reveal your password. This section shows how to change your password: Use the passwd command.

This is easy stuff. Just type passwd. As always, press Enter after typing the command. The passwd command asks you to type your current password to make sure that you are really you. (If it didn't do this, whenever you wandered

Ending command lines without hard feelings

Remember to end every command line by pressing Enter (or Return). UNIX is pretty dumb; in most cases, your pressing Enter is the only way UNIX can tell that you have finished doing something.

With a few programs, notably the text editors vi and emacs, you don't need to press Enter anywhere; we point out those exceptions. Everywhere else, remember to press Enter at the end of every line.

Don't turn off the computer if you make a typo!

To repeat something we have hinted at, if you make a mistake and all is not going well, do *not* turn off the computer, unplug it, or otherwise get unnecessarily rough. PC users get used to just turning the darned thing off if things aren't going well, but UNIX computers don't respond well to this approach.

Instead, suggest politely that UNIX stop doing whatever it is you don't like. To stop a command,

press Ctrl-C, or on some systems the Break key or the Delete key.

If the situation is out of control, UNIX is running a program you don't want, and you can't stop it, you can use some Advanced and Obscure Techniques to wrestle extremely recalcitrant programs into line. See Chapter 22 if you're desperate.

off to get some more coffee, someone could sneak over to your desk and change your password. Not good.) Type your current password and press Enter. The password doesn't appear on-screen as you type (security reasons — sorry).

Then passwd asks for your new password. (Chapter 1 has lots of sage advice about how to choose a password.) You have to type the new password twice so that passwd is sure that you typed it correctly. Assuming that you type the new password twice in the same way, passwd changes your password. The next time you log in, you are expected to know it.

If you forget your password, there is no way to retrieve it, not even by your system administrator. The administrator can assign you a new one, though, and you can change it again, preferably to something more memorable than the one you forgot.

Gimme a lista my files

This section discusses a command you use a lot: the ls command, which lists your files. Chapters 5 and 6 talk more about files, directories, and other stuff that ls helps you with; for now, here's ls Lesson 1. Type ls. The ls command lists the names of the files in the current directory. (Chapter 6 talks about directories.)

Oops!

If you're a world-class typist, you can skip this section. If you make thousands of typos a day, as we do, pay close attention. If you type something wrong, you can probably press Backspace to back up and retype it. If that doesn't work, though, all is not lost. Try Delete, the # key (Shift-3), or Ctrl-H (hold down the Ctrl key and press H). One of these combinations should work to back you up. To give up and start the line over again, press Ctrl-U. If that doesn't work, press the @ key (Shift-2).

Play it again, Sam

Sometimes, you may want to issue the same command again (it was so much fun the first time). If you use the C shell, type the following:

```
!!
```

If you use the BASH shell, press the up-arrow key to see the last command you typed and then press Enter.

In the Korn shell, you can type r to reissue a command.

If you use the Bourne shell, you are out of luck and must type your command over again.

The UNIX cast of special characters

One of the more exciting aspects of typing shell commands is that many characters are special. They have special meanings to UNIX; the next few chapters discuss some of them. Special characters include the ones in this list:

```
< >      '       "       *
{ }      ^       !       \
[ ]      #       |       &
( )      $       ?       ~
```

Spaces also are considered special because they separate words in a command. If you want to put special characters in a command, you must *quote* them. You quote stuff by putting quotation marks around it. Suppose that you have a file called c* (not a great idea, but sometimes you get these things by mistake). You can edit it by typing the following line:

```
e "c*"
```

You can use single or double quotation marks as long as you're consistent. You can even quote single quotes with double quotes, and quote double quotes with single quotes. Is that clear? Never mind.

Chapter 3

A Few Lines on Linux

*L*inux is the hottest thing to arrive in UNIX-land in years, a wildly popular, completely free version of UNIX. It is (quite deliberately) similar to other versions of UNIX, so for the most part, everything in this book that applies to other versions of UNIX also applies to Linux.

Out of the Frozen North

In 1992, a guy named Linus Torvalds took a then-popular small educational version of UNIX called Minix, decided it wasn't quite what he wanted, and proceeded to rewrite and extend it so that it was more to his taste. By mid-1993, his system had long since left its Minix roots and was becoming an actual usable version of UNIX. Linus's system was picked up with great enthusiasm by programmers and, later, users all over the Internet and spread like crazy to become the fastest-growing part of UNIX-dom.

Linux is popular for three reasons:

✔ It works pretty well, even on a small, cheap PC. A 386 PC with 4 megabytes of memory and a 40 megabyte disk is adequate. (John bought a computer like that for under $500, new, from a dealer who'd ordered more than he needed.)

✔ There are lots of enthusiastic people working on Linux, with wonderful new features and additions available every day. Many of them even work.

✔ It's free!

Linux's many developers proudly describe it as a "hacker's system," one written by and for enthusiastic programmers. (This is the classic meaning of "hacker," not to be confused with the other media-debased, "computer vandal" definition.) For this reason, being a Linux user is sort of like living in a house inhabited by a large family of carpenters and architects. Every morning when you wake up, the house is a little different. Maybe there's a new turret, or some walls have moved. Or perhaps someone has temporarily removed the floor under your bed. (Oops, sorry about that.)

What's Old, What's New

Linux was concocted from lots of existing free software, along with quite a lot of new work. The original guts of Linux was written from scratch by Linus Torvalds, and has since been greatly changed and extended by other people. Torvalds based it more or less on System V (descriptions of System V; there's no System V code). Most of the programs that people actually use (the shells and other commands) come from the GNU project, which modeled most of them after the Berkeley UNIX versions, so most of the commands are BSD-ish. The networking programs are adapted from the Berkeley ones, so they are all BSD-ish as well.

How free is free?

Linux is *free software.* In the UNIX software biz, "free" has a very concrete meaning that is different from public domain and different from shareware.

Linux is made available under the GNU General Public License (GPL), Version 2, the same license that the Free Software Foundation uses for most of its programs. It's seven pages of legalese, much of which is about where copyright notices have to appear and stuff like that, but the basic plan is simple. In short, it says:

✔ You can copy and distribute Linux and other GPL software, and you can charge for it.

✔ *But. . .* anyone to whom you distribute Linux has the right to give copies away for free.

✔ *And. . .* you must include the source code (or make it available for no more than a reproduction fee) in the distribution.

The idea is that people are permitted, even encouraged, to distribute copies of GPL software and to sell maintenance service, so long as the software itself remains freely available.

Free software shouldn't be confused with *shareware,* which is software for which you are supposed to pay the original author if you use it, nor with *public domain* software with which you can do anything you want.

The GPL was subject to considerable debate and a fair amount of ridicule when it first came out in about 1990, but it's worked pretty much the way its authors intended — GPL software (including Linux) is very widely available, and people do indeed constantly work on and improve it.

Like all UNIX systems, Linux systems can run various shells, various editors, and various other software. Most versions of Linux use BASH as the default shell because it's also new and snazzy.

Do keep in mind that Linux is a moving target, with frequent improvements to the programs, so the version of Linux you use is probably not exactly the same as the version described in any book, including this one. When we wrote this, the latest version of Linux was 1.2.5, but by now you can be sure that that version is long gone.

In Chapter 27 we describe a number of ways that you can get up-to-date information about Linux, including reading one of a number of Usenet newsgroups about Linux, or subscribing to a Linux magazine.

Where's Linux?

Linux development mostly happens on the Internet, and if you have an Internet connection, you can download the entire system at no charge. You do need either a very fast connection or great patience, since it's about 50 diskettes full of data, which, with a typical 14.4K bps on-line connection, would take about 15 hours to download. There are also quite a few bulletin board systems around the world with Linux code available. A more practical approach is to buy or borrow a CD-ROM version of Linux that you can install in an hour or so.

Sounds great, doesn't it? You can install a version of UNIX on your very own computer! But there's one tiny little snag — it makes *you* the system administrator. You'll have to learn how to create user accounts, deal with disks that fill up, and install and configure software. It's not impossible (far from it — John has done it for years), but you'll have a lot to learn.

The details of installing and setting up Linux are way beyond the scope of this book. For more details, take a look at *Running Linux,* by Matt Welsh and Lar Kaufman, published by O'Reilly & Associates, Inc.

Chapter 4
Pleading for Help

. . . .

In This Chapter
▶ When to plead for help
▶ Whom to ask
▶ How to ask
▶ Bribes and inducements

. . . .

Sooner or later, you run into a problem you can't solve on your own. If the time from when you start work until you give up is greater than 15 seconds, you have already beaten the averages.

You need to ask for help. In a perfect world, you pick up the phone, call someone, and describe what's wrong; the person tells you exactly the right thing to do. Of course, in that perfect world, there is also an Easter bunny. In the real world, the people you can call range from those who don't want to help you to those who couldn't help you even if they wanted to. You can get help as long as you carefully consider whom you ask for help and how you ask for it.

A Taxonomy of Possibly Helpful People

There are two general categories of people you can ask for help: normal people and abnormal people. The latter category is divided into Wizards (people who know more about UNIX than is healthy) and System Administrators (people whose job it is to keep the computer working).

Getting help from normal people

Usually, the best person to ask for help is some other, slightly more experienced user. There are several reasons for this approach. These people probably learned about this stuff just last week, so they're proud to show it off. They aren't so expert that they answer all your questions in incomprehensible gobbledygook. Statistically, there are many more normal users than wizards and system administrators, so they are much easier to find.

Getting help from UNIX wizards

No, a UNIX wizard is not a guy who has a pointy hat and who, for surgical reasons, cannot reproduce. It's someone who knows a heck of a lot about UNIX and has spent so long learning it that he (they're almost all male) has long since forgotten that not everyone knows this stuff.

Here are some of the pros and cons of asking a wizard for help:

Pro: A true UNIX wizard can answer any question about UNIX that you can possibly ask.

Con: The wizard is really busy and probably doesn't want to answer your question.

Con: Even if the wizard does answer your question, you may not understand the answer.

Getting help from system administrators

The system administrator is the person in charge of your UNIX system. UNIX systems generally are complicated enough that someone has the formal job of assigning user names and making sure that printers print, networks network, modems mo and dem, and so on. Traditionally, system administrators have been wizards also (they had to be). As demand for system administrators has increased and (strange but true) the job of managing UNIX systems has gotten easier, however, the typical system administrator doesn't know much about UNIX other than what's required to do administrative work. Not to belittle them; they surely know more than the average user does.

One thing all system administrators have in common is that they're extremely overworked. They have way too many systems to manage, no time to manage them, no budget, and so on. You can be sure that system administrators, no matter how nice they are in real life, will welcome your entreaties for help with about as much enthusiasm as they would greet a case of athlete's foot. But there are a few problems that only your system administrator can solve.

Every UNIX system has one user known as the *superuser.* (For historical reasons, the superuser's name is *root,* presumably because one of the original UNIX guys loved fine food and was a fan of Waverly Root, the food writer.) There are some jobs that only the superuser can do, such as adding and deleting users, installing new software, and rearranging disks to give you more disk space. Because the system administrator should be the only person who knows the password for the superuser, there's no one else to ask for help for these types of tasks. The system administrator is most likely to know the correct answer to other questions also, such as the version of the operating system you're using (sometimes essential for tracking down problems) and network-configuration questions. This information often changes weekly, and a user with last week's answer may inadvertently be lying to you.

Here are some pros and cons of asking the system administrator for help:

Pro: He or she is well informed about system configuration . . .

Con: . . . but overworked and will not welcome your question.

Getting help from help desks and the like

If you work for a large organization, it may have a help desk staffed by people whose job it is to answer questions from people within the organization. What the heck, give it a try. The quality of the help varies; if nothing else, these help sources have heard a lot of questions. Even an answer of "We have no idea how to solve your problem, but Mary in Purchasing had the same problem last week," can lead you in useful directions.

Getting electronic help

Most UNIX systems are attached to computer networks; you may be able to direct an electronic question to thousands of other people out there. It's worth learning how to use electronic mail; often you can get help faster from someone on the network thousands of miles away than you can from someone down the hall. See Chapter 19 for more details about using electronic mail.

Phrasing Your Plea

No matter who you ask, there are better and worse ways to ask for help. This section can steer you through some of these thorny areas.

Ask nicely

We hope that asking nicely is an obvious tip, but we know from bitter experience that it's not. Remember that no one really has to help you, despite what their job description says. And answers can range from the brutally short ("Type `kill -9 `ps | grep 123 | cut -f1`` and don't ask me why") to the truly useful. So be nice. And say *thank you* afterward, like your mother told you.

It's a ttyS034 running FrameMaker 11.72 and it just weirded out when I pressed F7

The more concretely you can phrase your question, the more likely you are to get useful help. If something didn't work the way you expected, what were you doing just before it screwed up? Remember the exact commands you typed and what messages were spat back. Did you do something different from the way you did it before? Did you use different files or programs? A different terminal? Do you know your terminal name? (See Chapter 1.) Do you know the names of the files and programs involved? If the answer to that last one is No, expect to encounter considerable rolling of eyes and deep, heartfelt sighs.

Don't ask the same question three times

Nothing wears out your welcome faster than asking the same question (or what seems to be the same question to the person you're asking) over and over again. You probably will find that, even after someone gives you a nice, clear answer you understand so that you can fix your problem and forge ahead, if you're not careful, you will forget what the answer was. The next time you run into the same problem, you won't remember what to do. Then you not only will ask the same question again, but also be beet red from embarrassment.

Don't let this happen to you! Many people find it helpful to write things down, preferably in a little notebook with something like "Jeff's Compleat Compendium of UNIX Hints and Tricks" written on the cover. (If your name isn't Jeff, feel free to adjust the title as necessary. Ours is called "Stupid UNIX Tricks.") In fact, we have found that, after you write down an answer or a hint, you never have to look it up; the act of writing it down is enough to commit it to memory.

Do write down solutions to your problems — unless you are absolutely, 100 percent sure that either you will never, never, run into that problem again or you have memorized the answer for all time. Then write it down anyway.

"Nothing changed, but . . ."

Never say this. There's nothing as exasperating to a UNIX wizard — or even to a genuinely helpful normal person — as someone who says, "Nothing changed, but now the `furble` command doesn't work anymore." Something must have changed. Different file? Terminal? Program? It's possible that your system administrator changed something behind your back, but it's far more likely you did something and didn't realize that something seemingly unimportant was indeed different.

Think of this as your key to power: If you screwed it up, you can probably fix it yourself! On the other hand, if it's broken, you may well have broken it.

Don't leap to confusions

Beware of the situation in which you think you're three-quarters of the way to solving a problem but you're heading down the wrong road. For example, one time we wanted to print a file with line numbers down the left side of the page. We had just learned about a UNIX program called sed (sort of a Swiss army-knife program for pushing around text in files) and decided that it was the natural way to print line numbers. We asked our local wizard how to get sed to insert line numbers, and he told us. It turns out that sed isn't very good at numbers, but if you stand on your head, hold your breath, whistle Dixie, and recite the Declaration of Independence in Bulgarian, you can, indeed, get sed to put line numbers in a file. (We exaggerate here, but not much.) So, with a couple of hours effort, we managed to get the job done.

What we didn't know, and what the wizard didn't tell us because we didn't ask, is that *another* program called nl does nothing but add line numbers to a file — no cleverness required — and we could have finished the entire job in two minutes. Oops.

When you ask for help, do yourself a favor and ask the question that you really want answered.

The Care and Feeding of UNIX Wizards

Your local helpful people (normal, wizardly, or even system-administratorish) are more likely to view your entreaties with favor if you make it worth their while. Cash is a little tacky, but you can express your appreciation in many other appropriate ways:

- Food is the most reliable bribe, discussed in greater detail later in this chapter.

- Flowers, silly little statuettes for the desk, novelty Post-Its, or other such items remind the guru of what a fine and appreciative user you are.

- If you're a member of the opposite sex, a nice hug or kiss on the cheek is sometimes appropriate, although the extremely nerdy are likely to overreact and respond with a sincere proposal of marriage. Use your discretion.

- It's appropriate, of course, to write an enthusiastic memo to the person's boss and exclaim what wonderful help you received. This method is *not* appropriate when giving help is not what the person is supposed to be doing. ("She's far too knowledgeable to be wasting her time talking to mere users.")

Nerds and Food

There is a widely held stereotype that technical types eat only food found in vending machines, particularly soda pop. In some cases, this is still true, but don't count on it. With the graying of the baby boomers, people who used to live on Jolt cola (the brand that "has all the sugar and twice the caffeine") often find that it now causes a variety of physical symptoms we don't need to describe in detail; they have switched to Perrier because it makes their kidneys feel better. A new generation of UNIX nerds are into granola and tofu.

A thank-you gift with a personal touch is always appreciated (brownies or cookies, for example). Real homemade cookies are the best, but even the kind made from a tube of dough you buy at the store can be pretty good.

If you use store-bought dough, be sure to remove the plastic before slicing it; otherwise, it's a dead giveaway. Some people won't notice, but don't count on it.

The most appreciated food for most UNIX technical types is pizza, particularly when it arrives at lunchtime on a day when the guru would have to go out for lunch in 34-degree weather when it's raining slush. With pizza delivery now available in all parts of the world, you don't have to go out in the slush either; just remember to make a phone call or two at 11:30 a.m. (Residents of Santa Cruz, California, don't even have to do that — they can order pizza over the Internet.)

Selection of pizza toppings is important. Some younger UNIX wizard types have a blanket policy to never eat anything green, ruling out all-star ingredients such as bell peppers and broccoli. Some highly educated technical types, particularly graduates of technical schools in Berkeley, California, and Cambridge, Massachusetts, have had their consciousness raised and don't eat any pizza unless the cheese comes from a free-will cooperative dairy owned by the cows themselves. On the other hand, we have known some strict vegetarians who, for the purposes of pizza design, have declared pepperoni an honorary vegetable. Your best bet, at least until you get to know your pizza lovers' tastes, is to order several different kinds of pizzas. The concept of too much pizza is unknown in technical circles, so let your wallet be your guide.

A possible alternative to pizza is Chinese food, another category that meets the criteria of food you can get delivered in 34-degree weather. But be careful: Many technical schools are surrounded by Chinese restaurants, so a typical MIT graduate knows an astonishing amount about Oriental cuisine and has little patience with third-rate Chinese food. Chinese food as a bribe or thank-you offering is a good idea only if it's really good; in this sense, pizza is much more reliable. It is possible to ruin a pizza by putting sauerkraut on it, something we discovered at a pizza joint, high in the Rocky Mountains, that was run by someone named Heidi (not an auspicious name for a pizza maker); other than that, though, pizza is foolproof.

Part II
Some Basic Stuff

In this part...

UNIX, like other computer systems, keeps your information in things called files. When you work with UNIX, you frequently need to make new files, rename existing ones, make copies of particularly interesting files, or get rid of files that have outlived their usefulness.

This section talks about files: what they are, what you can do with them, how to create them, how to print them, how to find them if you lose them, and how to blow them away. It also talks about your hardware — the computer itself.

Chapter 5

Files for Fun and Profit

· ·

In This Chapter

▶ Listing information about files

▶ Who has permission to use files

▶ Duplicating a file

▶ Erasing a file

▶ Renaming a file

▶ Looking at what's in a file

▶ Printing a text file

▶ Giving a file to someone else

· ·

A *file* is a bunch of information stored together, like a letter to your mom or a database of customer invoices. Every file has a name. You will end up with tons of them. This chapter explains how to work with files, including getting rid of the ones you no longer want.

Just as a reminder, you must log in before you can do any of the nifty things we talk about in this chapter (see Chapter 1). When you see the UNIX prompt (% or $), you are ready to rock and roll.

What Files Do You Have?

To see a list of your files (actually, a list of the files in the working directory, which we'll talk about in Chapter 6), type ls. (As ever, press Enter or Return at the end of the command line. This is positively the last time we'll nag you about that.)

This command stands for *list,* but could the lazy typists who wrote UNIX have used the other two letters? No-o-o . . . . This command lists all the files in your working directory. (Chapter 6 discusses directories and how to make lots of them.) The ls command just shows the names of the files in alphabetical order, like this:

```
bin/     budget-94 budget-95 budget-96 draft     jordan
Mail/    meg       news.junk zac
```

In Linux, if the directory contains subdirectories, the subdirectory names appear in a different color, which is very handy. In BSD UNIX, subdirectory names also have a slash after them. (Chapter 6 talks about subdirectories, if you are wondering what we are talking about.)

Let's see the nitty-gritty details

For more information about your files, use the `-l` option (*long form listing*):

```
ls -l
```

That's a small el, by the way, not a one. This option tells `ls` to display tons of information about your files. Each line looks like this:

```
-rw-r--r--   1 john1    users       250 Apr  6 09:57 junk3
```

Later in this chapter, in the section, "Who can do what?" we'll explain all the information in this listing. For now, just notice that the right-hand part of the line shows you the size of the file (250 characters, in this example), the date and time the file was last modified, and the filename.

Let's see 'em all

You may have more files in your directory than you think. UNIX lets you make things called *hidden files,* which are just like regular files except that they don't appear in normal `ls` listings. It's easy to make a hidden file — just start its filename with a period.

You can see your hidden files by typing

```
ls -a
```

Making a long listing stop and start when you're ready

If you have a lot of files, the `ls` listing may fly right off the top of your screen. If you have this problem, type the following line:

```
ls | more
```

The vertical bar is called a *pipe* (we talk more about the pipe in Chapter 7). The `| more` option after the basic `ls` command tells UNIX to stop listing information to the screen just before the first file disappears from view. Press the spacebar to see the next screen of filenames.

TIP

To switch or not to switch?

Lots of UNIX commands have *options*. (They are also called *switches* because you switch the options on and off by typing or not typing them when you type the command. True geeks call them *flags*.) Options make commands both more versatile and more confusing. Probably the most used option is the `-l` option for the `ls` command; it tells `ls` to display lots of information about each file. When you type a command with options, keep these rules handy:

✔ Leave a space after the command name (the command `ls`, for example) and before the option (the `-l` part).

✔ Type a hyphen as the first character of the option (`-l`, for example).

✔ Type a space after the option if you want to type more information on the command line after the option.

To see all the information about your hidden files, type

```
ls -al
```

This command combines the `-a` and `-l` options, so you see the long version of the complete listing of files.

Roger, I Copy

You can make an exact duplicate of a file. To do this, you must know the name of the file you want to copy, and you must create a new name to give to the copy. If a file contains your January budget (called `budget.jan`, for example) and you want to make a copy of it to use for the February budget (to be called `budget.feb`, for example) type this line:

```
cp budget.jan budget.feb
```

The lazy typists strike again. Be sure to leave spaces after the `cp` command and between the existing and new filenames. This command doesn't change the existing file (`budget.jan`); it just creates a new file with a new name, but with the same contents.

A good way to lose some work

What if a file named budget.feb *already* exists? Tough cookies; UNIX blows it away and replaces it with a copy of budget.jan. It truly is an excellent idea to use the ls command first to make sure that you don't already have a file with the new name you have chosen.

In Linux and UNIX System V Release 4, you can use the -i switch to ask cp to tell you whether a file with the new name already exists. If it does, the -i switch asks you whether to proceed. If you have this version of UNIX, type cp -i rather than just cp to use this nifty little feature.

If all goes well, and cp works correctly, it doesn't give you any message. Blessed silence on the part of UNIX usually means that all is well. You should use the ls command to check that the new file really does exist, just in case.

What's in a name?

When you create a file, you give it a name. UNIX has rules about what makes a good filename:

- Filenames can be pretty long; they're not limited to eight characters and a three-character extension, like some operating systems we could name. On older versions of UNIX, the limit is 14 characters for a filename; newer versions have a huge limit — in the hundreds — so you can call a file Some_notes_I_plan_to_get_around_to_typing_up_eventually_if_I_live_that_long.

- Don't use characters that mean something special to UNIX or a shell you may encounter. Stay away from these characters when you name files:

  ```
  <   >   '   "   *   {   }   ^   !   \
  [   ]   #   |   &   (   )   $   ?   ~
  ```

  Stick mainly to letters and numbers.

- Don't put spaces in a filename. Although some programs let you put them in, spaces cause nothing but trouble because other programs simply cannot believe that a filename might contain a space. So don't borrow trouble. Most UNIX people use periods to string together words to make filenames such as budget.jan.94 or pumpkin.soup. Underscores work too.

- UNIX considers uppercase and lowercase letters to be completely different. Budget, budget, BUDGET, and BuDgEt are all different filenames.

Nuking Files Back to the Stone Age

You can also get rid of files by using the command that the lazy typists call rm. To erase (delete, remove — it's all the same thing) a file, type the following:

```
rm budget.feb
```

If all goes well, UNIX reports nothing, and you see another prompt. Use ls to see whether the rm command worked and the file is gone.

Watch out! Usually there is *no way* to get a file back after you delete it.

To be safe, you can use the -i option to ask rm to ask you to confirm deletion of the file. This is a particularly good idea if you use wildcards to delete a group of files at once (see Chapter 7 for more on wildcards). For example, if you type

```
rm -i last-years-budget
```

UNIX asks

```
rm: remove 'last-years-budget'
```

Press y to delete the file or n to leave it alone.

Big, big trouble

If you delete something really, really important, and you will be called on to perform ritual seppuku if you can't get it back, don't give up hope. Your local UNIX guru probably makes things called *backups* on some regular basis. Backups contain copies of some or all the files on the UNIX system. Your files may be among those on the backup. Go to the guru on bended knee and ask whether the file can be restored. If the file wasn't backed up recently, you may get an older version of it, but hey — it's better than the alternative.

Even before you get yourself into this kind of pickle, ask your UNIX expert to confirm that regular backups are made. Make sure that your important files are included in the backups. If no one is making regular backups, panic. This is not a safe situation. See Chapter 9 for information about backup tapes and Chapter 21 for how to back up on another computer on your network.

Good housekeeping

You should get rid of files you no longer use, for several reasons:

- ✔ It gets confusing when you have all kinds of files lying around, and it's hard to remember which ones are important.

- ✔ The useless files take up disk space. Whoever is in charge of your UNIX system probably will bother you regularly to "take out the garbage," that is, to get rid of unnecessary files and free up some disk space.

On the other hand, it can be a good idea to make extra copies of files. If you've been working on a report for three weeks, it isn't a bad idea to make an extra copy every day or so. That way, if you make some revisions that, in hindsight, were stupid, you can go back to a previous revision.

What's in a Name (Reprise)

Having given a file a name, you may want to change it later. You can rename a file by using the `mv` (lazy typist-ese for *move*) command.

Suppose that you made a file called `bugdet.march`. Oops, dratted fingers . . . . Type the following line to correct the error in the filename:

```
mv bugdet.march budget.march
```

After `mv`, you type the current filename and then the name you want to change it to. It can be harder to retype the same typo than to type the name correctly!

Because you can't have two files with the same name in the same directory, if a file already has the name you want to use, `mv` thoughtfully blows the existing file away (probably not what you want to do). Type carefully. Linux and SVR4 users can use `mv -i` (like `cp -i`) to prevent inadvertent file clobbering.

Looking at the Guts of a File

We have been slicing and dicing files for a while now, but you still haven't seen what's inside one. There are two basic types of files:

- ✔ Files that contain text that UNIX can display nicely on-screen.

- ✔ Files that contain special codes that look like monkeys have been at the keyboard when you display the files on-screen.

The first type are called *text files;* spreadsheet files, database files, program files, and just about anything else comprise the second type. Text editors make text files, as do a few other programs.

To display a text file, type the following line:

```
cat eggplant.recipe
```

The `cat` stands for *catalog,* or maybe *catenate* — who knows? We're surprised the lazy typists didn't call it something like q. If you try to use `cat` with a file that doesn't contain text, your screen looks like a truck ran over it — but you won't hurt anything. Sometimes the garbage in the file can put your terminal in a strange mode in which characters you type don't appear, or they appear as strange Greek squiggles. See Chapter 22 to learn how to un-strange your terminal.

If the file is long, the listing goes whizzing by. (You learn how to look at the file one screen at a time in Chapter 7.) To see just the first few lines of the file, type

```
head eggplant.recipe
```

Most versions of the `head` command display the first ten lines.

You can ask UNIX to guess what's in a file with the `file` command. If you type

```
file filename
```

(replacing *filename* with the name of the file you are wondering about), UNIX takes a guess at what's in the file, by looking at it. It says something like this:

```
letter.to.jordan:    ascii text
```

or this

```
unix4d:    directory
```

Is This a Printout I See Before Me?

If a file looks OK on-screen by using the `cat` command, try printing it. If you use UNIX System V, type the following line:

```
lp eggplant.recipe
```

If you use BSD UNIX or Linux, type the following:

```
lpr eggplant.recipe
```

Assuming that you have a printer that's hooked up, turned on, and has paper, and that your user name is set up to use it, the `eggplant.recipe` file prints. If it doesn't, see Chapter 10 to straighten things out. If your computer is blessed with a network, the printed copy may come out down the hall or on another floor. If your printer isn't attached directly to your computer, you probably will have to ask for advice about where to pick up the printout. If you can print files on more than one printer, use the `-d` or `-P` option with the printer name to tell UNIX which one you want to use (see Chapter 10).

Who Goes There?

Unlike some operating systems we could name (like MS-DOS, f'rinstance), UNIX was designed from the beginning to be used by more than one person. Like all multiuser systems, UNIX keeps track of who owns what file and who can do what with each file. *Permissions* determine who can use which file or directory.

There are three types of permissions:

- **Read permission** lets you look at a file or directory. You can use `cat` or a text editor to see what's in a file that has read permission; you can also copy this file. Read permission for a directory lets you list its contents.

- **Write permission** lets you make changes to a file. Even if you can write (change) a file, you can't necessarily delete it or rename it; for those actions, you must be able to write in the directory in which the file resides. If you have write permission in a directory, you can create new files in the directory and delete files from it.

- **Execute permission** lets you run the program contained in a file. The program can be a real program or a shell script. If the file doesn't contain a program, execute permission doesn't do much good and can provoke the shell to complain bitterly as it tries (from its rather dim point of view) to make sense of your file. For a directory, execute permission lets you open files in the directory and use `cd` to make the directory your working directory.

Rock groups, pop groups, and UNIX groups

Every UNIX user is a member of a group. When the system administrator created your user name, she assigned you to a group. To see which group you are in, type `id`.

Groups usually indicate the kind of work you do. UNIX uses groups to give a bunch of people the same permissions to use a set of files. All the people who work on a particular project are usually in the same group so that they can look at and perhaps change each other's files.

If you are part of the accounting department, for example (it's a dirty job, but someone has to do it), you and the other accounting staff members might need read, write, and execute access to basically the same files. People in other departments should not have the same access to accounting programs and data. The system administrator probably made a group called something like acctg and put all you accounting guys and girls in it.

In Linux and BSD, you can be in several groups at a time, which is handy if you're working on several projects. To find out what groups you are in, type groups.

That's mine!

Every file and directory has an owner and a group owner. The owner is usually the person who made the file or directory, although the owner can sometimes change the ownership of the file to someone else. The group owner is usually the group to which the owner belongs, although the owner can change a file's group owner to another group. You can change who owns a file with the chown command (described later in this chapter).

Who can do what?

To see who can do what to a file, use the ls command with the -l option. Type

```
ls -l myfile
```

You see something like this:

```
-rw-r--r--   1 johnl    staff     335 Jan 22 13:23 myfile
```

If you don't specify a filename, UNIX lists all the files in the directory, which is often more useful. For every file, this listing shows all this information:

- ✔ Whether it is a file, symbolic link, or directory. The first character is a hyphen (-) if it is a file, an *l* if it is a symbolic link, and a *d* if it is a directory.

- ✔ Whether the owner can read, write, or execute it (as shown by the next three characters, 2–4, on the line). The first character is an *r* if the owner has read permission and a hyphen if not. The second character is a *w* if the owner has write permission and a hyphen if not. The third character is an *x* (or an *s*) if the owner has execute permission and a hyphen if not.

- ✔ Whether the members of the group owner can read, write, or execute the file or directory (as indicated by the next three characters, 5–7). An *r, w,* or *x* appears if that permission is granted; a hyphen appears if not granted.

✔ Whether everyone else can read, write, or execute the file or directory (as indicated by the next three characters, 8–10). An *r, w,* or *x* appears if that permission is granted; a hyphen appears if not granted.

✔ The link count, that is, how many links (names) this file has. For directories, this number is the number of subdirectories the directory contains plus 2 (don't ask).

✔ The owner of the file or directory.

✔ The group to which the file or directory belongs (group owner).

✔ The size of the file in bytes (characters).

✔ The date and time the file was last modified.

✔ The filename — at last!

Permissions by number

It is not too difficult to figure out which permissions a file has by looking at the collection of *r*s, *w*s, and *x*s in the file listing. Sometimes permissions are written another way, however: with numbers. Only UNIX programmers could have thought of this. (This is an example of lazy typists at their finest.) Numbered permissions are sometimes called *absolute permissions* (perhaps because they are absolutely impossible to remember).

When permissions are expressed as a number, it is a 3-digit number. The first digit is the owner's permissions, the second digit is the group's permissions, and the third digit is everyone else's permissions. Every digit is a number from 0 to 7. Table 5-1 lists what the digits mean.

Table 5-1	Absolute Permissions Decoded
Digit	**Permissions**
0	None
1	Execute only
2	Write only
3	Write and execute
4	Read only
5	Read and execute
6	Read and write
7	Read, write, and execute

If Mom says no, go ask Dad

If you own a file or directory, you can change its permissions. You use the chmod (for *change mode*) command to do it. You tell chmod the name of the file or directory to change and the new permissions you want the file to have for yourself (the owner), your group, and everyone else. You can type the numerical absolute permissions (like 440) or use letters.

To use letters to type the new permissions, you use a cryptic collection of letters and symbols that consists of the following:

- ✔ Whose permissions you are changing: u for user (the file's owner), g for the group, o for other (everyone else), or a for all three.

- ✔ If the permission should be + (on, yes, OK) or - (off, no, don't let them).

- ✔ The type of permission you're dealing with: r for read, w for write, and x for execute.

Type the following line, for example, to allow everyone to read a file called announcements:

```
chmod a+r announcements
```

This line says that the user/owner, group, and everyone else can read the file. To not let anyone except the user/owner change the file, type this line:

```
chmod go-w announcements
```

You can also use numeric (absolute) permissions with chmod. To let the user/owner and associated group read or change the file, type the following:

```
chmod 660 announcements
```

This sets the owner permission to 6 (read and write), the group permission to 6, too, and everyone else's permission to 0 (can't do anything).

You can change the permissions for a directory in exactly the same way you do for a file. Keep in mind that read, write, and execute mean somewhat different things for a directory.

Finding a new owner

When someone gives you a file, he usually copies it to your home directory. As far as UNIX is concerned, the person who copied the file is still the file's owner. In Linux and System V, you can change the ownership of a file you own by using the `chown` command. You tell `chown` the new owner for the file and the filename or filenames whose ownership you are changing. For example:

```
chown john chapter6
```

This command changes the ownership of the file named `chapter6` to `john`. Keep in mind that only you can give away files you own; if you put a file in someone else's directory, it's polite to `chown` the file to that user.

Another way to change the owner of a file is to make a copy of the file. Suppose Fred puts a file in your home directory, and he still owns it. You can't use `chown` to change the ownership; only the owner can do that (we have a chicken-before-the-egg problem here). You can get ownership of a file if you copy it. When you copy a file, you own the new copy. Then delete the original.

File seeks new group; can sing, dance, and do tricks

If you own a file or directory, you can change the group that can access it. The `chgrp` command lets you change the name of the group associated with the file. For example:

```
chgrp acctg billing.list
```

This command changes the group associated with the file `billing.list` to the group called `acctg`.

Chapter 6
Directories for Fun and Profit

● ●

In This Chapter

▶ Defining a directory

▶ Getting to the right directory

▶ Defining a home directory

▶ Making a new directory

▶ Erasing a directory

▶ Renaming a directory

▶ Moving a file from one directory to another

▶ Organizing your files

▶ A map of UNIX

● ●

*A*fter you begin working with UNIX, you will make more and more files. You will have files with important memos to coworkers and customers, programs that analyze productivity and costs, recipes for pumpkin soup, and programs that play battleship. All of this is very important stuff, so you don't want to lose anything. This chapter explains how to organize your UNIX files in directories and how to find things after you have done so.

Good News for DOS Users

We have good news about UNIX for you experienced DOS users. UNIX works almost exactly the same as DOS does when it comes to directories and files. Actually, it's the other way around — a guy named Mark added directories to DOS back in 1982, and ripped off, er, emulated, the way UNIX did things — with a few confusing changes, of course.

Briefly, DOS users should know the following things about UNIX directories:

✔ All those backslashes (\) you learned to type in DOS turn into regular slashes (/) in UNIX. No one knows why Mark decided that DOS slashes should lean backward. We're sure he had a very good reason, of course — maybe the / key was broken on his keyboard.

✔ The UNIX cd (change directory) command works (more or less) like the DOS CD command; remember not to capitalize it in UNIX.

✔ The UNIX command for making a directory is mkdir rather than the DOS MD command; to remove a directory in UNIX, you use the rmdir command rather than the DOS RD command. (Where were the lazy typists when we needed them?) These two commands also work (more or less) like the DOS versions. Don't capitalize them, either.

✔ As always, UNIX believes that capital and small letters have nothing to do with each other. They are completely different, so be sure to use the correct capitalization when you type directory names and filenames.

✔ If you really like DOS commands and want to make UNIX understand them, you can make shell scripts (the UNIX equivalent of DOS batch files) that let you type DIR or COPY while you are using UNIX. (Chapter 15 tells you how to make shell scripts.) Or, if you absolutely fall in love with UNIX commands — and who doesn't! — you can make DOS batch files on your PC so you can type ls and cp while you are using the PC.

What Is a Directory?

A *directory,* for you non-DOS people, is a group of files, or a work area. (Macintosh users call this a *folder.*) You give a directory a name, such as Budget or Letters or Games or Harold, and put in it as many files as you want.

The good thing about directories (also called *subdirectories,* for no good reason) is you can use them to keep together groups of related files. If you make a directory for your budget files, you see only those files while working in that directory. Directories make it easy to concentrate on what you're doing so that you're not distracted by the zillions of other files on the disk.

Divide and Conquer

Interestingly, a directory can contain other directories. You may have a directory called Budget, for example, for your departmental budget. The Budget directory may contain other directories (also called subdirectories), such as Year1996, Year1997, and Estimates. If a directory has so many files that you can't find things, you should create some subdirectories to divide things up.

Files and directories are stored on disks. Every disk has a main directory that contains everything on the disk. This directory is called the *root directory.* The designers of UNIX were thinking of trees here, not turnips, imagining an upside-down tree with the root at the top and the branches reaching down, as in Figure 6-1. This arrangement is called a *tree-structured directory.*

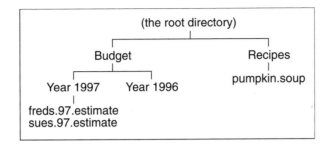

Figure 6-1: A tree-structured directory.

Strangely, you don't type root when you are talking about the root directory. Rather, you type /. Just like that: A single slash means "root" in UNIX-ese.

Paths to power

Unfortunately, UNIX never shows you the directory structure as a nice picture, like Figure 6-1. That would be too easy. Rather, to tell UNIX which file you want to use, you type its pathname. The *pathname* is the step-by-step map UNIX follows to get to the file, starting at the root. The pathname for the file named freds.97.estimate in Figure 6-1, for example, contains these steps:

/	The root, where you start.
Budget	The first directory on your way to the file.
/	Confusingly, this slash doesn't refer to another root; it separates one name from the next in the pathname.
Year1997	The next directory on your way to the file.
/	Another separator character.
freds.97.estimate	The filename you want.

When you type this pathname, you string it all together, with no spaces, like this:

```
/Budget/Year1997/freds.97.estimate
```

Luckily, you don't have to type big, long pathnames like this one very often because it's devilishly hard to get all that right on the first try!

You can also think of the tree structure of directories as a family tree. In this way of thinking, the Year1997 directory is a *child* of the Budget directory, and the Budget directory is the *parent* of the Year1997 directory. You will see these terms sometimes if you read more about UNIX.

Getting the big picture

If you have a UNIX workstation that's all your own, most or all the files on its hard disk are yours. If you have a terminal and share a UNIX computer with others, the computer's hard disk has files that belong to all the users. As you can imagine, we are talking about oodles of files. To keep the files — and the users! — organized, there are lots of different directories.

There are directories for the UNIX program files, program files for other programs, and other stuff you're definitely not interested in. Files that belong to users usually are stored in one area. A directory called /usr (or sometimes /home) contains one subdirectory for every user. If your user name is zacyoung, for example, the /usr directory has a subdirectory called zacyoung that contains your files.

Names for directories

Choose names for directories in the same way you choose names for files: Avoid funky characters and spaces, don't make the name so long that you will never type it correctly, and so on. Some people capitalize the first letter of directory names so that they can tell what's a directory and what's a file. When you use ls to list the contents of a directory, the command lists both filenames and the names of subdirectories. When you use capitalization to distinguish between directory names and file names, you can quickly tell which are which.

There's No Place Like Home

Every user has a home directory (sweet, isn't it) in which you store your personal stuff, mail, and so on. When you log in, UNIX starts you working in your home directory, where you work until you move somewhere else. Your home directory is your subdirectory in the /usr directory, so Zac Young's home directory is /usr/zacyoung. (Zac was only 5 months old when we wrote this book, but we're sure that he'll need a home directory shortly.)

Because most UNIX systems involve lots of people sharing disk space and files, UNIX has a security system to prevent people from reading each other's private mail or blowing away each other's work (accidentally, of course). Chapter 5 talks about the security system. In your home directory, you usually have the right to create, edit, and delete all the files and subdirectories. You can't do this in someone else's home directory unless they give you permission.

I've been working in the directory

Whenever you use UNIX, the directory you are currently working in is the *working* directory. Some people call it the *current* directory, which makes sense too. When you log in, your home directory is your working directory. Although you start in your home directory, you can move around. Move to the /Budget directory, for example, and the /Budget directory becomes the working directory. (Your home directory is still your home directory — it never moves.)

If you forget where you are in the directory structure, you can ask UNIX. Type pwd to ask UNIX where you are. This is short for *print working directory*. UNIX doesn't print the information on paper; it just displays it on your screen. For example, you might see:

/Budget/Year1997

When you use the ls command (or most other commands), UNIX assumes you want to work with just the files in the working directory. The ls command lists just the files in the working directory unless you tell it to look elsewhere.

To move to another directory to do some work (if you are tired of working on the budget and want to get back to that recipe for pumpkin soup, for example), you can change directories. To move from anywhere in the /Budget directory to the /Recipes directory, type the following line:

```
cd /Recipes
```

Remember that cd is the *change directory* command. After the cd (and a space), you type the directory to want to go to. You can tell UNIX exactly which directory you want in two ways:

- ✔ Type a *full pathname,* or *absolute pathname* (the pathname starting at the root, as you did earlier).
- ✔ Type a *relative pathname* (the pathname starting where you are now).

This is confusing, we know, but UNIX has to know exactly which directory you want before it makes the move. Because there can be more than one directory called Recipes on the disk, UNIX has to know which one you want.

When you type a full pathname starting at the root directory, the pathname starts with a /. When you type a relative pathname starting at the current working directory, the pathname doesn't start with a /. That's how UNIX (and you) can tell which kind of path it is.

If you are in the /Budget directory (on the /Budget branch of the directory tree) and want to go to the Year1997 subdirectory (a branchlet off the main /Budget branch), just type cd Year1997. To go to a different branch, or to move upward toward the root, you must use the slashes. To move from the

/Budget/Year1997 branchlet back to the main /Budget branch, type
cd |/Budget. To move from the /Budget branch to the /Recipes branch, for
example, type cd /Recipes.

If you try to move to a directory that doesn't exist, or if you incorrectly type the
directory name or pathname, UNIX says something like:

```
Dudegt: No such file or directory
```

I want to go back home to Kansas

If you move to another directory (/Oz, for example) and want to get back to
your home directory (/Kansas, that is), you can do so as easily as clicking the
heels of your ruby slippers together three times. (Or were they glass slippers?)
Just type cd. When you don't tell UNIX where you want to go, it assumes
that you want to go home.

Putting Your Ducks in a Row

As with everything else in life (if we may be so bold as to suggest it), it pays to
be organized when you are naming files and putting them in directories. If you
don't have at least a little organization, you will never find anything. Think
about which types of files you will make and use. (Word processing files?
Spreadsheet files?) Then make a directory for every type of file or for every
project you are working on. This section shows you how.

Making directories

Before you make a directory, be sure that you make it in the right place. Type
pwd to display your working directory (that is, the current directory).

The most likely place to make a subdirectory is in your home directory. If
you're not there already, type cd to go back home.

When you create a directory, you give it a name. To create a directory called
Temp to hold temporary files, type this line:

```
mkdir Temp
```

You can even go in there and look around:

```
cd Temp
ls
```

When you create a directory, it starts out empty (there are no files in it).

Most people have directories with names something like the following:

Mail   For electronic mail (see Chapter 19).

Docs   For miscellaneous documents, memos, and letters.

Temp   For files you don't plan to keep. Use Temp to store files you plan to throw away soon. If you put them in some other directory and don't erase them when you finish with them, you may forget what they are and be reluctant to delete them later. Directories commonly fill up with junk in this way. Make it a rule that any files left in the Temp directory are considered deletable.

bin   For programs that you use but that aren't stored in a central place. Your system administrator may have already made you your own bin directory. (See Chapter 15 for information about the bin directory and making your own programs.)

You can also make one or more directories to contain actual work.

Dot and dot dot

You can use two funny pseudo-directory names, especially with the cd and ls commands. One is . (a single dot), which stands for the current directory. Type the following line, for example, to tell UNIX to list the files in the current directory:

```
ls .
```

This is pretty pointless, of course, because typing ls does exactly the same thing.

OK, forget about . (the single dot). But .. (the double dot, or dot dot) can be useful. It stands for the parent directory of the current working directory. The *parent* directory is the one in which the working directory is a subdirectory. It is one level up the tree from where you are now. If you are in the directory /usr/home/zacyoung/Budget, for example, the .. (dot dot, or parent) directory is /usr/home/zacyoung.

When you type ls, you see a list of the files in the parent directory of where you are now. This can save you some serious typing (and the associated errors).

Neat operations to perform on directories

After you have some directories, you may want to change their names or get rid of them. You may also want to move a file from one directory to another.

Transplanting files

Chapter 5 describes the use of the mv command to rename a file. You can use the same command to move files from one directory to another. To get the mv command to move files rather than just rename them, you tell it two things:

- ✔ The name of the file you want to move.
- ✔ The name of the path where you want to put it.

You can rename the file at the same time you move it, but we'll keep things (comparatively) simple. Suppose you put the file allens.97.estimates into the /Budget/Year1996 directory rather than in /Budget/Year1997. The easiest way to move it is to go to the directory in which it is located by typing:

```
cd /Budget/Year1996
```

Use ls to make sure that the file is in the current directory. After you are sure that the file is there, you can move it to the directory you want by typing:

```
mv allens.97.estimates /Budget/Year1997
```

Be sure to type one space after mv and one space between the name of the file and the place you want to move it to. If you use ls again, you discover that the file is no longer in the working directory (Year1996). You should change to the directory to which you moved the file and use ls to make sure that the file is there. Make one typing mistake in a mv command and you can move a valuable file to some unexpected place.

Amputating unnecessary directories

You can use the rmdir command to remove a directory, but what about the files in the directory? Are they left hanging in the air with the ground blown out from under them? Nope, you must get rid of the files in the directory (delete them) or move them elsewhere before you can hack away at the directory.

To erase a directory, do the following:

1. **Use the rm command to delete any files you don't want to keep.**

   (See Chapter 5 for the gory details of using the rm command.)

2. **If you want to keep any of the files, move them to somewhere else by using the mv command (as explained in the preceding section).**

3. Move to another directory when the one you want to delete is empty.

UNIX doesn't let you delete the current working directory. The easiest thing to do is to move to the working directory's parent directory:

```
cd ..
```

4. Remove the directory by typing the following:

```
rmdir OldStuff
```

Replace OldStuff with the name of the directory you want to ax.

5. Use ls to confirm that the directory is gone.

You can delete a directory and all its files, and even all the subdirectories and files in them, but this is pretty dangerous stuff. You're usually better off sifting through the files and deleting or moving them in smaller groups.

Renaming a directory

If you have used DOS, you will be thrilled to learn that in UNIX you can rename a directory after you create it. (DOS doesn't let you do this, at least not in early versions.) Again, the mv command comes to the rescue.

To rename a directory, you tell mv the current directory name and the new directory name. Go to the parent directory of the directory you want to rename and use the mv command. To rename the /Budget directory as /Finance, for example, go to the / directory (type cd /) and then type this line:

```
mv Budget Finance
```

Remember to make sure first that a directory with that name isn't already there. If it is, UNIX moves the first-named directory to become a subdirectory of the existing directory. In other words, if a /Finance directory is already there, /Budget moves to become /Finance/Budget. Could be handy, if that's what you have in mind. Then again, it could drive you out of your mind.

A Map of UNIX

Most UNIX systems have thousands, or even tens of thousands, of files, stored in hundreds of directories. Luckily, you don't care about most of these directories, because they contain nothing but the files that make up the murky technical underbelly of UNIX. However, you may need to find something in some directory other than your own safe, well-lit home directory. Table 6-1 is a guide to some directories that you are likely to find on your UNIX system. (Not every UNIX system has all of these directories, but most do.)

Table 6-1	Popular UNIX Directories and What They Contain
Directory Name	*What It Contains*
/bin	Standard system commands.
/usr/bin	More standard system commands.
/usr/ucb/bin	Even more standard system commands (the ones written at Berkeley).
/usr/local/bin	Nonstandard, locally installed, system commands.
/dev	Contains connections to devices, such as tape drivers, rather than real files. UNIX uses a terribly clever trick, referring to hardware devices as if they were files.
/etc	Miscellaneous system files. Not interesting to non-weenies.
/home	Contains a home directory for each user. (If you don't see /home, try /usr.)
/lib	Program libraries and the like. (See comment about /etc.)
/usr/lib	More program libraries and the like. (Ditto.)
/usr/news	Usenet news articles, if stored on your system. (Even if you have the news *programs* discussed in Chapter 19, *articles* may be on another computer.)
/tmp	Small temporary files.
/usr/tmp	Larger temporary files.
/usr/src	On systems with source code, the source code to the system (fascinating to programmers, not so fascinating otherwise).
/var/src	Another place where source code can be found.
/usr/man; /usr/catman	Text of on-line manual pages.

Chapter 7
Cute UNIX Tricks

. . . .

In This Chapter

▶ Using redirection

▶ Viewing a file one screen at a time

▶ Printing the output of any command

▶ Working with groups of files

▶ Avoiding retyping commands, especially after typos

. . . .

*N*ow you know how to work with files and how to type some commands to UNIX (you type them to the shell, as you know, but let's not get bogged down in that here). UNIX has a clever way to increase the power of its commands: *redirection*. This chapter shows you how to use redirection and how to use wildcards to work with groups of files.

This Output Goes to Havana: Redirection

When you use a UNIX command like ls, the result (or *output*) of the command is displayed on-screen. The standard place, in fact, for the output of most UNIX commands is the screen. There is even a name for this: *standard output*. As you can imagine, there is also *standard input*, usually the keyboard. You type a command; if it needs more input, you type that too. The result is output displayed on-screen — all very natural.

You can pervert this natural order by *redirecting* the input or output of a program. A better word is *hijacking*. You say to UNIX, "Don't display this output on-screen — instead, put it somewhere else." Or, "The input for this program is not coming from the keyboard this time — look for it somewhere else."

The "somewhere else" can be any of these sources:

✔ **A file.** You can store the output of ls (your directory listing) in a file.

✔ **The printer.** Useful only for output; input from a printer is a losing battle.

✔ **Another program.** This gets really interesting, when you take the output of one program and feed it to another program!

Bunches of UNIX programs are designed primarily to use input from a source other than the keyboard and to output stuff to someplace other than the screen. These kinds of programs are called *filters*. Readers old enough to remember what cigarettes are may recall that the really advanced ones had a filter between the cigarette and your mouth to make the smoke smoother, mellower, and more sophisticated. UNIX filters work in much the same way, except that they usually aren't made of asbestos.

The only exception to redirection is with programs that take over the entire screen, such as text editors and spreadsheets. Although you can redirect their output to the printer, you won't like the results (nor will your coworkers, as they wait for a pile of your garbage pages to come out of the printer). Full-screen programs write all sorts of special glop (they give instructions) to the screen to control where stuff is displayed, what color to use, and so forth. These instructions don't work on the printer because printers use their own, different kind of glop. The short form of this tip is that *redirection and editors don't mix.*

Grabbing output

So, how do you use this neat redirection stuff, you ask? Naturally, UNIX does it with funny characters. The two characters ⟨ and ⟩ are used for redirecting input and output to and from files and to the printer. Another character (|) is used to redirect the output of one program to the input of another program.

To redirect (or *snag,* in technical parlance) the output of a command, use ⟩. Think of this symbol as a tiny funnel *into which* the output is pouring (hey, we use any gimmick we can to remember which funny character is which). To make a file called list.of.files that contains your directory listing, for example, type this line:

```
ls > list.of.files
```

UNIX creates a new file, called list.of.files here, and puts the output of the ls command into it.

If list.of.files already exists, UNIX blows away the old version of the file. If you don't want to erase the existing file, you can tell UNIX to add this new information to the end of it (*append* the new information to the existing information), by typing the following line:

```
ls >> list.of.files
```

The double ⟩⟩ symbol makes the command append the output of ls to the list.of.files file, if it already exists. If list.of.files doesn't exist already, ls creates it.

If you use > (single-angle) redirection, it blows away any previous contents of the file into which you redirect the output. For this reason, >> (double-angle) redirection is much safer. Some (but not all, of course) versions of the C shell check to see whether the file already exists and refuse to let you wreck an existing file with redirection. If your C shell works like this, then, to overwrite the file, use rm to get rid of the old version. The command that tells the C shell not to clobber an existing file when creating a new file from redirection is set noclobber. To turn this protection off, you can use the unset noclobber command.

Redirecting input

Redirecting input is less often useful than redirecting output, and we can't think of a single, simple example in which you would want to use it. Suffice it to say that you redirect input just like you redirect output, but you use the < character rather than the > character.

Gurgle, Gurgle: Piping Data

It can be really useful to redirect the output of one program so that it becomes the input of another program. This process is the electronic equivalent of whisper-down-the-lane, with each program doing something to the information being whispered.

To play whisper-down-the-lane with UNIX, you use a *pipe*. The symbol for a pipe is a vertical bar (|). Search your keyboard for this character. It's often on the same key with \ (the backslash). Sometimes the key shows the vertical bar with a gap in the middle, but the gap doesn't matter. If you type two commands separated by a |, you tell UNIX to use the output of the first command as input for the second command.

Gimme just a little at a time

When you have many files in a directory, the output of the ls command can go whizzing by too fast to read, which makes it impossible to see the files at the beginning of the list before they disappear off the top of the screen. A UNIX command called more solves this problem. The more program displays on the screen the input you give it, but it pauses as soon as it fills the screen and waits for you to press a key to continue. To display your list of files one screen at a time, type this line:

```
ls | more
```

This line tells the ls command to send the file listing to the more command. The more command then displays the listing. You can think of the information from the ls command gurgling down through the little pipe to the more command (we think of it this way).

The `cat` *and the fiddle, er, file*

As explained in Chapter 5, you can use the `cat` command to display the contents of a text file. If the text file is too long to fit on-screen, however, the beginning of the file disappears too fast to see. You can display a long file on-screen one screen at a time in these two ways:

- Redirect the output of the `cat` command to `more` by typing the following line (assuming, of course, that the file is called `really.long.file`):

```
cat really.long.file | more
```

- Just use the `more` command by typing this line:

```
more really.long.file
```

If you use the `more` command without a pipe (without the |), `more` takes the file you suggest and displays it on-screen a page at a time.

Sorting, sort of

A command called `sort` sorts a file line-by-line in alphabetical order. It alphabetizes all the lines according to the first letter(s) in each line. Each line in the file is unaffected, just the order of the lines changes.

Suppose you have a file of names called `bonus.recipients`. To sort it line by line into alphabetical order, type the following:

```
sort bonus.recipients
```

If you want to save the sorted list, type

```
sort bonus.recipients > bonuses.sorted
```

If you are sorting numbers, be sure to tell UNIX. Otherwise, UNIX sorts the numbers alphabetically (the sort of imbecilic and useless trick only a computer would do). To sort numbers, use the `-n` option:

```
sort -n order.numbers
```

For example, suppose your file of bonus recipients contained the bonus amounts, like this:

```
10000 Meg Young
8000  Shelly Horwitz
9000  Elana Kleiman
11000 Kate Henoch
8000  Timothy Kenny
```

When you alphabetize numbered items as letters, not as numbers, a 1 comes before an 8 no matter what, even if it's the first numeral of 10. When you alphabetize numbered items as numbers, 10 comes after 8, not before it. If you sort this file as letters, with this command

```
sort bonus.recipients
```

you get this:

```
10000 Meg Young
11000 Kate Henoch
8000  Shelly Horwitz
8000  Timothy Kenny
9000  Elana Kleiman
```

This does not show the bonus amounts in any useful order. If you sort the file as numbers, with this command

```
sort -n bonus.recipients
```

you get this more useful listing:

```
8000  Shelly Horwitz
8000  Timothy Kenny
9000  Elana Kleiman
10000 Meg Young
11000 Kate Henoch
```

If the file contains letters, not numbers, the -n option has no effect.

That's a take — print it

Being able to print the output of a command is terrifically useful when you want to send to a printer something that normally appears on-screen. To print a listing of your files, for example, type this line:

```
ls | lp
```

Users of Linux and BSD UNIX have to use the lpr command rather than lp. (Chapter 10 explains other stuff about printing.)

You can use more than one pipe if you want to be really advanced. To print a list of your files in reverse order, for example, use this convoluted command:

```
ls | sort -r | lp
```

Wild and Crazy Wildcards

When you type a command, you may want to include the names of a bunch of files on the command line. UNIX makes the typing of multiple filenames somewhat easier (as though we should be grateful) by providing wildcards. *Wildcards* are special characters — still more of them to remember! — that have a special meaning in filenames. There are two wildcards: ? means "any single letter" and * means "anything at all."

Pick a letter, any letter

You can use one or more ? wildcards in a filename. Each ? stands for exactly one character — no more, no less. To list all your files that have two-letter names, for example, you can type this line:

```
ls ??
```

Typing this command with the filename budget??, for example, matches all filenames that start with *budget* and have two — and only two — characters after *budget*, such as budget96 and budget97; the combination doesn't match budget1 or budget.draft.

Stars (***) in your eyes

The * wildcard stands for any number of characters. To list all your files that have names starting with a *c,* for example, type the following:

```
ls c*
```

This specification matches files named customer.letter, c3, and just plain c. The specification budget.* matches budget.1997 and budget.draft, but not draft.budget. The name *.draft matches budget.draft and window.draft, but not draft.horse or plain draft. By itself, the filename * matches everything. (Watch out when you let the asterisk go solo!)

Are kings or deuces wild?

Unlike some other kinds of operating systems (we won't name any, but one system's initials are *DOS*), UNIX handles the ? and * wildcards in the same way for every command. You don't have to memorize which commands can handle wildcards and which ones cannot. In UNIX, they all can handle wildcards.

Wildcards commonly are used with the ls, cp, rm, and mv commands.

Wildcards for DOS users

Although UNIX wildcards look just like DOS wildcards, and they work in almost the same way, they have a few differences:

> ✔ Because UNIX filenames don't have the three-letter extensions that DOS filenames use, don't use *.* to match all files in a directory. That will only match files that actually have a dot in their names. A simple * will do the trick.

> ✔ In DOS, you cannot put letters after the * wildcard — DOS ignores the letters following the asterisk. In DOS, *d*mb* is the same as *d**, for example. It's dumb, we know. The good news is that UNIX is not so dumb. In UNIX, *d*mb* works just the way you want it to.

Look before you delete!

The combination of wildcards and the rm command is deadly. Use wildcards with care when you delete files. You should look first at the list of files you are deleting to make sure that it is what you had in mind. Before you type the following command, for example, to delete a bunch of files

rm *.95

type the following line first and look at the resulting list of files:

ls *.95

Something may be worth keeping that you forgot about in that list of .95 files.

The most deadly typo of all is this one (*do not type this line!*):

rm * .95

There's a space between the * wildcard and the .95. Although you may have thought that you were deleting all files ending with .95, UNIX thinks that you have typed two filenames to delete:

* This "filename" deletes all the files in the directory.

.95 This filename deletes a file named .95 (yes, filenames can start with a period). Of course, by the time UNIX tries to delete this (nonexistent) file, it has already deleted all the files in the directory!

You end up with an empty directory and lots of missing files. Watch out when you use rm and * together!

UNIX Is History!

We make fun of the C shell a lot (and rightly so), but when Bill wrote it, he added a lovely feature called *history*. BASH does history too, even more nicely than the C shell. And the Korn shell has a way to do history which is clunky but serviceable. History lets you issue UNIX commands again without having to retype them, a big plus in our book. Bourne shell users might as well skip the rest of this chapter, since it'll just make you jealous (or it'll make you bite the bullet and switch to the BASH shell, by typing `bash`).

Here's how history works. The shell stores a list of the commands that you've given, in a *history list*. Then you can use the list to repeat commands exactly as you typed them the first time, or edit previously used commands so that you can give a similar command.

The C shell throughout history

In the C shell, you can type `!!` and Enter to repeat the last command you typed. The shell displays the command, then executes it.

You can also rerun the last command line that begins with a particular bunch of letters. If you type

```
!find
```

then the C shell repeats the last command line that began with the text *find*. You don't have to type an entire command; if you type

```
!fi
```

then it looks for the last command you typed that started with *fi*, which might be a `find` command or a `file` command.

To see the history list, type `history`. You see a list like this:

```
1  20:26    ls
2  20:26    ls -l
3  20:26    ls -al
4  20:26    history
5  20:26    cat junk3
6  20:26    cat .term
7  20:26    history
```

There are the commands you have just typed, in the order that you typed them. The list is numbered, so that you can refer to the commands by number. After the number comes the time that you typed the command (if you care), followed by the command you typed.

If you want to repeat a command, you can type a ! followed by the number of the command. For example, if you type

```
!3
```

then the C shell repeats command number 3 on the list (in this case, `ls -al`).

You can also repeat a command with a modification. For example, suppose you just typed this command:

```
find . -name budget.96 -print
```

Now you want to give the same `find` command, but this time looking for a file named `budget.97`. Instead of tediously, arduously retyping the line, character by character and keystroke by keystroke, worrying anxiously about a possible typo with every key you press, you can tell the C shell to repeat the last command, substituting *97* for *96*. The command is

```
^96^97
```

You type a caret (^), the old text, another caret, and the text to substitute. Voilà! The C shell displays the new command, then executes it.

BASH throughout history

BASH can do all the cool history tricks that the C shell can, with some additional acrobatics. When BASH displays your history list, it usually stores the last 500 commands you typed, so the list can be huge. To see it a page at a time, type

```
history | more
```

To see the last nine commands on the history list, type

```
history 9
```

Here comes the neat part — you can use the arrow keys to flip back through your commands. When you press the up-arrow (or Ctrl-P, for previous), BASH shows you the previous command from the history list. You can press Enter to execute the command. You can keep pressing the up-arrow or Ctrl-P until you get to the command you want. If you go past it, you can move back down your history list by pressing the down-arrow (or Ctrl-N, for next). This feature is useful and typo-saving! Of course, DOS 6.2 has it too, but who's counting.

Once you have displayed a command from your history list, you can edit it before you press Enter to execute it. Use the left- and right-arrow keys (or Ctrl-B and Ctrl-F for backward and forward) to move the cursor. When you type characters, BASH inserts them on the command line where the cursor is.

The folks at the Free Software Foundation who wrote BASH are big emacs fans (as we are) because you can use most emacs editing commands to edit the command on the command line. For example, Ctrl-A moves your cursor to the beginning of the line, Ctrl-E moves it to the end of the line, Esc-F moves it forward by a word, and so forth. For users who, for some reason, prefer vi to emacs, if you press Esc-Enter, BASH's editor changes to a vi-like editor, where you can press Esc and then use vi command letters such as j and k to move through the list of commands.

The Korn shell throughout history

We don't use the Korn shell much, because we're fond of BASH, but the Korn shell can do history too. The history command lists your history list, as does the more cryptic fc -l command. To repeat the last command, type r and press Enter. That's it — just r. To repeat the last cat command, type

```
r cat
```

To repeat the last command, but replace *96* with *97,* type

```
r 96=97
```

The Korn shell lets you edit your previous commands in all kinds of fancy ways, but it's confusing to do, so we suggest you switch to the BASH shell if you long to edit and reissue commands.

Instant script — just add water

For those of you who know what a shell script is, you can use the history command to create an instant script. (For those of you who don't, read the section, "Stuffing the bin," in Chapter 15 of this book, or read *MORE UNIX For Dummies,* Chapter 4, "An Introduction to Scripts.")

Here's how to use the history command to create a script. Give the commands that you want to include in the script, in the order in which you want them to occur. Then type history to display the list of commands. Note how many of the previous commands you want to include in the scripts, for example, the last eight commands. Type a command like this (for the C shell):

```
history -h 8 >myscript
```

If you use BASH, type this:

```
history 8 > myscript
```

In the Korn shell, type:

```
fc -l 8 > myscript
```

This command lists the last eight commands and stores the list in a file called myscript. It's a good idea to ask for more commands from your history list than you think you need, since you can always delete them from your script. You need to use a text editor to clean up the script anyway, deleting the command numbers and times.

Chapter 8
Where's That File?

*I*t's great to set up lots of different directories so that you can organize your files by topic, program, date, or whatever suits you. But after you have files in all those directories, it is also easy to lose them. Is that budget memo in your `Budget` directory, your `Memos` directory, your `ToDo` directory, Fred's `Budget.Stuff` directory, or somewhere else?

Two programs can help you find files: `find` and `grep`. Alternatively, you can use the `ln` command to create links to your files so that a file can appear in several directories at a time, with that many more opportunities to find it. This chapter offers the UNIX panoply of commands to try when you are looking for a file.

Beating the Bushes

The first approach to finding a lost file is to use the brute-force method. Starting in your home directory, use `ls` to search through each of your directories. In every directory, type the following line:

```
ls important.file
```

Obviously, replace *important.file* with the name of the file you are looking for. If the file is in the current directory, `ls` lists it. If the file isn't there, `ls` complains that it can't find it. This approach can take awhile if you have a lot of directories;

an additional drawback is that you won't find the missing file if it has wandered off to someone else's directory.

If you know — or think you know — that your file is nearby, you can use * (asterisk) wildcards in directory names. (Wildcards are covered in Chapter 7. They let you work with lots of files or directories at once.) To find *important.file* in any of the subdirectories in the working directory, type the following:

```
ls */important.file
```

This technique doesn't work if you have directories within directories; it looks only one level down.

When You Know the Filename

With luck, you know the name of the file you have lost. If so, you can use the find command to find it. When you use find, you tell it the name of the file and the place to start looking. The find command looks in the directory you indicate, and in all that directory's subdirectories.

Suppose that you are working in your home directory. You think that a file called chicken.soup is in there somewhere. Type this line:

```
find . -name chicken.soup -print
```

That is, you type these elements:

- ✔ find (just like you see it here).
- ✔ A space.
- ✔ The directory in which you want the command to begin looking. If it is the working directory, you can type just a period (which means "right here").
- ✔ Another space.
- ✔ -name, to mean that you will specify a filename.
- ✔ Another space.
- ✔ The name of the file you want to find (in this case, chicken.soup).
- ✔ Yet another space.
- ✔ -print, to tell UNIX to print (on-screen) the full name, including the directory name, to let you know where UNIX finds the file. If you omit this step, and find finds the file, it doesn't tell you. (We know that this is pretty stupid, but computers are like that.) If you use UNIX SVR4 or Solaris, you will notice that they fixed up the find command so that it warns you rather than runs the command pointlessly.

Links to shadow files

You may run into a situation in which a file seems to be in several directories at one time (*Twilight Zone* music here, please). DOS users know that this is patently absurd. Surprise! In UNIX, you *can* have a file in several places at the same time. It can even have several different names. It can be mighty useful, in fact, for a file to be in, for example, the home directories of several people at one time so that they all can easily share it.

To achieve this magical feat, you use *links*. We discuss links in the section, "A File by Any Other Name," later in this chapter. In the meantime, don't panic if you see a file lurking around in one place when you're sure that it belongs somewhere else.

The `find` command uses a brute-force approach to locate your file. It checks every file in all your directories; this can take a while. When `find` finds the file, it prints the name and keeps going. If more than one file — in different directories — has the name you gave, `find` finds and reports them all. After `find` has printed a found file, you usually will want to stop the command (unless you think that there is more than one match). Stop `find` by pressing Ctrl-C or Delete.

If the `find` command doesn't work, and you think that the file might be in some other user's directory, type the same `find` command and replace the . (dot) with a / (slash). This version tells `find` to starting looking in the root directory and to search every directory on the disk. As you can imagine, this process can take some time, so try other things first.

When You Know Where to Search

Rather than use a period to tell `find` to begin looking in the current working directory, you can use a pathname. You can type this line, for example:

```
find /usr/margy -name chicken.soup -print
```

This command searches Margy's home directory and all its subdirectories. (Her home directory name may be something different; see Chapter 6.) To search the entire disk, use the slash to represent the root of the directory tree:

```
find / -name chicken.soup -print
```

If your disk is large and full of files, a search from the root directory down can take a long time; as long as half an hour on a very large and busy system.

You can even search several directories. To search both Margy's and John's home directories for files named `white.chocolate.mousse`, for example, type this line:

```
find /usr/margy /usr/johnl -name white.chocolate.mousse -print
```

If you use the Korn, BASH, or C shell, rather than type the home directory name, you can type a tilde and the user name; the shell puts in the correct directory name for you:

```
find ~margy ~johnl -name white.chocolate.mousse -print
```

Well, I Know Part of the Filename

You can use wildcard characters in the filename if you know only part of the filename. Use ? to stand for any single character; use * to stand for any bunch of characters. There is a trick to this, however: If you use * or ? in the filename, you have to put quotation marks around the filename to keep the shell from thinking that you want it to find matching names in only the current directory.

You can search the entire disk for files that start with `budget`, for example, by typing this line:

```
find / -name "budget*" -print
```

If you leave out the quotation marks, the search may look like it worked, but `find` probably hasn't done the job right.

Directory Assistance

You can look for lost directories in addition to lost files. Give the `find` command the option `-type d`, like this:

```
find / -name "Budget*" -type d -print
```

This command searches the entire disk for directories that begin with `Budget`.

Remote Searches

If your system uses NFS (the grandiosely named Network File System, see Chapter 20), some or all of the directories and files on your machine may really be on other computers. The find command doesn't care where files are, and cheerfully searches its way into any directory it can get to. Getting to files over a network is about half as fast as getting to files stored locally, so telling find to look through a lot of files stored on a network can take a long time. Consider having a long lunch while it does its thing.

Suppose that you're looking for Tracy's famous stuffed squid recipe. The obvious way to look for it is with the following line:

```
find ~tracy -name stuffed-squid -print
```

But, if you know that Tracy's files are stored on machine xuxa, the following command can be much faster, because it runs the command on the machine where the files actually are:

```
rsh xuxa "find ~tracy -name stuffed-squid -print"
```

See Chapter 21 for details about the rsh command.

When You Find Them

After you find the file or files you were looking for, you can do more than just look at their names. If you want, you can tell the find command to do something with every file it finds.

Rather than end the find command with the -print option, you can use the -exec option. It tells find to execute a UNIX shell command every time it finds a file. For example:

```
find . -name "report*" -exec lpr {} ";"
```

This command tells the find command to look for files with names beginning with report. Every time it finds such a file, it runs the lpr command and substitutes the name of the file for the { }. (You type two curly braces, which was some nerd's idea of a convenient place holder.) The semicolon indicates the end of the UNIX shell command. (You have to put quotation marks around the semicolon or the shell hijacks it and thinks that you want to begin a new shell command. If that didn't make sense, take our word for it and put quotation marks around the semicolon when you use find.) Every time find finds a filename beginning with report, this command prints the file it found.

You can use almost any UNIX command with the -exec option, so, after you have found your files, you can print, move, erase, or copy them as a group. A slight variation is to use -ok rather than -exec. The -ok option does the same thing except that, before it executes each command, find prints the command it's about to run, followed by a question mark, and waits for you to agree that that would be a good thing to do. Type y if you want to do it, and n if you want it to skip that particular command.

By using find and -exec rm, you can delete many unwanted files in a hurry. But, if you make the smallest mistake, you can delete many important and useful files equally as fast. We don't recommend that you use find and rm together; if you insist, however, please use -ok to limit the damage.

It's Bigger Than a Breadbox . . .

"Hmm . . .I don't remember what the file is called, but I'm looking for a letter I wrote to Tonia, so it should contain her mailing address in the heading . . .that's 1471 Arcadia . . .How do I find it?"

This is a situation for grep — a great command with a terrible name. It stands for, if you can believe it, *g*lobal *r*egular *e*xpression and *p*rint, or some such thing. The grep command looks inside files and searches for a series of characters. Every time it finds a line that contains the specified characters, it displays the line on-screen. If it is looking in more than one file, grep also tells you the name of the file in which the characters occur. You control which files it looks in and which characters it looks for.

There are three grep commands: grep, egrep, and fgrep. They are very similar, so we will just talk about grep. (fgrep is faster but more limited, and egrep is more powerful and more confusing.)

To look in all the files in the working directory (but not in its subdirectories) for the characters 1471 Arcadia, type this line:

```
grep "1471 Arcadia" *
```

That is, type the following elements:

 ✔ grep (just as you see it here).

 ✔ A space.

 ✔ The series of characters to look for (also called the *search string*). If it consists of several words, enclose it in quotation marks so that grep doesn't get confused.

✔ A space.

✔ The names of the files to look in. If you type * here, grep looks in all the files in the current directory.

The grep command responds with a list of the lines it found, like this:

```
ts.doc: 1471 Arcadia Lane
tonia.letter: 1471 Arcadia La.
```

You can do lots of things with grep other than look for files. In fact, we could write entire (small) books about using grep. For our purposes, however, here are some useful options you can use when you use grep to look for files.

If you want just to see the filenames, and you don't want grep to show you the lines it found, use the -l (for *list*) option. (That's a small letter *l,* not a number *1.*) Suppose that you type this line:

```
grep -l "1471 Arcadia" *
```

The grep command responds with just a list of filenames, like this:

```
ts.doc
tonia.letter
```

It might be a good idea to tell grep not to worry about capital and small letters. If you use the -i (for *ignore case*) option, grep doesn't distinguish between uppercase and lowercase letters. For example:

```
grep -i DOS *
```

With this command, grep, which is extremely literal-minded, finds references both to DOS and to some "false hits":

```
fruit.study: salads; in Brazil, avocados are used in desserts.
chapter.26: DOS vs. UNIX
chapter.30: Dos and Don'ts
```

Finally, if you don't know the exact characters that occur in the file, you can use grep's flexible and highly powerful (that is, cryptic and totally confusing) expression-recognition capabilities, known in nerd-speak as *regular expressions.* The grep command has its own set of wildcard characters, sort of but not very much like the ones the shell uses to let you specify all kinds of amazing search strings. If you are a programmer, this can be very useful because you frequently need to find occurrences of rather strange-looking stuff. The reason we mention this is that grep's wildcard characters include many punctuation characters:

```
.  * [ ] ^ $
```

So, if you include any of these characters in a search string, `grep` doesn't do what you expect. To use these characters in a search string, precede them with a backslash. To search for files containing *C.I.A.,* for example, type this line:

```
grep "C\.I\.A\." *
```

Actually, the period (.) is `grep`'s wildcard character, like the question mark (?) in the shell. In this example, if you hadn't preceded the periods with backslashes, `grep` would have matched not only *C.I.A.* but also *CHIFAS* (a Peruvian dialect word meaning *Chinese restaurants,* in case you were wondering) and lots of other things. But don't press your luck — use the backslashes with punctuation marks to be safe.

Searching Is Slow!

Because `grep` and `find` can take a couple minutes to work, you may want to run them in the background (see Chapter 16). To do this, redirect their output to a file so that you can review the results of the search at your leisure; then end the command with an ampersand (&), which tells UNIX to run the command in the background. For example, you can type these two commands:

```
find / -name "budget*" -print > budget.files &
grep "chocolate mousse" * > mousse.recipe.files &
```

Quick 'n' dirty database

You can use `grep` to treat a text file like a quick and dirty database. Using a text editor, for example, you can make a file called `411` with names and phone numbers of your friends and associates, with one entry per line, like this:

```
Jordan Young, 555-4673
Meg Young, 555-5485
Zac Young, 554-8649
```

To look up someone's phone number, type:

```
grep Meg 411
```

The `grep` command displays the line or lines of the file with the name or names you asked for.

The `grep` command is used by UNIX enthusiasts to search all kinds of files for all kinds of information. As long as each item fits on one line, you can keep all sorts of data in this kind of cheap database file. One of our favorite files is called `restaurants` and has lines that look like this:

```
Chef Chung's Cheap 555-3864
```

So, if in the mood for something cheap, type

```
grep -i cheap restaurants
```

When the jobs end, type the following to see what the commands found:

```
cat budget.files
cat mousse.recipe.files
```

A File by Any Other Name

Sometimes it's nice for a file to be in more than one place. If you were working on it with someone else, it would be nice if it could be in both your home directory and your coworker's home directory; neither of you would have to use the cd command to get to it. A nice feature of UNIX (and you thought there weren't any) is that this is possible — even easy. A single file can have more than one name, and the names can be in different directories.

Take, for example, two authors working on a book together (a totally hypothetical example). The chapters are in John's directory: /usr/johnl/book. But what about Margy? It's annoying to have to type the following line every time work on the book begins:

```
cd /usr/johnl/book
```

Instead, it would be nice if the files could also be in /usr/margy/book.

How can you be in two places at once?

The way to do this is with the ln (for *link*) command. You tell ln two things:

✔ The current name of the file or files you want to create links to.

✔ The new name.

Margy wants to make a link to the file named chapterlog (the list of chapters). The file is in /usr/johnl/book. In her book directory, Margy types

```
ln /usr/johnl/book/chapterlog booklog
```

UNIX says absolutely nothing; it just displays another prompt. (No news is good news.) But it just created a *link,* or new name, to the existing chapterlog file. The file now appears also in /usr/margy/book as booklog.

After you create a link by using ln, the file has two names in two directories. The names are equally valid. It isn't as though /usr/johnl/book/chapterlog is the "real" name and /usr/margy/book/booklog is an alias. UNIX considers both names to be equally important links to the file.

How to delete links

To delete a link, you use the same `rm` command you use to delete a file. In fact, `rm` always just deletes a link. It just so happens that, when there are no links to a file, the file dries up and blows away. So when you `rm` a file that has just one name (link), the file gets deleted. When you `rm` a file that has more than one name (link), the command deletes the specified link (name), but the file remains unchanged, along with any other links it may have had.

How to call a link a lunk

You can use the old `mv` command to rename a link too. If Margy decides that it would be less confusing for the book-status file to have the same name in both places (as it stands now, it's `chapterlog` to John and `booklog` to Margy), she can type this line to change the name:

```
mv booklog chapterlog
```

You can even use the `mv` command to move the file to another directory.

How to link a bunch of files

You can also use `ln` to link a bunch of files at the same time. In this case, you tell `ln` two things:

- ✔ The bunch of files you want to link, probably using a wildcard character like `chapter*`. You can also type a series of filenames or a combination of names and patterns. (UNIX may be obscure, but it's flexible.)
- ✔ The name of the directory in which you want to put all the new links.

The `ln` command uses the same names that the files currently have when it makes the new links. It just puts them in a different directory.

The `chapterlog` business in the preceding example, for example, works so well that Margy decides to link to all the files in `/usr/johnl/book`. To make links in `/usr/margy/book`, she types this line:

```
ln /usr/johnl/book/* /usr/margy/book
```

This command tells UNIX to create links for all the files in `/usr/johnl/book` and to put the new links in `/usr/margy/book`. Now every file that exists in `/usr/johnl/book` also exists in `/usr/margy/book`. Margy uses the `ls` command to look at a file listing for her new `book` directory. It contains all the book files. This arrangement makes working on the files much more convenient.

Linking once and linking twice

Here's one caveat, though. The ln command in the previous example links all the files that exist at the time the command was given. If you add new files to either /usr/margy/book or /usr/john1/book, the new files are not automatically linked to the other directory. To fix this, you can type the same ln command every few days (or whatever frequency makes sense). The command tells you that lots of files are already identical in the two directories and makes links for the new files.

If you have linked to someone else's files, you may have permission to read those files but not to change or write to them. When you ask ln to make the new links, if it tries to replace a file you couldn't write to, it says something like this:

```
ln: chapter13: 644 mode?
```

See Chapter 25 for the exact meaning of this uniquely obscure message. Type y if you want to replace the file, which you probably do in this case, or n if you don't.

How to link across the great computer divide

All this talk about links assumes that the files you are linking to are on the same file system (that's UNIX-speak for *disk* or *disk partition*). If your computer has several hard disks, or if you are on a network and use files on other computers (through NFS or some other system, as explained in Chapter 20), some of the files you work with may be on different file systems.

Here's the bad news: The ln command can't create links to files on other file systems. Bummer. But there's good news for some readers: Linux, BSD, and SVR4 systems (that is, anything except older AT&T-ish systems) have things called soft links or symbolic links (symlinks for short) that are almost as good. *Soft links* let you use two or more different names for the same file. But, unlike regular links (or *hard links*), soft links are just imitation links. UNIX doesn't consider them to be the file's real name.

Making soft links (for users of Linux, UNIX BSD, and SVR4 only)

To make a soft link, add the -s option to the ln command.

Suppose that you want a link in your home directory to the recipe.list file in /usr/gita. In your home directory, you type this line:

```
ln /usr/gita/recipe.list gitas.recipes
```

Rather than respond with serene silence, UNIX responds with this line:

```
ln: different file system
```

Drat! Gita's home directory is on a different file system, perhaps even on a different computer. So you make a soft link by sticking a -s into the command:

```
ln -s /usr/gita/recipe.list gitas.recipes
```

No news is good news; ln says nothing if it worked. Now there is a file in your home directory called gitas.recipes. All through the magic of soft links.

Using soft links (for users of Linux, UNIX BSD, and SVR4 only)

You can look at, copy, print, and rename a soft-linked file as usual. If you have the proper permissions, you can edit it. But, if Gita deletes her file, the file vanishes. Your soft link now links to an empty hole rather than to a file, and you get an error message if you try to use the file. UNIX knows that the soft link isn't the file's "real" name. When you see a soft link in a long ls listing, UNIX gives the name of the soft link and also the name of the file it refers to.

If you try to use a file, and UNIX says it isn't there, check to see whether it's a dangling soft link. Type ls -l to see whether the file is a soft link. If it is, use another ls -l on the real filename to make sure that the file really exists. To get rid of a dangling soft link (a link to a nonexistent file), use the rm command to delete it.

Chapter 9

If I Wanted Hardware, I'd Go to the Hardware Store!

In This Chapter

▶ Parts of your computer and impressive nerdy terms that describe them

▶ Memories (thanks, and no thanks therefore)

▶ How to put disks into your computer and take them out

▶ Likewise for tapes

▶ Some other not-very-interesting parts of your computer

*T*his chapter talks about your *hardware* — well, actually, your *computer's* hardware. Hardware is all the stuff sitting around on your desk, or under your desk — the stuff related to your computer, that is. If you know all you want to know about this stuff, just skip this chapter. But if you are curious about what all these boxes and wires are, read on.

We're, by necessity, a little vague in this chapter (as though the rest of the book isn't) because UNIX runs on a huge variety of computers, from enormous multimillion-dollar IBM mainframes and Cray supercomputers to itty-bitty notebook-style portables about the same size as this book (but without the snazzy yellow-and-black cover). Fortunately, because all these computers have much more in common than you might expect, we forge ahead with a description of a generic UNIX computer.

Meet Mr. Computer

In all but the smallest computers, you can distinguish easily between the computer and the various pieces of attached equipment, known as *peripherals*. All the parts of the system that might be of some use to a human being, such as the keyboard, screen, mouse, and printer, are peripherals. The computer itself these days is just a boring box with maybe one light on it to show when it's turned on and a lot of wires coming out the back. People have different fancy names for the computer, like the *system unit*. A simple rule of thumb is that the part of the system that costs the most is probably the computer itself.

Storage devices, like disks and tapes, also are considered peripherals even though in smaller computers they're usually mounted inside the computer box.

Back in the good old days, the front of the computer had an attractive array of blinking lights. These lights told technicians what was going on and impressed people with what extremely important stuff the computer was doing. For an example of this, watch the old movie *Desk Set,* with Katherine Hepburn and Spencer Tracy. Kate believes that she's going to be replaced by a new computer, installed by Spencer, but she's not, of course, and gets to keep both her job and Spencer. The computer turns out to be a friendly ol' hunk of metal that would never put anyone out of a job, no way. The part of the computer is played by a 1950s IBM computer (IBM was never shy about getting publicity) that figures prominently in many scenes; the computer has a large panel several feet across, chock-full of impressive blinking lights. It didn't run UNIX, though, because UNIX wouldn't be written for another 15 years, so never mind.

Since the 1970s, the price of computer components has dropped so much that a humorless bean-counting bookkeeper discovered that the lights had become the most expensive part of the computer, so out they went. What a shame.

One Chip, Two Chips, Red Chip, Blue Chip

The heart of any computer is the central processing unit, or *CPU*. Nowadays, in all but the largest computers, the CPU is a single microchip (a little, plastic package that looks sort of like a robot built by centipedes). The kind of chip it has determines the computer's personality, such as it is.

Most CPU chips are named by using numbers, such as 80486 and 68000, while others have names, such as Pentium and Power PC. Technical people get into many arguments about the relative merits of different processor chips, but we'll let you in on a secret: They're all the same. That's right, the differences among the different chips are so nerdy that you don't care. The very largest machines, such as mainframes and supercomputers, haven't yet been squeezed into single chips, so this discussion doesn't apply to those very large machines.

TECHNICAL STUFF

Why RAM?

RAM stands for *random-access memory* because the CPU can fetch any particular piece of data stored there equally fast. Now you know. A long time ago, RAM was built from teensy little metal doughnuts called *cores,* so some hard-core nerds may still refer to something stored in RAM as being "in core."

Memory Lane

The other key component your computer needs, in addition to a CPU, is main memory, or *RAM*. Lots of main memory. The more, the better. Main memory is where the computer puts the programs and data it is working on now. Less urgent data goes on the disk (discussed later in this chapter). The contents of main memory evaporate when the power goes off; one of many reasons to be sure that everything is saved properly before you shut off your computer.

How much memory is enough?

Memory is measured in things called *bytes* (pronounced "bites"), as in "This here memory really bytes." Each byte is enough to store one letter, so the word *ketchup* takes seven bytes. A typed page of text is about 2,000 characters, so storing it takes about 2,000 bytes of memory. Memory sizes are measured in K, which stands for *kilobytes,* or about 1,000 bytes; M, or MB, which stands for *megabytes,* is about a million bytes; and G, or GB, which stands for *gigabytes* (sounds sort of like "giggle"), is about a billion bytes, which is a lot.

Actually, 1K is a little more than 1,000 bytes; it's 1,024 bytes, which happens to be an easy number to handle in a computer's internal binary code. A megabyte is 1K times 1K, which works out to 1,048,576 bytes; a gigabyte is 1K times 1K times 1K, which (as though you care) is exactly 1,073,741,824 bytes.

The earliest versions of UNIX used moderate amounts of RAM; one version needed only about 50K. As people have stuffed features into UNIX, its memory appetite has grown so that these days you can't even begin to run UNIX with less than 2 megabytes; many workstations have 100 megabytes or more of RAM.

More memory than I really have

UNIX also uses something called *virtual memory,* which enables you to run very large programs in small amounts of memory (although perhaps not as fast as you want). You may be familiar with other computers in which, for example, a 640K program won't run in a 512K computer. By using virtual memory, UNIX avoids that problem; although having extra RAM makes your computer faster, having less RAM doesn't prevent you from running large programs.

In reality, a program that has insufficient memory can slow down so much that it would have been a kindness if it hadn't bothered to run. We used to have a program that normally took about five seconds to start up, but when we tried to run it on a computer with a lot less RAM, it took 15 minutes to start. If your computer doesn't have enough RAM, you will know — it feels like someone poured a jar of molasses into it.

Every kind of computer has a maximum amount of RAM that can be installed. For PCs, the maximum may be as low as 8MB; for mainframes (big computers), it may be 1,000MB or more. For microcomputers and minicomputers — as long as you haven't reached the memory limit — it's technically straightforward for your system administrator to add more RAM (the hardest part is getting someone to pay for it). If your computer is chronically too slow, a RAM boost is usually the best way to fix it.

A Disk-usting Disk-ussion

The other kind of memory in UNIX computers is *secondary memory*. IBM calls the things that provide secondary memory *direct-access storage devices,* with the unpronounceable acronym DASD. (Maybe "dazz-dee"? Sounds like a diaper service.) The rest of us call them *disks* because that's what they are. There are two general kinds of disks: removable disks and permanently mounted disks.

Disks to go

Removable disks come in many varieties. They are called removable because (drum roll, please) you can take the disk out of the drive. They sometimes are also called *floppy disks* or *diskettes,* especially by PC and Macintosh users. CD-ROMs, which look like the CDs that you play in your stereo, can store lots more information than diskettes can, but you can't change what's on them.

Diskettes are used primarily for moving information from one computer to another. UNIX software is often distributed on CD-ROMs.

If your UNIX machine uses diskettes or CD-ROMs, you should warn UNIX before taking a disk out of its drive. To get the disk out, first wait for the computer to finish with the disk; that is, wait until the light on the disk unit is off and the disk unit stops humming. For some kinds of UNIX, before you can take the disk out, you must give an "unmount" command to tell the system to finish writing all its updated information to the disk.

Some CD-ROM drives can also play music CDs, which is usually the real reason that people want these kinds of players on their workstations. Music can make you much more productive when you are using a computer. At least, it can make you less destructive; you're unlikely to throw the thing out the window in annoyance while you are singing along to "Hound Dog."

TECHNICAL STUFF

Disregard this hopelessly technoid discussion of virtual memory

The way virtual memory works is, in principle, very simple. (Paying off the national debt is, in principle, very simple, too.) Every running program is divided into 4K chunks, called *pages*. At any given moment, the program really uses only a small fraction of the pages it has been assigned. UNIX copies to the disk all the pages of memory that haven't been used lately and removes them from RAM. If the program later needs one of the pages out on the disk, the program freezes, UNIX quickly scurries around and finds some other unused page in RAM, copies the page to the disk, drags the newly needed page back into RAM, and lets the program continue. Amazingly, this entire shell game takes only about a tenth of a second. As long as this process doesn't happen often, the program runs *virtually* (that word) as though all its pages were really in RAM. The more pages that really *are* in RAM, of course, the less often the shell game is required and the faster the program runs.

I-never-get-to-go-anywhere disk storage

Most of the data in your computer is stored on *permanently mounted* (fixed) *disks*. Fixed disks range in size from Maytag-size down to some nearly as small as matchboxes. The most common models are about the same size as a telephone. They don't look like disks; they look like metal boxes. The disks are permanently mounted inside the metal boxes, but we still call them disks.

The amount of data you can store on a fixed disk ranges from 80MB up to about 20GB for the largest models attached to mainframes. Sometimes the disk is mounted physically inside the computer. If there isn't enough space inside the computer box, the disk goes in a separate shoebox-sized case. (Computer wonks call these cases *shoeboxes*. Are they creative or what?)

Because fixed disks are permanently sealed at the factory, there isn't much you can do to break one, other than to drop it off a table. Most people put shoebox cases on the floor, forestalling this problem.

That disk doesn't look so scuzzy to me

You may hear people talking about *scuzzy disks.* This doesn't mean that the disks need to go in the dishwasher. It means Small Computer Systems Interface, abbreviated SCSI and pronounced *scuzzy,* except in certain parts of California where they pronounce it *sexy.* Hmmmm.

SCSI defines some rules for the way disks and tapes and computers plug together, so if you take any SCSI-compatible disk or tape and plug it into a computer with a SCSI connector on the back (most workstations, many PC clones, and most Macs have these connectors), it will in all likelihood work. This is an astonishing degree of compatibility for the computer industry, so you'll be relieved to hear that committees are hard at work on mutant versions of SCSI with names like *SCSI-2* and *Fast and Wide SCSI.* There will soon be plenty of opportunity for things not to work.

In the meantime, the fact that all SCSI disks are pretty much interchangeable has made the disk market very competitive; disk prices get significantly cheaper from one month to the next.

Don't Scotch That Tape

One problem with permanently mounted disks is that if one breaks, the information on the disk is permanently gone. This is why people make backup copies of data that is on the fixed disk, as insurance against a disaster of unthinkable proportions. Although you could, in principle, make backup copies of the fixed disk onto floppy disks, a typical 300MB fixed disk would take 300 floppies; it's hard to find people willing to sit around and feed 300 disks into a computer.

Tapes largely solve this problem. Computer tapes come in various sizes. The most common tape comes in a plastic cartridge about the same size as an old eight-track tape. (Remember them?) There are also smaller tapes a little bigger than a cassette. The big old reels of tape you may remember from old movies are almost completely obsolete because cartridge tapes hold more stuff and cost a lot less.

Tape capacities range from 20MB for the oldest varieties to 10GB for the newest kind of cassette-style variety. The tape units are quite small; if you have a shoebox containing a fixed disk, it probably also contains a tape unit.

If you're lucky, you'll have a diligent System Administrator who arranges to copy all the system's data to backup tapes every night. If this is true, in a disaster you'll never lose more than one day's work. Most of us are not so lucky, however, and you may have to do some of your own backing up.

Backup procedures are, wildly inconsistent from one system to another. Ask a local Wizard to write you a little two-line program that copies all your files to a backup tape, something the Wizard can probably do in about a minute and a half. Then have your expert walk you through putting the tape into the tape unit, running the program, taking the tape out, and putting it on the shelf. Back up your data *every single day* before you go home. You'll be glad you did. It's not a bad idea to ask the Wizard for help in getting a file or two from the backup tape, just to be sure that you have all the stuff on the tape you think you do.

Many people think that backing up all that data is a pain. It's true, it is. Of course, you have to compare that to the pain you're going to feel when your disk breaks and all your data disappears. We can tell you from experience that there are few smug grins quite as smug as the one you'll grin when your disk breaks, and you know that all your precious stuff is safe on tape on the shelf.

For a stern lecture on backups and more information about how to make them, see Chapter 23.

Swinging from the Net

Most UNIX systems are attached to networks. *Networks* are highly sophisticated electronic communication facilities through which you can exchange gossip, innuendo, rumors, lies, slander, and other important information with your coworkers. Even if you have no personal interest in the network, you'll probably have to learn something about it because, in many cases, the disks that contain your files are in fact on some computer somewhere else on the network. Without the network, your computer will get a severe case of amnesia. You may also want to use the network's electronic mail program. We talk more about networks and files in Chapter 20, but here are a few helpful network tips.

Your friendly neighborhood network

Networks that connect a bunch of computers in the same building, or nearby buildings, are called *local area networks,* or *LANs.* The most common kind of LAN is something called *Ethernet.* Ethernet lets you connect together an almost unlimited number of computers, including both UNIX and non-UNIX computers. Computers on the Ethernet can share files on each other's disks and print things on each other's printers. You can have computers with super-big disks (*file servers*) so everyone can store files there. You can have computers with fancy, expensive printers so everyone can print their resumes out in the evenings with the highest possible print quality (these computers are called *print servers*). And you can have plain old computers like the one on your desk that are used to get work done. All the computers on the network are called *nodes.* (Don't you love all this fancy tech talk?)

The great thing about networks is you can share expensive disks and printers, share files, and send and receive electronic mail (see Chapter 19 for how). The bad thing about networks is that if someone kicks a network connector out of a socket in a cubicle on the other side of the building, you can't get any work done until they fix it. Centralization, as always, has its drawbacks.

We'll talk about finding out who is on your network in Chapter 18, using e-mail in Chapter 19, and sharing files over the network in Chapter 20.

The information supercollider

The other kind of network your computer may be connected to is the Internet. The Internet is a vast, worldwide collection of networks that are all connected together. If your computer is on the Internet, you have access to an unimaginable array of information: free software, searchable libraries, multimedia pages of data, ongoing discussions on thousands of different topics — you name it. So much for getting any useful work done!

We talk a bit about finding out who's out there in Chapter 18 and sending e-mail to the Internet in Chapter 19. For more information about surfing the Net (as they say in the lingo), see *The Internet For Dummies* and *Internet Secrets,* as well as *More UNIX For Dummies,* which has a bunch of chapters on the topic.

Getting wired

If the network fails (you can tell when this happens because your computer largely freezes up and starts mumbling incomprehensible complaints about network servers not responding), the most likely problem is that the network wire has come unhooked from the computer.

Look at the back of your computer. If the Ethernet cable has come unhooked, you can plug it back in.

(Unlike practically every other part of the computer, networks are designed so that computers can be plugged and unplugged into the network while they are running. Wow!)

If replugging or wiggling the network connector doesn't help, you're out of luck and will have to call for help.

Chapter 10
Printing (the Gutenberg Thing)

● ●

● ●

*U*nless you happen to work in the paperless office of the future (reputed to be down the hall from the paperless bathroom of the future), from time to time you will want to print stuff. The good news is that it's usually easy to do so. The bad news is that nothing is as easy as it should be.

The major extra complication is that the way to print things is different on UNIX BSD and System V systems. (Remember which one you have? Refer to Chapter 2 if you don't. You may have written it on the Cheat Sheet in the front of the book.) We start by explaining how you print something already in a file; then we go on to the fancy stuff.

There's a Daemon in System V

If you use UNIX System V, the way you print stuff is, in theory, simplicity itself: You use the lp command. If you have a file called myletter, for example, you print it by typing this line:

```
lp myletter
```

UNIX responds with this important information:

```
request id is dj-2613 (1 file)
```

Usually, this is all you need to do. UNIX responds to your request by telling you the request ID of the print job, which you probably don't care about. Sometimes you will want to pretty up the way the printout looks by leaving wider margins; we talk about that later in this chapter.

The lp command doesn't print the file. That would be much too simple. What it does is leave a note for another program buried deep inside UNIX, and this buried program prints your file. The theory behind this arrangement is that a bunch of people may want to use the printer, and it'd be a pain if you had to wait for the printer to be free. So lp puts your file on a list; the other program (called a *daemon,* pronounced "demon") runs down the list and does the printing so you don't have to wait. The *request ID* is the name lp gives to the note it leaves for the daemon. You can ignore it unless you change your mind and decide that you don't want to print that file after all.

More Daemons in BSD and Linux

If you use Linux or BSD UNIX, printing is just as easy as printing with System V, except that you use the command lpr rather than lp. If you have a file called myletter, for example, you print it by typing this line:

```
lpr myletter
```

Some systems, notably SVR4 and Solaris, have both the lp and lpr commands. If you have these versions of UNIX, either command should work equally well. Notice that the lpr command doesn't report a request ID.

Finding Your Printout

As far as UNIX is concerned, its only job is to send your file to the printer. Now the real work begins: finding your printout.

If your UNIX system is attached to a network, chances are your printer is attached to some other computer than your own. This means you may have to go looking for it to find your printouts.

You may have to ask people in nearby cubicles, or stand very still in the center of the office and listen for the sound of printing (a gentle whir and click from most laser printers). If all else fails, ask your system administrator. Your UNIX system may use more than one printer, so your system administrator may be the only person who can tell you which printer your printout is on.

Printers, printers everywhere

A reasonably large installation probably has several printers, because there's too much work for one printer or because there are different kinds of printers. When you use the lp or lpr command, UNIX picks one printer as the default. If you use lp, you use the -d option (that's a lowercase *d* — remember that UNIX cares about these things) to identify the printer. To print your file on a printer called draft, for example, you type this line:

```
lp -ddraft myletter
```

If you use lpr, the analogous option is -P (that's a capital *P*):

```
lpr -Pdraft myletter
```

In either case, don't type a space between the -d or -P and the printer name.

Calling all printers

The list of available printers depends entirely on the whims of the system administrator. Typically, one day she gets tired of putting up with the slow, illegible, or chronically broken previous printer, storms into the boss's office, gets the necessary signature, and buys the first printer available. Sometimes the old printer is thrown away, sometimes not.

It's generally not too difficult to get a list of printers known to the system. If you use the lp command to print, type this line to get a list of available printers:

```
lpstat -a all
```

This line means roughly, "Show me the status of all active printers." The lpstat program lists the status of all available printers, one per line, like this:

```
dj accepting requests since Thu Apr 25 13:43:50 1991
```

In this case, there is only one printer; its name is dj. The listing also shows the vital fact that it was installed on a Thursday afternoon in April, 1991. Whoopee.

If you use the lpr command to print, try typing this line to get the same information (unfortunately, not all versions of lpq support this):

```
lpq -a
```

With luck, the lpq program responds with a similar list, like this:

```
lp:
Rank      Owner     Job       Files          Total Size
1st       john1     7         longletter     4615 bytes
ps:
no entries
```

The lpq command stands for something like *l*ine *p*rinter *q*uery, and -a means *a*ll printers. In this case, there are two printers, named lp and ps, and something is printing on the first one.

Keep in mind that not every printer that the lpstat and lpq commands report is usable. Frequently, system administrators put in the table of printers some test entries that don't really represent printers you can use.

Help! I've Printed, and It Won't Shut Up

The first time you print something large, you suddenly will realize you don't want to print the file because you have found a horrible mistake on the first page. Fortunately, you can easily tell UNIX that you have changed your mind.

If you tell UNIX to print a file that does not contain text, such as a file that contains a program or a database, in most cases UNIX prints it anyway. In a classic example of Murphy's Law (anything that can go wrong, will go wrong), files like that tend to print about 12 random letters on each of 400 pages. Every page has just enough junk on it so that you can't use it again. As you might expect, people who print a lot of files like that tend to become unpopular, particularly with coworkers whose 2-page memos are in line behind the 400 pages of junk.

Cancel the order, System V

If you used lp to print the file in the first place, you use cancel (we don't know how that name slipped past the lazy typists) to cancel the print job. You have to give the cancel command the request ID that lp assigned to the job. If you're lucky, the lp command is still on your screen, and you can see the request ID. If that information has vanished from your screen, remain calm. Remember that the lpstat command lists all the requests that are waiting for the printer, displaying a list like this:

```
dj-2620              john1            34895    Dec 23 21:12 on dj
```

This list tells you that your request was named dj-2620, that is was done on behalf of a user named john1, that the size of the file to be printed is 34895, and that the print command was given on December 23. You can cancel the request with the following command:

```
cancel dj-2620
```

UNIX responds with the following line:

```
request "dj-2620" cancelled
```

Woodsman, spare that file!

When you tell UNIX to print a file, the file doesn't print immediately. UNIX makes a note to print the file and remembers its filename.

What if you delete the file before UNIX has a chance to print it? If you print with `lp`, you get a nasty message because UNIX can't find the file. If you print with `lpr`, the file is printed normally because UNIX makes a copy of the material to print.

To force `lp` to copy the file, use the `<` command-line operator. To send a copy of the file `myfile` to the printer, for example, type this line:

```
lp < myfile
```

You can then delete or change `myfile` and not affect the printout.

If you're printing a large file, `lpr` can take awhile to make a copy of the file (which it doesn't really need to do because it's already in a file in the first place, isn't it). You can use `lpr -s` to tell UNIX to print from the original file to save time and disk space. If you use the `-s` option, be sure not to delete or change the file until it's printed.

You can tell `lpr` to delete the file when it has finished printing it. This capability is sometimes useful when you made the file in the first place only so that you could print it. Use the `-r` option to remove the file after printing:

```
lpr -r myfile
```

For large files, you can use `-r` and `-s` together:

```
lpr -s -r myfile
```

UNIX has a surprisingly convenient (surprising for UNIX, anyway) shortcut you can use. If you give the name of a printer, UNIX cancels whatever is printing on that printer. If you remember that the local printer is called `dj`, you can type this line to cancel whatever `dj` is printing:

```
cancel dj
```

Cancel the order, Linux (or BSD)

If you made your printing mistake with the `lpr` command, you use `lpq` to find out the request ID, which — to add confusion — is called a *job number*.

UNIX responds with a list of print jobs:

```
Rank    Owner       Job  Files                    Total Size
1st     johnl       12   blurfle                  34895 bytes
```

You need to note the job number (12, in this case). Use that number with the `lprm` command, which, despite its name, removes the request to print something and not the printer itself:

```
lprm 12
```

The lprm command usually reports back something about "dequeued" lines; this information is meant to be reassuring, although it's not clear to whom. In response to the lprm 12 command, for example, UNIX displays this message:

```
dfB012iecc dequeued
cfA012iecc dequeued
```

Some final words about stopping the printer

Most printers have something called an *internal buffer* in which data to be printed resides before the printer prints it. An internal buffer is good and bad: It's good because it keeps the printer from stopping and starting if the computer is a little slow in passing your file to it; it's bad because, after data is in the buffer, there's no way the computer can get it back. So, even after you cancel something you want to print, some of it may still be in the buffer — as much as 2 pages of normal text or about 20 pages of the junk that results from printing a non-text file.

There's no easy way to keep from printing the stuff in the printer buffer. One really bad idea is to turn the printer off in the middle of a page. This method tends to get the paper stuck and, on laser printers, lets loose a bunch of black, smeary stuff that gets all over your hands and on the next 1,000 pages the printer prints. If you insist, push the printer's Stop or Off-Line button and wait for the paper to stop moving; then you can turn the printer off relatively safely.

After your print request is canceled, the printer probably still has half a page of your failed file waiting to print. You can eject that page by pushing a button on the printer labeled something like Form Feed or Print/Check or even Reset.

Prettying Up Your Printouts

If you send a file full of plain text to the printer, the result can look ugly: no margins, titles, or anything else. You can use the pr command to make your file look nicer. Use it only with plain text files, not with PostScript files, document files from a word processor, or files from a desktop publishing program.

Titles and page numbers make your printouts look much more official

The simplest thing you can do with the pr command is to add titles and page numbers to your printout. By default, the title is the filename and the date and time it was last changed. You can use a pipe (defined in Chapter 7 as the vertical bar, |) to format with pr and print in a single line:

```
pr myfile | lpr
```

(Remember to use the lp command rather than lpr, if appropriate.) This command tells the pr program to pretty up the file and to pass the results to the lpr program.

You can set your own heading by using the -h option with the pr command:

```
pr -h "My Deepest Thoughts" myfile | lpr
```

The pr command assumes that printer pages are 66 lines long. If that's not true for you, instead of the title appearing at the top of every page, it sort of oozes down from page to page. You can override the standard page length with the -l. For example, if the page length is 60 lines, you type

```
pr -l60 myfile | lpr
```

Why you don't want to know about PostScript

You may have what's known as a PostScript printer. There are two general camps of laser-printer design: the Hewlett-Packard camp and the PostScript camp. Hewlett-Packard-type printers just print whatever text is sent to them, but PostScript printers expect to get a program written in a PostScript programming language that tells them exactly what to print. If you want to print a page of text on a PostScript printer, you send with the text a program that tells the printer what fonts, lines, boxes, margins, and other printer-type stuff to use.

PostScript has two problems that may bite you. The first is sending a regular file to a PostScript printer. Usually, UNIX printer software is smart enough to figure out automatically that it send along a PostScript program with the file to tell the printer to print it. If the printer software is not that smart, another program can do the PostScriptization. Adobe, the originator of PostScript, sells a widely used package called Transcript; Transcript includes a program called enscript that prints plain files. If the plain lp or lpr command doesn't work, try using the enscript command before you run for help.

The other problem you may encounter is that a file contains PostScript but prints like a regular file. PostScript files look like incomprehensible programs written in an obscure programming language, because that's what they are. The tip-off is that the first two letters on the first line are %!. To see what the file is supposed to look like, you must send it to a PostScript printer that can run the program in the file and print whatever the file contains. If you print the PostScript program instead, most likely you're sending the file to a printer that doesn't speak PostScript.

Lacking a PostScript printer, you still may not be out of luck. A program from the Free Software Foundation called Ghostscript can read PostScript files and translate them into something that your local printer can print. We discuss Ghostscript later in this chapter. Ghostscript also has a cousin called Ghostview which lets you preview PostScript documents on the screen.

To use pr and not have any heading at the top of the page, use the -t option:

```
pr -t myfile | lpr
```

(This example doesn't do anything interesting to myfile; later, though, you will see that it really is useful when you combine with the margins and stuff.)

Marginally yours

You may frequently put printouts in three-ring binders. Normally, because printing starts very close to the left side of the page, the hole punch may put holes in your text and make the page difficult to read — not to mention look stupid. The -o option (that's a lowercase letter *o*, for *offset*, not a zero) pushes the stuff you print to the right, leaving a left margin. To leave five spaces for a left margin, for example, type the following command:

```
pr -o5 myfile | lpr
```

Sometimes it's nice to leave a wider margin at the bottom of the page. You can do that by combining the -l option (described in the preceding section to set a page length) with the -f option that tells pr to use a special *form-feed character* to make the printer start a new page *now*! (Normally, the -l option uses blank lines to space to the next page, like a typewriter.)

```
pr -o5 -l50 -f myfile | lpr
```

This command tells UNIX to print just 50 lines per page, indented 5 spaces. That should be enough space in the margin for anyone.

Seeing double

The -d option tells pr to double-space the printout:

```
pr -d myfile | lpr
```

This command also puts a title on every page; use -d -t to avoid that:

```
pr -d -t myfile | lpr
```

One column can't contain me

If the lines in your file are short, you can save paper by printing in multiple columns. To print your file in two columns, for example, type the following:

```
pr -2 myfile | lpr
```

Astute readers probably can guess what the options -3, -4, and up to -9 do. (If you're not feeling that astute today, these options specify the number of columns you want.) Columns normally run down the page, as they do in newspapers. If your file contains a list of items, one per line, and you want to print them in columns, you may want to change the order in which the lines print. If you want to print items across the page, then move down to the next line, and so on (which is nowhere near as cool), and use the -a option in addition to the -2 or -3 option.

For a truly baffling effect, you can arrange to print several files side by side with the -m option:

```
pr -m firstfile secondfile | lpr
```

This command prints the first line of every file on the first line of the printout, the second line of every file on the second line, and so on. You can specify as many as nine filenames and have them print side-by-side in skinny little columns. We never have been able to figure out much of a use for this option, but it is definitely a way to produce really odd printouts.

Seeing Ghosts

Earlier in this chapter we talked about PostScript, the fabulously complicated printer language that lets you print fabulously complex documents on PostScript printers. But what if you don't have a PostScript printer?

These days, the short answer is "Get one." PostScript printers used to cost a lot more than other printers, but you can now buy a perfectly decent PostScript laser printer for under $1,000. Nonetheless, there are still lots of PostScript-free sites, where Ghostscript comes to the rescue.

Ghostscript is a free GNU (see "What's GNU?" in Chapter 2) version of PostScript, written by L. Peter Deutsch, a very skillful programmer from way back who surely should have been doing something else when he wrote it.

When Ghostscript runs, it reads its PostScript input either from a file or from the keyboard (not very useful unless you're trying to learn PostScript), and produces its output on one of a zillion possible output devices. If you want to see what the PostScript document looks like, you can tell it to send its output to an X Window System window, and if you want to print the document, you can send its output to your printer.

The default place for Ghostscript to send its output is to an X Window, although there's a nicer program called Ghostview that makes on-screen Ghostscript easier to deal with.

If you're lucky, your system manager will have installed Ghostscript so it's semi-automatically called when you print a PostScript file. You typically use the -v flag, something like this:

```
lpr -v floogle.ps
```

Failing that, to run Ghostscript, type its name, gs, and the name of the PostScript file to display:

```
gs floogle.ps
```

If you just type that, Ghostscript will open a new X Window and display the first page of floogle in that window, probably not what you want. Press Ctrl-C once or twice to stop it. To get Ghostscript to do something useful, you need to use switches. Lots and lots of switches:

```
gs -sDEVICE=deskjet -dNOPAUSE -sOutputFile=floogle.lj floogle.ps quit.ps
```

What's going on here is that we set the output device (DEVICE) to *deskjet,* a popular inkjet printer, we tell it not to pause between pages, we tell it what output file to create, then tell it the PostScript file to print, and then give it another file from the Ghostscript library (quit.ps) which contains a one-line command telling Ghostscript that it's done. You can tailor this as needed; run gs -h to see the available printers.

We expect that you'll find this all a wee bit complicated. In practice, unless your system manager has set up Ghostscript to run automatically, your best bet is to find a local expert who can tell you the exact command to use. Lacking an expert, you can still look at PostScript on the screen by using Ghostview.

Part III
Of Mice and Computers

The 5th Wave   By Rich Tennant

"Here at MIC, leaders in OEM, it's SOP to wish a happy retirement to a great MIS like Douglas U. Hodges, or DUH, as we came to know him."

In this part...

*I*t's a new world here in UNIX-land! You may have to deal with a GUI (graphical user interface), a mouse, and cute little icons, which can be almost as cryptic as the commands they are designed to replace.

This part explains the newfangled concepts using the GUIs and tells you how to use the most popular UNIX GUI — Motif.

Chapter 11
I'd Rather Be GUI Than a WIMP

*T*o answer your first question, GUI stands for *graphical user interface* and really *is* pronounced "gooey." We prefer the term WIMP, which stands for *windows, icons,* and *mouse pointing,* but for some reason the term never caught on. Fast-track executives would rather be gooey than wimps, we suppose.

A GUI combines a graphics screen (one that can show pictures in addition to text), a mouse, and a system that divides the screen into several windows that can show different things at the same time. All GUIs work in more or less the same way because they're all based on the same original work done at Xerox about 20 years ago; the details differ enough, though, to make you want to tear your hair out.

The Big GUIs (the Big Gooey Whats?)

Most UNIX systems that have any sort of GUI use one based on the X Windows system. Older Sun workstations use systems called SunView or NeWS; NeXT machines use NeXTStep. (Are tHoSE wOrDS cAPiTaLlzed corREctlY?) Other than those exceptions, however, you almost certainly will get X Windows. NeWS systems also support X (*X* is lazy author-ese for X Windows); there are frequently used X-under-NeXTStep packages too.

X has many advantages as a windowing system:

✔ It runs on all sorts of computers, not just those that run UNIX.

✔ It is *policy independent:* A program can make the screen look any way it wants; the screen is not constrained to a single style, as it is on the Macintosh or with Microsoft Windows. (As you might imagine, this capability is not an unmitigated blessing. More about this subject later.)

✔ It uses a networked client-server architecture (love those buzzwords). You can run X on one computer, but the programs that display stuff on-screen can be on entirely different computers connected by a network.

✔ MIT gives it away for free.

You can imagine which of these important advantages is the one that really made all the computer makers choose X. Even though MIT gives away the base version of X, unless you happen to be using the exact same kind of computer the guys at MIT use (or you feel like compiling and debugging a gazillion lines of C code), you don't get it for free. You must buy a version tailored for the particular kind of screen and adapter on your computer.

How your screen looks depends on which GUI you use. This chapter talks about things that are the same for all GUIs. Chapter 12 tells you how to tell which GUI you are using, and how to do things that work differently for each GUI.

Basic Mouse Skills

You have to know how to use a mouse to get anything done under X. Fortunately, mouse wrangling is pretty easy. Make friends with your mouse. One of us built a little mouse hole in the wall next to the computer desk, with a basket where the mouse can rest when it's not working, but that's probably excessive.

Mice (or mouselike things, such as trackballs) have a way to tell when you have moved them and some buttons you can push to tell the computer you want to do something. Different mice have different numbers of buttons. If your mouse has fewer than three buttons, it is a pain in the neck to use because many programs assign functions to the third button. The first button, by the way, is the one on the left (unless someone has configured your mouse to be left-handed, and then the first button is the one on the right).

When you move the mouse on the pad or on your desk, a *cursor* (a little doohickey on-screen) moves along with it. You can pick up the mouse and put it back down somewhere else on the pad or desk without moving the cursor. This capability comes in handy when you find that you have moved the mouse to the edge of the pad and that the cursor is still in the middle of the screen;

just pick up the mouse and move it to a more convenient part of your desk. If your mouse lives on a mouse pad printed with a grid of lines, it works only when you move it on the pad.

When you move the mouse, try to keep it square to the desk, with the cord (or the tail, depending on whether you're willing to put up with another cute term) pointing away from you. Particularly when the mouse is off to the side of your desk, it's easy to turn the mouse at an angle. Because the computer can't tell that you have done that, you find that you move the mouse down but that the cursor moves up because the mouse is twisted around. Fortunately, you get used to mousing pretty quickly and all this becomes second nature.

With a click-click here

The two key mouse skills are clicking and dragging. Clicking is easy; you move the mouse until the cursor is on a screen item you want to activate and then you quickly press and release one of the mouse buttons, generally the first (the left) button. In window-ese, this process is called *selecting* the screen item; it means that you want to do something with the item you just clicked on.

Sometimes you need to *double-click* (click the same button twice quickly) to tell the screen item to do something particularly important. It can take some practice to train your finger to click the button quickly enough for the computer to recognize it as a double-click rather than one click and a second click, made when the nerve impulses finally get back to your finger. If you had practiced the piano when you were a kid, like your mother told you to, you would have the finger dexterity to do this the first time. (Really.) To keep your children from being at a disadvantage in the highly computerized land of the future, be sure that they take piano lessons and practice. Or maybe saxophone lessons would do as well and offer more upward political mobility. But we digress. Back to mouse skills.

And a drag-drag there

Dragging the mouse is a slightly more complicated procedure. You move to a point of interest, press a mouse button, *hold it down,* move the mouse as you hold the button, and then let go of the button.

You use dragging in two main ways. The first is for *pop-up menus.* When you press one of the mouse buttons, a menu appears, with a list of possible things to do. While you are holding down the button, drag the cursor to the item on the menu you want and then let the button go. If you change your mind and don't want to do any of the things on the menu, drag the cursor entirely off the menu before letting go of the button.

The second way to use the drag technique is to outline some part of a window. You move to one corner of an area you want to select, press a mouse button, drag to the opposite corner of the area, and let go; at this point, a box on-screen shows the area you outlined.

Window Treatments

Now that you're a mouse expert, we discuss a few of the basic things you can do with X Windows. Suppose that you have two or three windows on your screen. How do you tell UNIX which window you want to use? The answer is — wait, no, how did you know this was coming? — *it depends.*

Most commonly, to select a window, you just move the mouse cursor into the window you want to use. You can tell when a window is *active* because the border around it changes color. Some systems are configured to use the "click to type" window-selection technique, in which you have to move the mouse to the window you want and then click one of the buttons to activate the window.

If you have to "click to type" and really hate it — or don't and really want to — a guru skilled in the ways of X (naturally called an X-pert) can change some parameters and turn "click to type" on or off. We recommend that you live with whatever you have; there are so many changeable parameters that, after you begin fiddling with them, it can become X-asperating to figure out X-actly how your X-pert left them, and you will utter an X-cess of X-pletives. (If you're feeling adventurous, Chapter 16, "Mutant Motif," of *MORE UNIX For Dummies* tells you how to turn "click to type" on and off in the popular Motif window system.)

Chapter 12

Motif and Other Schools of Windowing Theology

In This Chapter

▶ How to tell which theology you subscribe to

▶ Window-wrangling skills

▶ How to log out

Most windowing systems on most kinds of computers make programs use a consistent style. All Macintosh programs, for example, look pretty much the same: They all use the same menu, the same little window when you want to select a file, similar windows to turn options on and off, and so forth. One Microsoft Windows program looks a lot like all the others: They all use similar sets of windows. But do all X Windows programs have a consistent look? Of course not — that would be too easy. (This is what the X crowd means by *policy independence:* no enforced window-appearance policy.)

Let's Go Window Shopping

Competing window "looks" are on the UNIX market, the best known being Motif. To tell which one you are stuck with, er, have the pleasure to use, look at the border around the windows on your screen. If the windows have 3-D-style borders with sharp corners, as shown in Figure 12-1, you're using Motif. If they have rounded corners, as shown in Figure 12-2, you're using OPENLOOK. If they have a thin border around the sides and bottom, and top borders like those shown in Figure 12-3, you're using a program called TWM, which comes with the base version of X and is still sometimes used because it is simple and small.

After several years of window system warfare, Motif has emerged as the clear favorite window system, so that's the one that we concentrate on here.

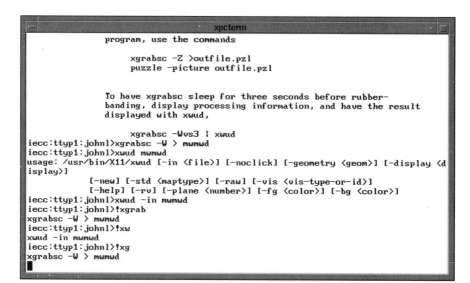

Figure 12-1: A typical Motif window.

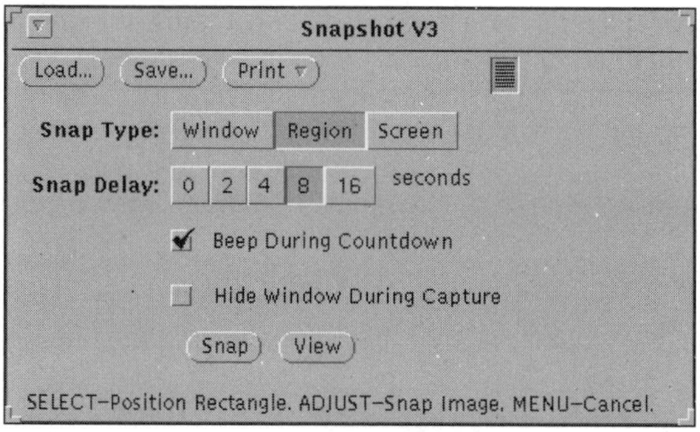

Figure 12-2: A typical OPENLOOK window.

You can and do mix different window styles on the same screen. If one of the programs you run is written with Motif and another is written with the original Athena toolkit that comes with X, each one displays its own windows by using its own style. The border around the windows, on the other hand, is controlled by a separate program called a *window manager;* if you have the Motif window manager, you can have a Motif border around an Athena window. This arrangement can look pretty strange, but fortunately it usually works smoothly.

```
┌─────────────────────────────────────────────────────────────────────────────┐
│ ⊠ xpcterm                                                                  凹 │
├─────────────────────────────────────────────────────────────────────────────┤
│ iecc:ttyp1:johnl>who -a                                                       │
│         .    system boot   Dec 12 12:32                                       │
│         .    run-level 2    Dec 12 12:32      2      0    S                    │
│ bcheckrc     .              Dec 12 12:33   0:20      5    id=bchk term=0   exit=77 │
│ brc          .              Dec 12 12:33   0:20     15    id= brc term=0   exit=0 │
│ brc          .              Dec 12 12:33   0:20     19    id=  mt term=0   exit=0 │
│ rc2          .              Dec 12 12:49   0:20     23    id=  r2 term=0   exit=0 │
│ root         console        Dec 29 20:16   0:01  17956                         │
│ sleep        .              Dec 12 12:49   0:20    130    id=  wt term=0   exit=0 │
│ johnl        vt01           Dec 21 15:19   0:01   5938                         │
│ LOGIN        vt02           Dec 29 20:16  20:48  17955                         │
│ LOGIN        ttyd1          Dec 30 16:24   0:52   2827    492-3869             │
│ faxserve     .              Dec 26 11:45   0:20  24871    id=  F2              │
│ johnl        ttyp2          Dec 30 17:16      .   3053    id=  p2 term=112 exit=2 │
│ johnl        ttyp1          Dec 30 16:55      .   3054                         │
│ johnl        ttyp0          Dec 30 16:55   0:15   3055                         │
│ johnl        ttyp3          Dec 30 16:56   0:20   3086    id=  p3 term=112 exit=2 │
│ johnl        ttyp4          Dec 30 16:12   1:04  19342    id=  p4 term=112 exit=2 │
│ johnl        ttyp5          Dec 23 18:41    old  11186    id=  p5 term=112 exit=2 │
│ LOGIN        .              Dec 15 15:28   0:20  25517                         │
│ LOGIN        .              Dec 15 15:30   0:20  25532                         │
│ LOGIN        ttyd2          Dec 17 18:55    old   5561    id=  02 term=15  exit=0 │
│ iecc:ttyp1:john                                                               │
│ iecc:ttyp1:johnl>xgrabsc -W > twmwd                                           │
│ ▮                                                                             │
└─────────────────────────────────────────────────────────────────────────────┘
```

Figure 12-3: A typical TWM window.

Opening a New Window

When you run a new X program, generally speaking, it opens a new window. In some cases, you tell a program that's already running to open another window (for a word processor, for example), but the way that you do that is specific to each program; you have to read the manual — gasp! — for the program.

You usually have at least one terminal window running. A *terminal window* isn't as sinister as it sounds; it's a window that acts like a terminal. The usual program is called xterm; it acts much like a DEC VT100 terminal. Most systems also have a modified terminal program that acts like the computer maker's favorite terminal. Hewlett-Packard systems have hpterm, for example, which acts like an HP terminal, and some PC UNIX systems have xpcterm, which acts like a PC console. For most purposes, all these terminal programs act the same. They start up running a UNIX shell, and you type commands just as we describe in this book.

There are two ways to start a new program that opens a new window: the GUI-oriented user-friendly way and the easy way.

Follow these steps for the GUI-oriented user-friendly way:

1. **Move the cursor so that it's not in any of your current windows.**

2. **Click the Menu mouse button.**

   This button is the last one (the rightmost button unless you have a left-handed mouse) in TWM and the first button otherwise.

3. **Drag the mouse up and down the menu that pops up until you find the program that you want.**

4. **Let go of the button.**

   Sometimes you have nested menus; when you pick an item from the first menu, a second menu pops up, and you must pick an item there too.

The easy way to start a program has only one step:

1. **Go to a terminal window and type the name of the program that you want to run.**

This approach is the same one you use to run any other program or to give a command. To display another terminal window, type xterm or the name of the terminal program you use.

Then there's the issue of where on-screen the new window appears. Some programs and window managers have strong opinions of their own, and the new window appears wherever the program or window manager thinks that it should. With other, less-opinionated programs, you make the call: A ghostly window that appears floats near the middle of the screen. You move the ghost around with the mouse and click when the window is where you want it. At that point, the ghost materializes into the regular window. This latter scheme is usually more convenient because the locations that the opinionated programs choose for window placement are rarely where you want them. Beware of one thing, though: While the ghost is on-screen, all other windows are frozen. If you leave the ghost on-screen for a long time (while you're at lunch or overnight), all the others can get rather constipated waiting for the screen to unfreeze so that they can update their windows. If you're using Motif, your local guru can switch your system between opinionated mode and floating ghost mode. If you're feeling brave, we tell you how to do it yourself in Chapter 16, "Mutant Motif," of *MORE UNIX For Dummies.*

Some systems have desktop manager programs (unrelated to window manager programs) that attempt to make it easier to handle programs and files. Desktop managers have sets of icons that you click on to start common programs; they let you click on filenames to edit the file — sort of like the Macintosh Desktop. Opinions vary on how useful these desktop managers are. We haven't been crazy about them, but it's worth trying them for a few minutes because some people find them much easier to use than menus and shell commands.

Icon Do This with a Picture

GUIs are crazy about pictures (they're graphical, after all), especially cute, little ones. The cutest, littlest ones you run into are icons. An *icon* is a little picture in a little box on-screen that represents a window. When you tell X Windows to "iconify" a window, the window disappears, and an icon remains. When you double-click (or single click, if you're not using Motif) on the icon, the window comes back just as it was before. Being able to reduce windows to icons lets you shove programs out of the way and not lose what you were doing — one of the best things about window systems. Figure 12-4 shows a pair of icons, one for an electronic-mail program and one for a terminal program. If new mail arrives, the little flag on the mail icon flips up, which is almost useful enough to make up for its X-treme cuteness.

Figure 12-4: Icons are windows in a miniature disguise.

Rearranging Windows

You frequently will find that you don't like the way the windows on your screen are arranged. You can do lots of things to alleviate this problem and simultaneously waste lots of time. In fact, we have found that, by giving your dedicated attention to window management, you can spend the entire day at the computer apparently working but not accomplishing anything. A little rearrangement is inevitable, so the following sections are thumbnail sketches of what you can do and how to do it with Motif.

The chic window dresses in layers

To bring a window to the front of a stack of windows, move the cursor to the bar at the top of the window (known as the *title bar* because it shows a title for the window) and click the first mouse button. Motif also lets you do this: Move the cursor into the window, hold the Alt or Meta key, and press the F1 key.

You can also banish a window to the back of the pile. In Motif, you do this by holding the Meta or Alt key and clicking the first mouse button in the title bar; alternatively, hold Meta or Alt and press F3.

Where, oh where, has my window gone?

In Motif, put the cursor in the title bar, press the first mouse button, and drag the window to where you want it (that is, move the window as you hold the mouse button). This action also brings the window to the front because you use the same button to do that.

You can move windows so they are partially off the edge of the screen, sort of like pushing papers to the side of your desk so they hang over the edge (except that windows are less likely to fall on the floor). This ability is sometimes useful if the interesting stuff in the window is all at the top or all on one side.

Stashing your windows

The title bar of the window has little things on it that you can click.

Motif puts a bunch of strange-looking blobs in a window's title bar. On the left is a box that contains a little bar; if you click on it, a menu of window operations pops up. (You can do all the window-management tricks by using that menu, but there are easier ways to do them all.) Near the right of the title bar is a little box that contains a small dot; when you click on it, the window turns into an icon. To the right of that box is a third little box we discuss in the next section (don't be impatient, we're writing as fast as we can).

When the window disappears, an icon appears and replaces it. The icon is located either where the window used to be or off in one corner of the screen that has been made into an icon ghetto. You move icons the same way you move windows: In Motif, drag them with the first mouse button.

To get the window back, double-click on the icon with the first mouse button.

Curiouser and curiouser: resizing windows

The last little bit of window magic involves changing window sizes. Motif has gone to a lot of trouble to let you change the size of your windows, which tells us that they gave up trying to make them the right size in the first place. Oh, well. Little "grab bars" are in each corner of most windows. (The few windows you can't resize don't have the grab bars.) You move the cursor to one of the grab bars, click the first mouse button, drag the corner to where you want it (make the window larger or smaller), and release the button. Then do it again two or three times because you never get it right on the first try. Motif also has grab bars on the top, bottom, and sides of every window that let you change the height of a window without changing the width or vice versa.

Motif has a shortcut to let you expand a window to fill the entire screen. Click on the little box-in-a-box at the right end of the title bar. If you do the same thing again, the window shrinks back to normal size.

In practice, we never blow windows up to the full screen, because UNIX programs aren't written to take advantage of the entire screen very well. The full-screen option was a lot more important when screens were smaller.

Getting Rid of Windows

Your screen often becomes cluttered with windows you no longer need. You already know how to turn them into icons to get most of the screen space back, but sometimes you just want to make the program go away.

Remember that if you have 57 different programs running, even if most of them are snoozing behind their icons, it can put enough of a load on your computer to slow down the ones you want to use.

Most programs have a natural way to exit. In terminal windows, you log out from the shell by typing exit or logout in the terminal window. Real windows-oriented programs usually have menus of their own with a Quit or Exit entry that cleans up and makes the program stop. But because some programs just won't die, you have to take drastic measures.

In Motif, click on the little bar in the box at the left end of the title bar; a menu of window operations pops up. (The program can tell Motif not to show that little box, and then you display the window-operations menu by holding Meta or Alt and pressing the spacebar). From that menu, select Close, either with the mouse or by typing c. The window and its associated program go away.

Motif uses confusing and inconsistent names in the window-operations menu. Close means to destroy the window and the program, and Minimize turns the window into an icon.

Ta-Ta for Now

The last little detail is how to tell X Windows you're finished with it. The way you do that (we're getting tired of saying this) varies from one system to another. You have to stop the startup program, which is usually a terminal window named `login` or else the window manager itself. If there is a window named `login` or `console`, go to that window and type `exit` or `logout` to exit that shell, or kill it as explained in the preceding section.

If your startup program is the window manager, you must persuade the window manager to exit. You can't kill it the way you kill other programs because the window manager doesn't have a particular window. In Motif, you move the cursor outside any window, press the last mouse button, and select the item labeled Quit from the menu that pops up. Motif will pop up another box, incredulous that you claim that you want to leave a program as wonderful as itself, so you have to click on OK to assure it you are indeed such an ingrate.

Terminal Happenings

Even though X Windows allows you to run all of the coolest, gnarliest, newest, most graphicalest programs, guess what program people use the most? It's called `xterm` and all it does is to act like the kind of VT100 dumb terminal that window systems are supposed to save us from. Such are the ways of progress.

`xterm` is one of the oldest programs that runs under X, and it has the greasy fingerprints of generations of programmers. As the README file in its source code notes, "This is undoubtedly the most ugly program in the distribution." So, although `xterm` has over 70 exciting options on the command line alone, we won't tell you about them.

Click, click

One place where `xterm` acts a little better than the dumb terminal it purports to emulate is in mouse handling. You can select text with the mouse, and then paste the selected text into either the same or a different `xterm` window.

To select some text, move the mouse to the beginning of the text, press down the first (left) mouse button, and move the mouse to the end of the text that you want to select. As you move the mouse, the selected text will change color. When you've selected it all, let go of the mouse button. Normally, `xterm` selects text character by character, but if you double-click rather than just pressing the mouse button, it'll select by word, and if you triple-click, it'll select by line. For users who don't believe in walking and chewing gum at the same time, there's an alternate way to select text: move to the beginning of the selection, click the left button, then move to the end of the selection and click the right button.

Either way, once you've selected the text, move the mouse to the window where you want to paste and click the middle button. If after you've selected the text, a program erases the window, you won't be able to see the selection anymore, but it'll still be there, and you can still paste it.

Most other programs that have text type-in areas use the same mouse conventions that xterm does, so you can select text from an xterm and paste it into other programs, and vice versa.

Coming in for a save

The other thing that makes xterm occasionally useful is that you can save a transcript of what goes on in the window into a file, a *log file*. To turn on logging, move the cursor into the xterm window, hold down the Ctrl key with your non-mouse hand, press and hold the left mouse button to get a little menu like the one in Figure 12-5, move the mouse down to Log to File, and let go of the mouse. (This sequence isn't quite as hard as it sounds, fortunately.) There are a bunch of other options on that menu, none of which we recommend other than the self-explanatory Redraw Window and Quit.

```
Main Options
Secure Keyboard
Allow SendEvents
Log to File
Redraw Window
Send STOP Signal
Send CONT Signal
Send INT Signal
Send HUP Signal
Send TERM Signal
Send KILL Signal
Quit
```

Figure 12-5: A few xterm menu options.

After that, everything you type in that window, including the backspaces and other correction characters to remind you of what a rotten typist you are, and everything that UNIX types back, get written to a file. What file? The answer varies, but usually, it's a file in your home directory called XtermLog.12345 where the last five digits are unique. Type ls Xterm* and you'll probably find it. When you're done logging, do the same Ctrl and mouse dance and select Log to File again (it'll be checked to remind you that logging is on) to turn the log off.

Logging is an optional feature of xterm, and some systems have logging permanently turned off. In that case, if you try to turn on logging, the terminal will just beep.

One last stupid xterm *trick*

If you find the text in your xterm window to be insufficiently or excessively legible, you can make the type larger or smaller. Hold down the Ctrl key and press the right mouse button to get the xterm VT Fonts menu, on which you can select font sizes ranging from Unreadable to Huge. We recommend the Unreadable font, which will take your typical 80 x 40 character text window and scrunch it down to a one-inch square that is indeed unreadable. When you tire of that, select the Default font to return things to normal.

Part IV
Getting Things Done

The 5th Wave   By Rich Tennant

"SURE, HE'S A LITTLE DIFFERENT, BUT HE WORKS HARD, AND KEEPS THE SYSTEM FREE OF BUGS."

In this part...

Well, so far, we have talked about the computer, UNIX, the shell, files — you name it. What about getting some real work done?

To get useful work done, you need software. This part talks about some useful programs that come with UNIX, including text editors. It also discusses buying and installing other programs.

Chapter 13
Writing Deathless Prose

• •

In This Chapter

▶ What is a text editor?

▶ What is a text formatter?

▶ What is a word processor?

▶ What is a desktop publishing program?

▶ How to use ed if you don't have anything better

▶ How to use vi if you absolutely have to

▶ How to use emacs, which is not that bad, really

▶ How to use pico, which is pretty nice

• •

*I*n the land of UNIX, many programs handle text. Where you come from, you may be accustomed to the idea of using a word processor when you want to type something and print it. Not in UNIX. There are four kinds of programs to do this, just to keep things interesting.

Just the Text, Ma'am

A text editor lets you create a file full of text and edit the text.

You can print the file by using the lp or lpr programs, described in Chapter 10, but text editors can't do boldface, running headers or footers, italics, or all that other fancy stuff you need in order to produce really modern, over-formatted, professional-quality memos.

You may want to use a text editor to write letters and reports. You certainly will use one to send electronic mail (see Chapter 19).

The most commonly used text editors in the land of UNIX are ed, vi, emacs, and pico. We have strong opinions about editors, which is abundantly clear in the later sections of this chapter, where we tell you how to use them.

Text Formatters Aren't Really Editors

Text formatters are programs that read text files and create nice-looking format-ted output. You use a text editor to make a text file that contains special little commands only the formatter understands; the .IT command, for example, makes something italic. When you run the text formatter, it reads the text file, reads the special little commands, and creates a formatted file that you then can print. You use pr or lpr to print the output of the text formatter.

The most common UNIX text formatter is troff, pronounced "tee-roff." Some people use nroff ("en-roff"), an older version of troff, groff ("gee-roff"), the GNU version of troff, or TeX, pronounced "teccccch" (like yecccccch). With luck, you will never have to use any of them.

Cuisinarts for Text: Word Processors

Word processors combine the capabilities of text editors and text formatters. Most word processors are (or try to be) *WYSIWYG* (an acronym for *w*hat *y*ou *s*ee *is w*hat *y*ou *g*et) so you can see on-screen how documents (that's what they call their files) will look when you print them.

Word processors for UNIX include WordPerfect (available also for PCs and Macintoshes) and Microsoft Word (available for at least XENIX and SVR4 as well as for Macs and PCs). Most UNIX users think that word processors are for wimps (*w*hat *y*ou *s*ee *is a*ll *y*ou've *g*ot) because they like the unintelligible and unmemorable commands used by text formatters and prefer to imagine what their text will look like when it is printed rather than be able to see it on-screen. Text formatters can do more complex things than word processors can, like formatting complicated mathematical expressions, laying out multi-page tables, and fetching reference citations from a database. But that's probably not your problem. (We used troff to write drafts of this book, then Microsoft Word to revise it, so it just goes to show ya.)

Desktop Publishing Does It All

A desktop publishing program (DTP) resembles a fancy word processor. It can do everything a word processor can, plus things you need only if you are printing a book, newsletter, or something else that looks fancy. DTPs include facilities for creating tables of contents and indexes, maintaining cross-refer-ences — you name it. For writing an occasional memo, a desktop publishing program is definitely overkill.

The most common desktop publishing programs for UNIX are Interleaf (available for PCs also) and FrameMaker (available for PCs and Macintoshes also).

TeX and some versions of troff are available for free, which explains why they remain so popular. (Big surprise, eh?) All word processors and desktop publishers are commercial products that cost extra. Lots extra.

ed *and* vi *and* emacs *and* pico *Are Your Friends*

The rest of this chapter explains how to use each of the Big Four text editors (ed, vi, pico, and emacs). Even if you use a word processor or desktop publishing program, you may need to use a text editor to do things like these:

- ✔ Write electronic mail (see Chapter 19).
- ✔ Create or edit text files called *shell scripts* to allow you to create your own UNIX commands (see Chapter 15).
- ✔ Create or edit special text files that control the way your UNIX setup works (see Chapter 28).
- ✔ Write C programs — just kidding!

Talk to Mr. ed

The ed program is the original editor that has been a part of UNIX since the beginning of time. When you use it, you begin to appreciate how far software design has progressed since 1969. The ed program is a *line editor,* which means that ed assigns line numbers to the lines in the file; every time you do something, you must tell ed which line or lines to do it to. If you have used the EDLIN program in DOS, ed should look familiar.

If there is *any way* — repeat — *any way* you can get another text editor to use, do it. If you don't think that ed can really be that bad, just peruse the next few pages and you will run screaming to your system administrator for vi , pico, or emacs (preferably pico or emacs).

Some systems have a program called ex that is similar to but not quite as horrible as ed. Try typing ex to see what happens.

To run ed, type this line:

```
ed important.letter
```

(Type the name of your file rather than *important.letter*.) If no file has the name you specify, ed makes one. UNIX responds to this command with a number, which is the number of characters (letters, numbers, punctuation, and spaces) in the file, just in case you are getting paid to write by the letter.

If you receive an error message when you try to run ed, talk to your system administrator. Congratulate her on getting rid of that Neanderthal text editor and find out which text editor you *can* use.

Hey, Wilbur, which command was that?

All ed commands are one letter long (as in h). Remember *not* to capitalize ed commands unless we specifically say to; ed commands are almost all small letters.

The ed program is always waiting for either commands or text (a.k.a., input). When ed is waiting for a command, it is in *command mode*. When it is waiting for text, it is in *input mode*. Normally, it is up to you to figure out which mode ed is in at any particular moment (it doesn't give you a clue). Whether ed is waiting for a command or for text input, it just displays a blank line — truly among the most unhelpful, not to say hostile, programs ever designed.

At the time that the lazy typists who created UNIX wrote ed, they were using old, slow, noisy Teletype terminals and wanted to save themselves from having to type any character they could avoid. But why should that be your problem?

Emergency exit from ed

To get the heck out of ed — in case someone used your computer and left it running — follow these steps:

1. Type a period on a line by itself and press Enter (or Return). This action gets you into command mode in case you are in input mode. If you were already in command mode, a line of the file prints on-screen. Ignore it.

2. Type q and press Enter.

If changes to the file have been saved or if there were no changes, this action quits ed, and you see a UNIX shell prompt. If changes to

the file haven't been saved, ed displays a question mark, meaning, "Yo, you're about to throw away your changes. Are you cool with this?" Type q again and press Enter again. This time, ed exits. If someone has used your computer and run ed, and didn't save the work, to heck with it. And if *you* ran ed by mistake and are fighting to get out, you probably don't want to save any changes anyway.

In most versions of ed, you can also use the capital Q command, which means, "*Quit* — and don't ask any questions!"

Relatively recent versions of ed (since, oh, about 1983) have a P command (that's a capital *P,* one of the few uppercase commands) that turns on a prompt. If you type P and press Enter, ed prompts you with an asterisk when it's in command mode and waiting for a command. Is that incredibly user-friendly or what? It actually allows you to determine when you are in command mode! Must have snuck that one in when the lazy typists weren't looking.

If you are in input mode and want to give a command, type a period (.). That's just a single period on a line by itself; it switches ed to command mode.

In the remainder of this discussion about using ed, whenever we tell you to type a command, it works only if you are in command mode. If you are not sure, type a period and press Enter first.

If you are in command mode and want to type some text, you switch to text input mode. But first you must decide whether you are going to *append* (by using the a command) after the current line the lines of text you will type or *insert* (by using the i command) the lines of text before the current line.

Help, Wilbur!

The ed program has a fascinating and totally self-explanatory error message that you see if you type anything wrong:

?

That's it — that's the whole thing. Luckily, you can humbly ask ed for more information about what went wrong. Just type h and press Enter.

The ed program displays a short message that gives you a hint about the problem. In most versions of ed, if you type a capital H, ed not only explains the current complaint but also any others that occur later on. Be warned: The explanations are not as helpful as they might be, but what did you expect?

What's my line?

The ed program thinks (if we may anthropomorphize a bit) of your file as a series of lines of text. It numbers the lines, starting at 1 for the first line, and works with them one at a time. And so must you, to get anything done using ed.

For most commands, you tell ed which line or lines to work with. When you insert lines, for example, you tell ed before which line to insert the new lines.

If you don't specify the line or lines you want to work on, ed assumes that you want the *current line.* The current line is the line you last worked with. If you last worked with a bunch of lines, it's the last one of the bunch. When you start using ed, the current line is the last line in the file.

Mr. ed *gets lunch*

To create a file and feed some text to it, start the process by typing this line:

```
ed eating.peas
```

You can name your file something other than `eating.peas`, if you want. UNIX responds with a question mark, just to keep you on your toes. (This time, the question mark tells you that `ed` just created a new file for you.)

To add (append) new lines of text to the end of the file — in this case, the end of the file is the same as the beginning because the file is empty — type a.

UNIX responds by saying absolutely nothing, which is your indication that `ed` is now in input mode and waiting for you to type some text. Type some pearls of wisdom, like this:

```
I eat my peas with honey,
I've done it all my life.
It makes the peas taste funny,
but it keeps them on the knife.
.
```

When you finish typing text, type a period on a line by itself to switch `ed` from input mode back to command mode. Not that `ed` gives you a hint that this is going on, unless you have used the P command to tell it to prompt you.

The lines of text are now in your file. This would be a good time to save the file, just in case you kick the plug of your computer out of the wall in your frustration at having to use such a brainless program.

Save me from this stupid program!

The w command saves your text in a file with `ed`. If you are in input mode, remember to type a period on a line by itself to switch to command mode before giving this command. UNIX responds with the number of characters in the file. Be sure to give this command before leaving `ed` so that your deathless prose is saved in the file, in this case, `eating.peas` (or whatever filename you used when you ran `ed`).

Show me the file, please

Now that you have text in the file, how can you see it or change it? By using the p (print) command. This command doesn't print anything on the printer, it just displays it on-screen — another example of superb software engineering. (Well, it printed on those old Teletypes.) If you type the p command by itself, `ed` displays the current line.

TIP

What if ed commands end up in my text?

If you are in input mode and type an ed command, ed doesn't do the command. Instead, it thinks that you are typing text and stores the letter or letters of the command as just some more text in your file.

If this happens, delete the lines you don't want (we explain how to delete lines later in this chapter). The next time you want to enter a command, be sure to type a period on a line by itself first.

In the case of the sample `eating.peas` file, the current line is the last line in the file. You can also tell ed which lines to display by typing their line numbers. To display lines 1 through 4, for example, type this line:

```
1,4p
```

You can also use the $ symbol to stand for the line number of the last line in the file (in case you don't know how many lines are in the file); the following command always displays the entire file:

```
1,$p
```

Take a number, please

We know — you shouldn't have to see line numbers when you just want to write a simple memo or whatever, but, because ed uses line numbers with its commands, displaying line numbers can be useful. To display lines with line numbers, use n rather than p. Type the following line, for example, to see a complete listing of your file with line numbers:

```
1,$n
```

The result is something like this:

```
1       I eat my peas with honey,
2       I've done it all my life.
3       It makes the peas taste funny,
4       but it keeps them on the knife.
```

Now you see it, now you don't

To delete the current line of text, type d.

Watch out when you type lines that start with the letter *d* whenever you are using ed! If ed decides that you are in command mode when you type a *d*, ed

> # Accidental input
>
> Most other lowercase letters are ed commands, too. (We just didn't think that you would want to know about them.) When you are in command mode, typing almost any letter (or even some other symbols) tells ed that you want to do a command. So, watch what you type when you're in command mode.

deletes the current line (or whatever lines you specify) with no warning or confirmation. We suggest that you use the p and n commands a lot as you go along, to see what your file looks like.

After you add or delete lines, ed renumbers the lines in the rest of the file. Use the n command often to find out your line numbers.

You can specify the lines you want ed to delete by typing the line number or numbers, like this:

```
4d
```

Or like this, to delete lines 1 through 2:

```
1,2d
```

The comma tells ed to delete lines starting with 1 and ending with 2, inclusive.

A miserable way to edit

You can change the contents of a line of text with ed, but it involves giving commands like this:

```
12,13s/wrong/right/
```

This command substitutes right for wrong in lines 12 through 13, inclusive. Totally primitive and painful, isn't it. For the amount of editing you probably do in ed, it is almost easier to delete the line with the typo and insert a new line. We recommend that you immediately ask for a better text editor.

Make me better again, doctor

But wait — there is one useful, humane command in ed after all! The u command lets you "undo" the last (and only the very last) change you made to the file. If you delete a line by mistake with the d command, for example, you can type u to undo the deletion.

Be sure that you don't make any other changes before using the u command; it undoes only the very last thing you did.

Give my regards to Broadway, ed

When you finish making changes and you want to leave ed (or even if you're not finished making changes and you want to leave ed anyway), type q. If you are in input mode, first type a period on a line by itself to get into command mode. Then type q to quit.

If you haven't saved your work by using the w command, ed just doesn't quit. Instead, it displays a question mark to tell you that it was expecting a w command first. To save your changes, type w and then q. If you don't want to save the changes to the file, type q again at the question mark. This time, ed believes that you really want to leave and exits. Not a moment too soon!

Shy vi, *the princess of text editors*

The vi text editor is head and shoulders above ed in every way. It is a *screen editor* rather than a line editor; it shows you as much of the file as it can fit on-screen. You don't have to beg it to display bits and pieces of your file — definitely a step forward.

The bad news is that, command-wise and mode-wise, vi works just like ed because deep down it's just a souped-up version of ed: two modes with no clue about which one you are using, cryptic one-letter commands — the works. You're still better off learning emacs or pico, but vi really is better than ed.

The vi program is available on almost all UNIX systems, the major reason it is so widely used.

To run vi, type this line:

```
vi eating.peas
```

Substitute the name of the file you want to create or change for eating.peas. If the file you name doesn't exist, vi creates it. So to make a new file, just type vi and the new filename.

Screens full of text

The vi program shows you a full-screen view of your file. If the file isn't long enough to fill the screen, vi shows tildes (~) on the blank lines beyond the end of the file. Figure 13-1, for example, shows the file eating.peas (created in the preceding discussion about ed) as it would appear in vi.

The cursor (the point at which you are working) appears at the beginning of the first line of the file.

✔ If you get an error message when you try to run vi, talk to your system administrator.

✔ If the screen looks weird, your terminal type may not be set right — another reason to talk to your system administrator.

```
I eat my peas with honey,
I've done it all my life.
It makes the peas taste funny,
But it keeps them on my knife.
~
~
~
~
~
~
~
~
~
~
~
~
~
~
~
~
~
~
~
"eating.peas"  4 lines, 114 chars
```

Figure 13-1: Tildes fill up the blank lines on the vi screen.

Royal commands and edicts

Nearly all vi commands are one letter long (like ed commands). Some are lowercase letters and others are capital letters. When you type vi commands, be sure to use the correct capitalization.

The vi program has two modes, just like ed: command mode (waiting for a command) and input mode (waiting to accept text input). You have to keep track of which mode you are using because vi doesn't tell you. If you are in input mode and want to give a command, press the Escape (or Esc) key.

Yikes, it keeps displaying lines!

If you are in command mode and press Enter without having typed any command, ed assumes that you want to see the next line of the file. It moves down one line in the file and displays that line — rather convenient, really, if you are expecting it.

Also, if you are *already* in command mode and you type a period on a line by itself — are you following this? — ed displays the current line in the file, since a period means the current line number.

Emergency exit from vi

To escape from vi, do the following:

1. Press Escape at least three times. The computer should beep. Now you are in command mode for sure.

2. Type the following line and press Enter:

   :q!

   This line tells vi to quit and not save any changes.

Whenever we tell you to type a command, it works only if you are in command mode. If you are not sure which mode you're in, press Esc first. If you are already in command mode, pressing Esc just makes vi beep.

To switch from command mode to text-input mode, you tell vi to add the text after the character that the cursor is on (by using the a command) or to insert the text before the current cursor position (by using the i command). You can see where the cursor is in your file, which is a big improvement over ed.

Because vi deep down is still a souped-up version of ed, you can use the same commands we talked about earlier in this chapter in the section about ed. Here's how to issue ed commands to vi: press the Esc key to get to command mode and then type a colon (:) followed by the ed command. With rare exceptions, this isn't worth the effort.

Help! I need somebody!

The guy who wrote vi (remember Bill, the grouchy guy who's 6'4" and in excellent physical condition — same guy) didn't believe in help, so there wasn't any.

Fortunately, vi has been used in so many introductory computing courses that Bill eventually relented and added a "novice" mode. Rather than type vi to run the editor, type vedit to get the same editor with some allegedly helpful messages. In particular, whenever you're in input mode rather than command mode, vi displays a message like INPUT MODE, APPEND MODE, CHANGE MODE, or OPEN MODE at the bottom of your screen. All these messages mean the same thing (except to Bill, evidently): text that you type when these messages can be seen is added to the file rather than interpreted as commands.

Easy text-entry techniques

To make a new file with some more deathless prose, run vi and make a new file:

```
vi madeline
```

To add text after the current position of the cursor, type a. (We tell you how to move the cursor in a minute.) Because v i is a full-screen editor, you do *not* press Enter after a command. You can type a, for example, to add this text to a newly created madeline file:

```
In an old house in Paris
All covered with vines
Lived twelve little girls
In two straight lines.
```

To get back to command mode, press Esc. Press Esc whenever you finish typing text so that you are ready to give the next command.

Other commands you can use to enter text include i to insert text *before* the current cursor position, A to add the text at the end of the line that the cursor is on, and 0 to add the text on a new line before the current line.

All around the mulberry bush: moving the cursor

You can use dozens of commands to move the cursor around in your file, but you can get to where you want with just a few of them:

- ✔ The arrow keys (←, →, ↑, and ↓) usually do what you would expect: They move the cursor in the indicated direction.

  Sadly, there are terminals on which v i does not understand the arrow keys. If this is true for you, use h to move left, j to move down, k to move up, and l to move right. Bill chose these keys on the theory that, because those keys are close to a touch typist's home position for the fingers on the right hand, you can save valuable milliseconds by not having to move your fingers. Really. In some versions of v i, arrow keys work only in command mode; in others they work also in input mode.

- ✔ Enter or + moves to the beginning of the next line.

- ✔ The hyphen (-) moves to the beginning of the preceding line.

- ✔ G (the capital letter) moves to the end of the file.

- ✔ 1G moves to the beginning of the file. (That's the number 1, not the letter *l*. Why ask why?)

A makeover for v i

To modify the text you have typed, follow these steps:

1. **Move the cursor to the beginning of the text that you want to change.**

2. **To type over (on top of) the existing text, type** R.

3. **Type the new text.**

   What you type replaces what is already there. Press Esc when you finish replacing text.

4. **To insert text in front of the current cursor position, type** i.

5. **Type the new text.**

   What you type is inserted without replacing any existing text. Press Esc when you finish inserting text.

Take a little off the top

To delete text, follow these steps:

1. **Move the cursor to the beginning of the text that you want to delete.**

2. **To delete one character, type the letter** x.

   To get rid of five characters, type xxxxx. You get the idea.

3. **To delete text from the current cursor position to the end of the line, type a capital** D.

4. **To delete the entire line the cursor is on, type** dd **(the letter *d* twice).**

I liked it better the way it was

Like ed, vi has a way to "undo" the most recent change or deletion you made. Type u.

If you type a capital *U*, vi undoes all changes to the current line since you moved the cursor to that line.

Write me or save me, just don't lose me

To save the updated file, type :w (be sure that you have pressed Esc so that you are in command mode first). That's a colon and a *w;* then press Enter. This command is the same one you used in ed to save (or write) a file. You should give this command every few minutes, in case the confusing nature of vi commands makes you delete something important by mistake.

Good-bye, vi

To save your changes (if you made any) and leave vi, type ZZ.

Be sure to press Esc a few times so that you are in command mode before giving this command. To quit and not save the changes you have made, type :q!. Then press Enter. This means, "Leave vi and throw away my changes. I know what I'm doing."

Most other letters, numbers, and symbols are vi commands too, so watch what you type when you are in command mode.

I just love vi *!*

If you just love vi and want to learn more about it, read Chapter 11, "Oy, Vi!" in *MORE UNIX For Dummies*. Or try emacs or pico, and see if you still love vi.

A novel concept in editing: emacs *makes sense*

Not to get your hopes up, but emacs is much easier to use than ed or vi. The reason is that it doesn't have the mysterious modes that require you to remember at every moment whether the program is expecting a command or text.

On the other hand, commands in emacs aren't exactly intuitive. But we like them better. In case you are wondering, the name *emacs* comes from *editor macros* because the original version of emacs was written as an extension to an early text editor called teco, an editor that makes ed look like the winner of the Nobel Prize for user-friendliness. (Scary thought, isn't it?)

Although emacs doesn't come with UNIX, a popular version called GNU Emacs is distributed for free, so most systems have it or can get it. Also available are commercial versions of emacs, including Epsilon and Unipress Emacs.

To run emacs, type the following line:

```
emacs eating.peas
```

You replace eating.peas with the name of the file you want, of course. If the file you name doesn't exist, emacs creates it. Like vi, emacs displays a full-screen view of your file (as shown in Figure 13-2). On the bottom line of the screen is the *status line;* it tells you the name of the file you are editing and other less interesting information.

> ✔ If you get an error message when you try to run emacs, ask your system administrator what's up. The emacs program may have another name on your system. If your system administrator says that you don't have emacs, plead with him to get it.
>
> ✔ If emacs looks or acts weird (weirder than usual, that is), your terminal type may not be set correctly. Again, ask your system administrator to straighten this out.

How to Meta-morphose emacs

Rather than have two modes, as do ed and vi, emacs treats normal letters, numbers, and punctuation as text and sticks them in your file when you type them. (Pretty advanced concept, huh?) Commands are usually given by

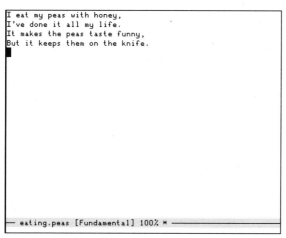

```
I eat my peas with honey,
I've done it all my life.
It makes the peas taste funny,
But it keeps them on the knife.
```

`eating.peas [Fundamental] 100% *`

Figure 13-2: At the bottom of the screen, `emacs` displays the filename and other mysterious information on the status line.

pressing combinations of the Ctrl (or Control) key and a letter. You also give some commands by pressing the Meta key and a letter.

On most computers, the Meta key is the Esc key. If your keyboard has an Alt key, it may be the Meta key. In this section, we tell you to press Esc.

Another novel concept: type to enter text

To enter text, just start typing! The text is inserted wherever your cursor is.

Tripping hither, tripping thither

To move the cursor around in your text, use the following keys:

✔ Arrow keys usually move the cursor up, down, left, and right.

In a few situations, `emacs` doesn't understand the arrow keys. If this is true for you, use Ctrl-B to move backward a character, Ctrl-F to move forward a character, Ctrl-P to move to the preceding line, and Ctrl-N to move to the next line. At least they tried to make them mnemonic.

✔ Ctrl-A moves to the beginning of the line (you hold Ctrl and press A).

✔ Ctrl-E moves to the end of the line.

✔ Esc-< (press Escape and then hold Shift and press the comma key) moves to the beginning of the file.

✔ Esc-> (press Escape and then hold Shift and press the period key) moves to the end of the file.

A small change

Even though emacs is a better text editor, you still make typos, change your mind, and think of brilliant improvements to your text. To change text, follow these steps:

1. **Move the cursor to the beginning of the text that you want to change.**

2. **Type the new text.**

   The text is inserted wherever the cursor is.

3. **Delete any text you don't want.**

It's that simple. No weird commands required.

More than one way to delete a character

There are several commands for deleting stuff:

- To delete the character that the cursor is on, press Ctrl-D (hold the Ctrl key and press D).

- To delete text from the cursor to the end of the word (up to a space or punctuation mark), press Esc and then D.

- To delete from the cursor to the end of the line, press Ctrl-K.

Someone saved my file tonight (sorry, Elton!)

To save the text in the file, press Ctrl-X Ctrl-S (press and hold the Ctrl key, press XS, and then release the Ctrl key). You should save your work every few minutes. Even though emacs isn't as frustrating as ed or vi, lots can still go wrong.

Emergency exit from emacs

To stop using emacs, follow these steps:

1. Hold the Ctrl (or Control) key and press X.

2. Hold Ctrl and press C.

This procedure doesn't save any changes you made to the file in emacs. It just gets you out. Some versions of emacs may ask whether you want to save the file that the editor was looking at, or say something like "Buffers not saved. Exit anyway?" (Translation: "Do you really want to quit without saving your changes?") Press y for yes or n for no, as appropriate. If you just want to get out, say n to the "Do you want to save" question or y to the "Buffers not saved" question. GNU Emacs is very skeptical that you'd want to do such a thing, so you have to type out yes to escape.

TIP

Moving text in emacs

Although this discussion is beyond the scope of this quick introduction to emacs, here's how to move text from one place to another in the file. It turns out that when you use Ctrl-K to kill the text from the cursor to the end of the line, it stores the killed information in a temporary place called the *kill buffer.* You can copy the information from the kill buffer back into your file by pressing Ctrl-Y (*yank* it back into the file). To move some text, kill it with Ctrl-K, move to the new location, and press Ctrl-Y to insert the text where your cursor is.

Bidding emacs *adieu*

When you finish editing and want to leave emacs, press Ctrl-X Ctrl-C (press and hold the Ctrl key, press XC, and then release the Ctrl key). You leave emacs and see the UNIX shell prompt.

If you didn't save your work, emacs politely points out your "buffers" (the stuff you have been working on) aren't saved and asks whether you really want to exit. It suggests n as the safe default in case you want to save the file. To leave without saving, press y (or in GNU emacs, type yes) and Enter.

The pico *the crop*

One other editor has become popular: pico. As the Pine mail program has spread like wildfire, the editor that comes with it, pico, has taken off, too. pico is the easiest to use of the four text editors we describe in this chapter, if not the most powerful. It was written by folks at the University of Washington.

To run pico, type this command:

```
pico eating.peas
```

As usual, type the name of the file that you actually want to edit, instead of *eating.peas.* If you type a filename that doesn't exist, pico makes a file by that name just for you.

Your system may not have pico; if not, ask your system administrator if she can get it for you. Assure her that if she doesn't, you'll be back ten times a day for a year for help with ed or vi.

The pico screen looks like Figure 13-3. Amazing — pico actually shows you a menu of the most commonly used commands at the bottom of the screen! What will they think of next?. . .

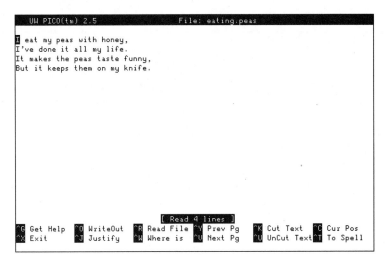

Figure 13-3: pico actually offers some hints.

You're my type

Typing text into a file using pico is a breeze. Just type. That's all. No modes, commands, or anything strange.

You move me

If your cursor keys work in pico, great. If not, you can use Ctrl-F to move forward one character, Ctrl-B to move back one character, Ctrl-N to move the next line, and Ctrl-P to move to the previous line. The following keys also move you around the screen:

- Ctrl-A moves to the beginning of the line.
- Ctrl-E moves to the end of the line.
- Ctrl-V moves forward one screen of text. (F8 also does this.)
- Ctrl-Y moves back one screen of text (as does F7).

You're a big help

To get help about pico's commands, press Ctrl-G. If your keyboard has an F1 key, that should work, too. You see pages of helpful information about the program. Press Ctrl-V to see more, or Ctrl-X to return to pico.

Time for a change

It's also easy to edit your text in pico. Whatever you type is inserted wherever the cursor is. You can use these commands to edit stuff:

✔ Ctrl-D deletes the character that the cursor is on.

✔ Ctrl-^ (that's Ctrl-Shift-6) marks the beginning of text that you want to work with. You use this command to select a bunch of text to delete or move.

✔ Ctrl-K (or F9) deletes ("kills") the text from the mark to the current cursor position. Blammo — the text is gone, and stored in an invisible holding tank somewhere.

✔ Ctrl-U (or F10) "uncuts" or "pastes" the last text that you cut, making it reappear where the cursor is now.

Thanks for saving my file

To save the text in a file, press Ctrl-O (or press F3). pico asks for the filename to write the text into, suggesting the filename you used when you ran pico in the first place. You can change the name, so that the text is written out to a new file, or leave it as is, to update the existing file. When you press Enter, pico writes the information into the file.

I'm outta here

When you are done editing and want to leave pico, just press Ctrl-X. If you haven't already saved your file, pico asks you whether you really want to leave, since leaving will lose any changes you made to the file since you last saved it. Then you're out, and you see the shell prompt.

pico doesn't claim to be an editor with the power of emacs or vi. After all, you can't edit ten files at once, read your mail, and rename files from pico. But who cares? It's a nice, easy program for editing text. Isn't that what a text editor is supposed to be for?

Chapter 14
Umpteen Useful UNIX Underdogs

* *

In This Chapter

▶ A grab bag of useful programs

▶ Sorting and comparing files

▶ Stupid calendar tricks

▶ Squashing files to make them smaller

▶ Some other odds and ends

* *

*W*ebster's defines an underdog as a victim of injustice or persecution; we certainly have been persecuting UNIX in this book. But UNIX actually has some fairly handy programs lying around. In this chapter, we look briefly at some of them. All these programs have a severe case of what is known as Feature Disease (closely related to the greasy fingerprints mentioned in Chapter 2): They all are bristling with features and options. Most of the features and options aren't worth mentioning, so we won't.

Comparing Apples and Oranges

When you have used your UNIX machine for a while, you have piles of files (say that six times quickly) lying around. Often, many of the files are duplicates, or near duplicates, of each other. Two comparison programs can help sort out this mess: cmp and diff.

The simplest comparison program is cmp; it just tells you whether two files are the same or different. To use cmp to compare two files, type the following line:

```
cmp onefile anotherfile
```

You replace onefile and anotherfile with the names of the files you want to compare, of course. If the contents of the two files are the same, cmp doesn't say anything (in the finest UNIX tradition). If they're different, cmp tells how far into the files it got before it found something different. You can compare any two files, regardless of whether they contain text, programs, databases, or whatever, because cmp cares only whether they're identical.

A considerably more sophisticated comparison program is `diff`; this program attempts to tell you not only whether two files are different but also how different they are. The files must be plain text, not word processor documents or anything else, or else `diff` gets horribly confused. Here's an example that uses two versions of a story one of us wrote. We compared files `tse1` and `tse2` by typing the following command:

```
diff tse1 tse2
```

Enter the name of the older file first and the name of the new, improved file second. The `diff` program responds with the following:

```
45c45
< steered back around, but the sheep screamed in panic and reared back.
---
> steered back around, but the goats screamed in panic and reared back.
46a47
> handlebars and landed safely in the snow.
```

The changes between `tse1` and `tse2` are that, in line 45, the *sheep* changed to *goats,* and a new line 47 was added after line 46.

In its first line of output, `45c45`, `diff` reports that there are changes (that's what the *c* stands for) in lines 45 through 45 (that is, just line 45). Then it displays the line in the first file, starting with a <, and the line in the second file, starting with a >. We think of this as `diff`'s way of saying that you took out the lines starting with < and inserted the lines starting with >. Then `diff` reports that there is a new line between lines 46 and 47 of the original file, and it shows the line that was inserted. This is a great way of seeing what changes have been made when you get a new revision of a document you have written.

BSD versions of `diff` can compare two directories to tell you which files are present in one and not in the other and to show you the differences between files with corresponding names in the two directories. Run `diff` and give it the names of the two directories.

Assorted Files

Computers are really good at putting stuff in order. Indeed, there was a day when a third of all computer time was spent sorting. UNIX has a quite-capable sorting program, cleverly called `sort`, that you may have met briefly in Chapter 7. Here, we talk about some other ways to use it.

`Sort` sorts the lines of a file into alphabetical order. From `sort`'s point of view, a line is anything that ends with a carriage return (that is, you pressed Enter). If you have a file containing a list, with one item per line, this program alphabetizes the lines.

The easiest way to use sort is to sort one file into another. That is, you take the original file and tell sort to place the sorted version in another file. This way, you don't risk screwing up the original file if the sort runs amok. To sort the original myfile into a second file called sortedfile, type the following:

```
sort myfile > sortedfile
```

Although you can sort a file back into itself, you can't do it in the obvious way. The following line, for example, doesn't work:

```
sort myfile > myfile
```

The problem with this command is that the UNIX shell clears out myfile before the sort starts (with the result that, when sort tries to sort something, it finds that myfile is empty). You can use the -o (for *output*) option to tell sort where to put the results, like this:

```
sort myfile -o myfile
```

This command works because sort doesn't start to write to the output file until it has read all its input.

Normally, sort orders its results based on a strict comparison by the internal ASCII code the computer uses. The good news is that this command sorts letters and digits in the correct way, although there are some peculiarities: Normally, uppercase letters sort before lowercase letters, so *ZEBRA* precedes *aardvark*. You can use the -f (for *fold* cases together) option to sort regardless of uppercase and lowercase letters:

```
sort -f animals -o sortedanimals
```

Although we could have used the > redirection symbol here, with sort it's safer to use -o. You can use several other options also to tell it to sort:

-b Ignore spaces (blanks) at the beginning of the line.

-d Use dictionary order and ignore any punctuation. You usually use this option with -f.

-n Sort based on the number at the beginning of the line. With this option, 99 precedes 100 rather than follows it, as it does in usual alphabetical order. (Yes, the normal thing the computer does is pretty dumb. Surprised?)

-r Sort in the reverse order of whatever would have been done otherwise. You can combine this option with any of the others.

We find sorting to be particularly useful in files in which every line starts with a date. For example:

```
0201      Margy's birthday
1204      Meg's birthday
1102      Zac's birthday
0510      John's birthday
```

We can type sort -n to sort this file by date. Notice that we wrote February 1 as 0201 and May 10 as 0510 so that a numeric sort would work.

You can do much more complex sorting and treat every line as a sequence of "fields" that sort uses to decide the final sorted order. If you really need to do this, talk to someone who knows something about sorting.

Time Is Money — Steal Some Today!

All UNIX systems have internal clocks. You can ask it what the date and time are with the date command.

UNIX responds with the following information:

```
Mon Jan   4 15:43:50 EST 1993
```

Many options let you tailor the date format any way you want. Don't waste your time. UNIX has an idea about the time zone too, and even does daylight savings time automatically.

You can schedule things to be done later with the at command. You say something like this:

```
at 5:15pm Jul 4
sort  -r myhugefile  -o myhugefile.sort
pr  -f  -2 myhugefile.sort | lp
```

And then you press Ctrl-D to indicate that you're finished giving commands.

You give the at command and specify a time and date. Then you enter the commands you want to run at that date and time; press Ctrl-D on a separate line to tell UNIX that you're finished listing tasks. In this example, we sort a huge file and then print it in two columns, all on the Fourth of July when presumably no one will be around to complain that it's taking too long. If you omit the date, UNIX assumes that you mean today if the time you give is later than the current time; otherwise, UNIX assumes that you mean tomorrow.

Any output that normally goes to the terminal is sent back to you by electronic mail; you should at least skim Chapter 19 to find out how to read your mail.

Many UNIX systems are set up so that only certain users can use the at command. If your system is set up that way, and you're not on the list, you'll get a message like "execute permission denied." In that case, you'll have to ask (politely, of course) to be added to the at user list.

Calendar Games

Another handy program is calendar, which keeps a "tickler" file of important dates. You keep a file, also called calendar, in which every line has a date and an event. The date format is quite flexible:

```
Feb 1     Margy's birthday
1/15,March 15,6/15,Dec 15    Pay estimated taxes
```

When you run calendar, it looks in the current directory for a file called calendar and prints any lines that have that day or the next day's dates (that day or Monday's dates, if a weekend intervenes). If you have a calendar file in your home directory, the system automatically runs the calendar program every day at midnight; if any lines are printed, UNIX sends them to you through electronic mail.

If you want to see a calendar for the current month, type cal.

UNIX responds by displaying the following:

```
July 1995
 S  M Tu  W Th  F  S
                    1
 2  3  4  5  6  7  8
 9 10 11 12 13 14 15
16 17 18 19 20 21 22
23 24 25 26 27 28 29
30 31
```

UNIX can do calendars for any month and year, back to the year 1. You can type cal 1993 to display all 12 months of 1993 or cal 7 1776 to display July, 1776. (The fourth was a Thursday.) If you type cal 93, you get a calendar for the year 93 A.D., which is probably not what you want. In a typical bit of UNIX over-implementation, because cal knows that the calendar in use in the United States changed from the Julian to the Gregorian calendar in September, 1752, cal 9 1752 produces a most peculiar calendar missing the 11 days by which the calendar was adjusted at that point. We suggest that you not point that out to your friends unless they have pocket calculators hanging from their belts.

A final time-related command is sleep. You use it to delay something for a while. If you're going out to lunch, for example, and want to print something ten minutes later, type the following command:

```
sleep 600 ; lpr bigfile
```

The 600 is 600 seconds, or 10 minutes (the sleep command insists on taking the sleep time in seconds). The semicolon separates two commands on the same line; it works for any shell commands. While UNIX is sleeping, you can't use it (for GUI users, you can't use the window that is sleeping). For delays of more than an hour or so, or if you want to do something with your computer in the meantime, it's easier to use the at command. If you change your mind and decide that you didn't want to wait after all, you can interrupt sleep with the usual keystrokes, usually Del or Ctrl-C.

Squashing Your Files

One problem that is common to all UNIX systems — indeed, to nearly all computer systems of any kind — is that there is never enough disk space. UNIX comes with a couple of programs that can alleviate this problem: compress and pack. They change the data in a file into a more compact form. Although you can't do anything with the file in this compact form except expand it back to the original format, for files you don't need to refer to very often, it can be a big space saver.

You use compress and pack in pretty much the same way. To compress a file called sleuth1.doc, for example, type the following line:

```
compress -v sleuth1.doc
```

The optional -v (for *verbose*) option merely tells UNIX to report how much space it saved. If you use it, UNIX responds with the following information:

```
sleuth1.doc: Compression: 49.79% — replaced with sleuth1.doc.Z
```

The compress program replaces the file with one that has the same name with .Z added to it. The degree of compression depends on what's in the file, but 50 percent compression for text files is typical. On a few files, the compression scheme doesn't save any space, in which case compress is polite enough not to make a .Z file.

To get the compressed file back to its original state, use uncompress:

```
uncompress sleuth1.doc.Z
```

This command gets rid of sleuth1.doc.Z and gets back sleuth1.doc. You can also use zcat, a compressed-file version of the cat program, which sends an uncompressed version of a compressed file to the terminal, without storing the uncompressed version in a file. It is rarely useful by itself but can be quite handy with programs such as more or lp:

```
zcat sleuth1.doc.Z | more
```

This command lets you see what's in the file one page at a time. Unlike uncompress, zcat does not get rid of the .Z file.

A similar but older program that uses a different compacting scheme is pack. To use it, type the following line:

```
pack sleuth1.doc
```

UNIX responds with the following information:

```
/usr/bin/pack: sleuth1.doc: 37.1% Compression
```

You get packed files back with unpack; you can look at packed files with pcat. Packed files end in .z (that's a lowercase *z*, to confuse the innocent). Like compress, pack leaves the file untouched if packing doesn't save any space. In most cases, pack doesn't save as much space as compress does, although it occasionally does better. Sometimes it's worth it to try both.

Zippedy day-tah

PKZIP and WINZIP are widely used compression programs among DOS users to create *ZIP* files containing one or more files compressed together. You may run into ZIP files if you get information from the Internet or on a DOS disk. Fortunately, a number of volunteers (led by a perfectly nice guy who goes under the enigmatic handle of Cave Newt) have written free zipping and unzipping programs called zip and unzip. They're both available for free over the Internet, so no UNIX system should be without them.

To unzip a ZIP file, you use unzip, for example:

```
unzip flurgle.zip
```

Unzip has a whole bunch of options, the most useful of which is -l, which tells the program to list the contents of the zip file without actually extracting anything. To find out what all the options are, run unzip with no arguments.

If you need to create a ZIP file, you can use the equally boringly named `zip`.

```
zip flurgle *.txt
```

This says to create a file called `flurgle.zip` (it adds the `.zip` part if you don't) containing all of the files in the current directory whose names end in `.txt`. `Zip` also has a lot of options, the most useful of which are `-9`, meaning to compress as well as possible even though that's slow (`-1` means as fast as possible, other digits give results in between), and `-k`, which means to make the file look just like one created on a DOS system, not using any lowercase filenames or other UNIX-isms. We use `zip -9k` to create ZIP files to copy to DOS systems.

What's GNU, zip department

The people at the Free Software Foundation, who we met in Chapter 2, have their own compression programs, GNU Zip and Unzip, known to UNIX as `gzip` and `gunzip`. The GNU programs use the best up-to-date compression techniques, so they do a better job than `compress` and its ilk. Also, unlike `compress` and `zip`, `gzip` and `gunzip` use 100 percent, publicly available, non-patented algorithms. They handle one file at a time, so you use them pretty much the same way you use `compress`:

- ✔ `gzip floogle` replaces *floogle* with *floogle.gz*.
- ✔ `gunzip floogle.gz` gets back *floogle*.
- ✔ `gcat floogle.gz` shows what's inside *floogle.gz*.

Although `gzip` only makes GNU ZIP files, `gunzip` knows how to unpack files created by pretty much every compression program around, so if you have a mystery compressed file, let `gunzip` try to unpack it.

What's in That File?

Sometimes you have a bunch of files and no recollection of what they contain. The `file` command can give you a hint. It looks at the files you name on the command line and makes its best guess about what's in the files.

To have `file` try to figure out what's in the files in the working directory, type the following line:

```
file *
```

UNIX responds with the following bunch of seemingly incomprehensible information:

```
sleuth1.doc: data
sleuth1.ms: [nt]roff, tbl, or eqn input text
tse1: ascii text
tse2.Z: compressed file - with 16 bits
```

This mess says that file figured out that the sleuth1.ms file is a text file coded for input to the troff text formatter (those other programs are some of troff's helpers), that tse1 contains text, and that tse2.Z is compressed. (The "16 bits" stuff tells which version of compress was used; it doesn't really matter because current versions of compress can read any compressed file.) The file program guesses "data" whenever it has no idea what's in a file. The first file, sleuth1.doc, is a Microsoft Word document, something file doesn't know about, so it guessed that it's data.

A Desk Calculator

UNIX comes with a severely over-implemented desk calculator program called bc. You run it and then type arithmetic expressions to which UNIX gives answers. To run it, type bc.

It doesn't say anything, so it's ready for you to type a formula. If you type 2*3

It responds with

6

You can use parentheses to tell bc the order in which to perform the calculations. If you type

```
(2+9)*3
```

It says

33

You can ask bc to do things with really big numbers, like this:

```
238735743473874874857485748547*9297264355406956849479586958596656
```

It responds

2219589318161235893764880347174617659766790965431481791 9832

Answers can get so long that they don't fit on one line. If you type

```
2^900
```

you get

```
8452712498170643941637436558664265704301557216577944354047371344426786\
2440907597751590676094202515006314790319892114058862117560952042968596\
0086236554070332305341869439840813466997042828228230568483877265313790\
14466368452684024987821414350380272583623832617294363807973376
```

That last example is 2 to the 900th power (2 multiplied by itself 900 times). The bc program doesn't believe in rounding off. By golly, if the answer to some calculation is a 14,000-digit number, it computes all 14,000 digits exactly, even if it takes a while. The people in your accounting department who are always after you to explain the missing 17 cents on your expense report will like this feature of bc.

To leave bc, type quit or press Ctrl-D.

A Really Dumb Program

Lest we leave you with the impression that UNIX is full of useful programs, we end this chapter with banner. If you type this line, for example

```
banner "Eat at" "Joe's"
```

UNIX responds with the following:

```
######
#          ##     #####              ##     #####
#         #  #        #             #  #        #
#####    #    #       #            #    #       #
#        ######       #            ######       #
#        #    #       #            #    #       #
######   #    #       #            #    #       #
         #                  ###
         #    ####   ######  ###    ####
         #   #    #   #       #    #
         #   #    #   #####   #    ####
#        #   #    #   #               #
#        #   #    #   #           #    #
 #####    ####    ######          ####
```

All banner does is print words in large, ugly letters. If you want it to print two words together with a space, put them in quotation marks, like we did. Perhaps this program was useful at one point for printing separator pages on the printer. Then again, perhaps not.

Chapter 15

I'm Not a System Administrator — I Can't Install Software!

. . . .

In This Chapter

▶ Where does software come from, the software stork?

▶ Where to put software

▶ Writing shell scripts, or files full of commands

▶ Writing aliases for your favorite commands

. . . .

*H*ey, calm down. No, we're not about to train you to be a system programmer. Every user has a few favorite programs, and you will wear out your welcome quickly if you go off to your local wizard every time you want to use a new program. In many cases, installing new programs is easy enough that you can do it yourself.

If you are a DOS or Macintosh user, you probably are thinking just the opposite: "Sure, I can install new programs. What's the big deal? I just stick in a floppy disk and type INSTALL, right?" No. In UNIX, it's not that simple, of course. There are issues of paths, permissions, and other technical-type stuff we have been protecting you from.

The Software Stork

Interesting software comes from many places:

✔ Some other user on the same machine already has it for his or her own use, and you want to use it too.

✔ Some other machine on the network has a program that you want for yourself. See Chapters 20 and 21 for the gory details of copying it from other machines on the network.

✔ Someone sends programs through electronic mail. (Yes, it's possible.)

✔ You create files that contain frequently used commands so that you don't have to type them repeatedly. In UNIX-speak, these files are called *shell scripts*. In essence, you make your own multipurpose UNIX commands.

First, let's talk about where you should put your own software; then we can go into more detail about the mechanics of putting it there.

You've bin *Had*

Every UNIX user should have a bin directory. It's just a directory called bin in your home directory. If it's not there, you can make it by going to your home directory and typing this line:

```
mkdir bin
```

The thing that's special about bin is that the shell looks for programs there. Most system administrators automatically set up a bin directory for users. If not, and you had to create it yourself, you may have to do some fiddling to tell the shell to look for programs there. See the sidebar entitled "Your search path" for the bad news.

To put programs in your bin directory, you just copy them there by using the cp command. Alternatively, you can move them there by using the mv command, a text editor, or any other way to create or move a file.

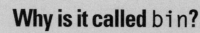

Why is it called bin?

Early on, *bin* was short for *bin*ary, because most programs that people put there were, in fact, compiled binary code. In the late 1970s, a famous professor of cognitive science at the University of California published a paper called "The Trouble with UNIX," in which he complained bitterly about how difficult it was to use UNIX. One of the items on his list was that bin was difficult to remember. One of the UNIX guys at Bell Labs published a witty rebuttal and pointed out that many of the allegedly "more natural" command names that the professor suggested were merely the names that the computer system at his university used. The UNIX guy reported that many Bell Labs users thought that a bin was the obvious place to stash their programs. So, it's still a bin.

The famous professor now works for a large Silicon Valley computer maker and is even reputed to use UNIX now and then, although he probably shuts his office door so no one can see.

A bin *of Shells*

You can make your own commands (that is, shell scripts) to put in your bin directory. A shell script is a text file that contains a list of shell commands — the same commands you type at the shell prompt. You can store a list of commands as a shell script, and run the commands at any time by typing the name of the shell script. Here's how.

You too can be a scriptwriter

To create a shell script, use any text editor (see Chapter 13). Enter the commands one per line, just as you would type them at the shell prompt. Save the file in your bin directory.

Here's an example — if you frequently search for files with names that begin with *budget,* you probably are tired of typing this command over and over:

```
find . -name "budget*" -print
```

(Check out Chapter 8 to see how the find command works.) Instead, you can put this command in a shell script and perhaps call the script findbud. To do this, create a text file named findbud that contains just one line: the command.

First you move to your bin directory, because that's where your programs live, by typing

```
cd bin
```

Then you use a text editor to create a text file containing the commands you want in your script. In this example, we use ed, a creepy editor, but you can use the editor of your choice. Type

```
ed findbud
```

UNIX responds with the following line:

```
?findbud
```

or maybe

```
findbud: No such file or directory
```

Either way, you are editing the findbud file. Type a to tell ed to start appending text to the end of the findbud file. (Remember that because you're using ed, you have to type weird commands.)

Then type these two lines:

```
find . -name "budget*" -print
.
```

The dot on a line by itself tells ed to return to command mode. To save the file, type w.

UNIX responds with the information that you have saved a file with 30 (or so) characters.

Quit ed by typing q. You see the shell prompt again. Great! You've created a shell script!

Making a screenplay from a text file

Now you must tell UNIX that the text file you have created is executable — that it's more than a mere text file. To do this, type the following line:

```
chmod +x findbud
```

This line marks the findbud file as *executable* (a script that the shell can run).

Take 1

To run the shell script, just type its name:

```
findbud
```

Voilà! You have just created your own UNIX command! UNIX runs the find command to look for your budget files.

You may not quite be finished, though. Observe what happens when you go to another directory. Type the following two commands to go to your home directory and give the findbud command:

```
cd
findbud
```

If UNIX responds with this message:

```
findbud: Command not found.
```

To get UNIX to do what you want type rehash.

Now when you type findbud, it works.

What's going on? Well, it's Mr. too-smart-for-his-own-good shell. Because programs don't appear and disappear very often, when the shell starts up, it makes a list of all the commands it can access and where they are. Because there are frequently five or six command directories, this process saves considerable time (the alternative is to check every directory for every command every time you type one). The rehash command tells UNIX to rebuild its list (known in geekspeak as a *hash table*) because you have added a new command. (The findbud file is really a command, remember?) If the command still doesn't work, you will have to fiddle with your search path — not a pretty job. See the sidebar titled "Your search path."

In the C shell, type rehash to tell the shell that you have added a new command and that you want it to rebuild its list of available commands to include this one. If you don't give the rehash command and you change directories, you can't use the newly created shell script during this login session.

We could write an entire book about shell scripts (others have). In fact, we wrote several chapters about them in *MORE UNIX For Dummies.* The finer points naturally vary depending on which shell you use, but this explanation gives you the general idea. Shell scripts aren't limited to one line; they can be as long as you want, which is handy when you have a long list of commands that you want to run regularly.

Don't give me any arguments!

Shell scripts can be complete programs. Every shell program has lots of swell programming features you don't want to know about. But one is so useful that we're going to tell you anyway: Your shell scripts can use information from the command line. That is, if you type *foogle dog pig*, your script called *foogle* can see that you ran it saying *dog* and *pig*. The things on the line after the name of the command are called *arguments*. The word *dog* is the first argument, and *pig* is the second one. In shell scripts, the first argument is called $1, the second $2, and so forth. In shorthand, $* means "all the arguments."

Suppose that you want to write a script called 2print that prints files in a two-column format. (You do that by using the pr command, described

in Chapter 10.) Create a file called 2print that contains the following line:

```
pr -f -2 $* | lpr
```

Then use the chmod and (if need be) rehash commands to make 2print an executable script. If you want to print several files, one right after the next, in two-column format, you can type this line:

```
2print onefile anotherfile
    yetanotherfile
```

In reality, you are saying this:

```
pr -f -2 onefile anotherfile
    yetanotherfile | lpr
```

This line prints all three files in two-column format. (Note that you may need to use lp rather than lpr in this shell script. Refer to Chapter 10.)

Your search path

You can ignore this section unless you have put a command in your `bin` directory and the shell can't find it. Still reading? Sorry to hear it. The shell has a list of directories that contain commands; this list is known as the *search path*. On any sensible UNIX system, the `bin` directory is already in your search path. If it's not, you have to put it there. There are two stages: putting it in once and putting it in permanently.

To see what your current search path is, type this line if you are using the C shell:

```
echo $path
```

If you have the Bourne or Korn shell or BASH, type this line:

```
echo $PATH
```

Yes, one's uppercase and one's lowercase. Arrgh. The C shell responds with something like this:

```
/bin /usr/bin /usr/trufax/bin /
    usr/local/bin
```

The other shells show something like this:

```
/bin:/usr/bin:/usr/trufax/bin:/
    usr/local/bin:.
```

What you have to do is add your `bin` directory to the path.

If you use the C shell, type this magical incantation:

```
set path=($path ~/bin)
```

That's a tilde (~) in the middle. This tells the C shell to set the path the same as the current path (`$path`), plus the `bin` subdirectory of your home directory (~).

If you use one of the other shells, type this even more magical incantation:

```
PATH=$PATH:$HOME/bin
```

```
export PATH
```

Notice that in the first command, when you type `PATH` the second time as well as when you type `HOME`, you put a dollar sign ($) in front of them. This tells the shell to set the path the same as the current path (`$PATH`), plus the `bin` subdirectory of your home directory (`$HOME`). Same song, different words.

Now you should be able to run your new script regardless of which directory you're using.

This new, improved path lasts only until you log out. To put your `bin` directory on the path every time you log in, you must add the incantation to the end of the shell script that runs automatically when you log in. If you use the C shell, add it to the `.login` file. If you use the Bourne or Korn shell or BASH, add it to the `.profile` file.

Yes, these filenames begin with periods. Filenames that start with periods usually don't show up in file listings, which is why you haven't noticed these files in your home directory. Type the following to list all your files, including these hidden ones:

```
ls -a
```

In principle, to add your `bin` directory permanently to your path, you only have to edit the file, go to the end, and add the necessary lines. In practice, it's easy to screw up, so — unless you're feeling particularly brave — you're probably better off asking for expert assistance.

Borrowing Other People's Programs

Lots of times, someone else has a cool program that you want to be able to use. There are two approaches to getting what you want, and both are pretty easy. Suppose that your friend Tracy has a program called `pornotopia` in the `bin` directory. (No, we don't know what it does, either.) How can you run it?

The long way

If you use the C shell, Korn shell, or BASH, you can run the program from his directory by typing this line:

```
~tracy/bin/pornotopia
```

If you use the Bourne shell, you can type this line:

```
/usr/tracy/bin/pornotopia
```

The easier way

It is a pain to type this long string of letters and symbols every time you want to run the program. A better way is to put a *link* to the cool program in your `bin` directory so that you can run it directly. (Links are described in Chapter 8.) You use the `ln` command to create a link, which makes the file appear to be in your own `bin` directory, too.

Try the direct approach. Move to your home directory and create a link:

```
cd
ln ~tracy/bin/pornotopia bin/pornotopia
```

With any luck, this method will work, creating a link from Tracy's file to the name `pornotopia` in your `bin` directory. You're all set. (C shell users need a quick `rehash`.)

However, the `ln` command doesn't work if you and Tracy have files on different disks. (This is all explained in Chapter 8 and 20.) In this case, you may get this unhelpful message:

```
ln: different file system
```

If you get this message, it's time for Plan B. BSD, Linux, and SVR4 systems have things called *symbolic links* that work across different disks (explained in Chapter 8, too). Try this line:

```
ln -s ~tracy/bin/pornotopia bin/pornotopia
```

If it works, it makes a symbolic link to the file you want. You're all set. The link to pornotopia refers to Tracy's version; after a rehash, you're ready to go.

Using an alias

Well, if you were named pornotopia, you probably would want an alias too. Fortunately, the BASH, Korn, and C shells give you the ability to invent a short name for a long command. (Bourne shell users, you are out of luck. Skip to the next section.)

In the BASH and Korn shells, type this line:

```
alias dobudget='/usr/tracy/bin/pornutopia'
```

This line tells the shell that, when you type dobudget, you really want to run Tracy's program. Heh, heh. To avoid inadvertent ease of use, the C shell's alias command works in almost the same way, but it is punctuated slightly differently:

```
alias dobudget '/usr/tracy/bin/pornutopia'
```

(In both cases, the quotes are optional if the command doesn't contain any spaces or special characters, but it never hurts to use them.)

You can define aliases for any frequently used one-line command. The alias can contain spaces, pipes, and anything else you can type on a command line. In BASH, for example, you can type:

```
alias sortnprint='sort -r bigfile | pr -2 | lpr'
```

This line makes the new sortnprint command sort your bigfile in reverse alphabetical order, format it in two columns with pr, and send the result to the printer. Aliases can also be useful if you are subject (as we are) to chronic miswiring of the nerves in your fingers. We always type mroe when we mean more, so an alias fixes it:

```
alias mroe=more
```

(That's the BASH version; the C shell would have a space rather than an equal sign between mroe and more.)

Aliases you type directly to the shell are lost when you log out. If you want them to be available permanently, you must put the alias commands in your .login or .profile file, in the same way we mentioned earlier, in the "Your search path" sidebar.

The last resort

If this method doesn't work either, try Plan D to use Tracy's program: a one-line shell script. Although we use the ed program because it's easier to show, you should use a real editor. Start by revving up ed:

```
ed bin/pornotopia
```

You get the following helpful response, or something like it:

```
?bin/pornotopia
```

Now tell ed to add some text to the file by typing a.

You are now in append mode. Type the command line that you want to include in the shell script, followed by a dot (period) on a line by itself:

```
/usr/tracy/bin/pornotopia
.
```

The dot on a line by itself switches back to ed's command mode. Then type w.

This writes the new shell script file and prints the size of the file. Type q to quit ed.

Type this command to make your new shell script "runnable":

```
chmod +x pornotopia
```

C shell users give the rehash command.

Now your script named pornotopia will run Tracy's original program called pornotopia. At least one of these four plans should work for any program lying around anywhere on your system.

We don't even discuss software copyrights, licenses, and ethics here, but if you use a copyrighted program, you should pay for it unless you like to think of yourself as a thief.

Sneaking Software through the Mail

It is possible to disguise programs as mail messages so that you can mail them around. This method is often the only way to do samizdat software distribution when networks and system administrators are uncooperative. Two methods are commonly used: shar messages and uuencoded messages. Here's the low-down on both methods.

Sneaky shar

For short programs and shell scripts, the usual way to send stuff is as a *shar message,* a shell script that, when you run it, re-creates the files in question. (If you care, shar rhymes with cigar and is lazy-typist-ese for *sh*ell *ar*chive.) Shar files are also a convenient way to mail groups of text files as a unit.

Shar messages usually start with lines like this:

```
#!/bin/sh
# This is a shell archive (produced by shar 3.49)
# To extract the files from this archive, save it to a file, remove
# everything above the "!/bin/sh" line above, and type "sh
file_name".
#
# made 01/05/1995 19:41 UTC by johnl@iecc
# Source directory /usr/johnl/bin
```

Recovering the files is a three-step process:

1. **Save the message in a separate file, something like** incoming-shar.

   See Chapter 19 for instructions about how to do this.

2. **Use any text editor to delete all the lines from the beginning of the file to the first line that starts with a #.**

   If you delete a few of the # lines, don't worry; the shell ignores them anyway.

3. **Feed the edited file to the shell by typing this line:**

   ```
   sh incoming-shar
   ```

This command runs the script in the file and creates the program files, or whatever else is in the shar file. (Near the front of most shar messages is a manifest that lists the files contained in the file.) When you see the UNIX prompt, it is done. Delete the incoming-shar file and move the files it created to the appropriate place, probably to your bin directory.

WARNING!

Shar files are major security gaps. Nothing stops them from doing something nefarious to your system. We recommend running shar files only if you know the sender. Uuencoded files are far safer.

Sneaky you-you

Shar files don't work well for binary programs, so a widely adopted scheme called uuencode disguises them as text. If you receive a file coded in uuencode, the message looks something like

```
begin 775 pornotopia
M3'$$'!C?&RN:4@"0',"!P"P$+'Q"S"P"#'9"#X"Q"$"-"""<
M#4"+G1E>'Q"#X""T"",PL"#X"'-I1'"'("""YD
```

Recovering the binary file from the uuencode file is a two-step process:

1. **Save the message in a file with a name something like** uu-incoming.

2. **Feed the file to the** uudecode **program by typing the following line:**

```
uudecode uu-incoming
```

You don't have to edit the encoded file to delete the first lines in the file because uudecode ignores them for you. When you see the UNIX prompt, it is done. Then get rid of the uu-incoming file and move the created binary file to the appropriate place.

Making your own sneaky e-mail

What if you want to send a program or other binary file by e-mail? You too can create uuencoded files, just like the big guys. Not surprisingly, you use the uuencode program. Here's how.

1. **Type this command:**

```
uuencode pornotopia strange-program > temp
```

In this command, replace pornotopia with the file you want to uuencode, strange-program with the name that you want the file to have when it is uudecoded, and temp with any temporary filename (junk is another perennial favorite). This command creates a uuencoded file named temp which, when uudecoded, will create a file named strange-program with the same contents as your pornotopia file.

2. **Include this uuencoded file at the end of an e-mail message.**

   The message should say that it contains a uuencoded file and what it's for. (See Chapter 19 for how to send e-mail.)

Sneaking MIMEly

If you use the Pine mail program, you don't have to go through all this nonsense to mail files. Pine handles something called MIME, which is a new standard way to mail arbitrary files around. To mail a file with Pine, just tell it to *attach* the file to a mail message. For an incoming message, Pine recognizes the file automatically. See Chapter 14 of *MORE UNIX For Dummies* for Pine details.

Chapter 16

How to Run a Bunch of Programs at a Time

*1*f you have a plain, old terminal with no windowing system, you may be envious of users with fancy window systems who can pop up a bunch of windows and run umpteen programs at a time.

Well, don't be. Any UNIX system lets you run as many programs simultaneously as you want; nearly all the systems let you stop and restart programs and switch around among different programs whenever you want.

If you're used to an old-fashioned, one-program-at-a-time system, such as DOS (without Windows) you might not see the point of doing several things at a time. Suppose, however, that you're doing something that takes a while and that the computer can manage with little or no supervision from you, such as copying a large file over a network (which can take 10 or 15 minutes). There's no reason for you to sit and wait for that process to finish — you can do something useful while the copying runs in the background.

Or suppose that you're in the middle of a program and want to do something else: You're writing a memo in a text editor and need to check an e-mail you received to make sure that you spell someone's name right. One way to do that is to save the file, leave the editor, run the mail program, leave the mail program, start the editor again, return to the same place in the file, and pick up where you left off. What a pain. UNIX lets you stop the editor, run the mail program, and resume the editor where you left it. For that matter, you can run *both* the editor and the mail program and flip between them.

In the interest of fairness, we must point out that *job control,* the feature that lets you flip back and forth, was written by Bill, the same guy who wrote the C shell, vi, and NFS. In contrast to our opinion of some of his other efforts, we think that job control is pretty cool.

If you have a program that has run amok, see Chapter 24 to find out how to kill it.

So What Is a Process, Anyway?

All the work that UNIX does for you is done by UNIX *processes.* When you log in, the shell is a process. When you run an editor, the editor is a process. Pretty much any command you run is a process.

Processes called *daemons* lurk in the background and wait to do useful things without manual intervention — when you use lp or lpr to print something, for example, a daemon does the real work of sending the material to the printer.

Normally, this process stuff happens automatically, and you don't have to pay much attention to it. But sometimes a program gets stuck, and you can't make it go away. If you use a PC running DOS or a Macintosh, the usual response to a stuck program is to restart the computer. When you run UNIX, resetting the computer is a little extreme for a single stuck program. For one thing, other running programs and other people who are logged in do not appreciate having their computer kicked out from underneath them. Also, it can take UNIX a while to restart from a forced reboot (it takes our system about 20 minutes to check all the disks), and you run the risk of losing files that were being updated.

Any Processes in the House?

The basic program you use to find out which processes are around is ps (for *process status*). The details of ps (wait! — how did you know?) vary from one version of UNIX to another, but there are two main kinds of ps: the System V kind and the BSD kind. (SVR4 uses the System V kind of ps, even though SVR4 has a lot of BSD mixed in. Linux uses a ps that looks more or less like BSD.)

Mind your ps (and qs)

If you run plain ps, no matter which version of UNIX you have, you get a list of the processes running from your terminal (or window, if you're using X Windows). The list looks something like this:

```
PID    TTY      TIME COMMAND
24812  ttyp0    0:01 -csh
25973  ttyp0    0:00 ps
```

The PID column gives the *process identification,* or *process ID.* To help keep processes straight, UNIX assigns every process a unique number as an identifier. The numbers start at 1 and go up. When the PIDs get inconveniently large (about 30,000 or so), UNIX starts over again at 1 and skips numbers that are still in use. To get rid of a stuck process, you need to know its PID to tell the system which process to destroy.

The TTY column lists the terminal from which the process was started. In this case, ttyp0 is the terminal, which happens to be pseudo terminal number 0. (Because UNIX systems were written by and for nerds, they tend to start counting at 0 rather than at 1.) A *pseudo terminal* is what UNIX uses when you're logged in from an X window or from a remote system through a network, rather than through a real, actual, drop-it-on-your-foot-and-it-hurts terminal. For our purposes, all terminals act the same, be they real, pseudo, or whatever.

The TIME column is the amount of time the computer has spent running this process. (The time spent waiting for you to type something or waiting for disks and printers and so forth doesn't count.)

The COMMAND column shows the name of the command that started the process, more or less. If the process is the first one for a particular terminal or pseudo terminal, the command name starts with a hyphen.

Why processes are not programs and vice versa

Programs and processes are similar, but they're not the same. A *process* is, more or less, a running program. Suppose that you're using X Windows or Motif, have two windows on-screen, and are running vi in both of them. Although the same program is running in both windows, they're different processes doing different things (in this case, editing different files).

To add to the confusion, some programs use more than one process apiece. The terminal program cu, for example, uses two processes: one to copy what you type to the remote computer, and the other to copy stuff from the remote computer back to your screen. Sometimes there are "hidden" processes: Many programs have a way you can execute any UNIX command from inside the program. (In ed, for example, you type ! and the command you want to run.) In addition, a separate process usually interprets each shell command you type.

In most cases, it is easy enough to tell in a list of processes which one is which, because each one is identified by the command that started it.

The Linux ps

Linux's ps command adds one additional column to the list of processes running, like this:

```
PID  TTY   STAT  TIME COMMAND
1797 pp5   S     0:00 -bash
1855 pp5   R     0:00 ps
```

The STAT column shows the status of the process. According to the man page for the command, R means runnable, S means sleeping, D means uninterruptible sleep, T means stopped or traced, and Z means a zombie process. Wow! For our purposes, Z means it's already finished, and the other stuff doesn't matter much.

Fancier ps *(and qs)*

If you're logged in on several terminals or in several windows, you may want to see all your processes, not just the ones for the current terminal. With the System V version of ps, you can ask to see all processes for a given user by typing:

```
ps -u tracy
```

This command lists all processes belonging to user tracy. You can ask to see any user's processes, not just your own. You can get a full listing for that user too:

```
ps -fu tracy
```

System V has other, less useful switches for ps, notably -e, which shows every process in the entire system.

Berkeley ps *(and qs)*

You can ask for a particular terminal's process list by using the -t option, as in this example:

```
ps -tp4
```

With the -t option, you have to use the same two-letter terminal abbreviation ps uses. Have fun guessing it. Try the two-letter abbreviations that appear in the TT column of the ps listing.

There are lots of other useless options for the BSD version of ps, including -l for a *long* technoid listing, -a for *all* processes, not just yours, and -x to show processes not using a terminal. There's no way to ask for all processes

Why cd isn't a process

People always ask us (well, someone asked once) why the cd command doesn't always act the way they expect it to. The problem is what is called in erudite circles *Lamarckian Heritability,* but what we call "you look like your mother."

When a parent process creates a child process, the child inherits many characteristics from its parent, such as the user name, the terminal, and (this is important) the current directory. The child, ungrateful for its heritage as all children are, can change many of these things. Inheritance goes only one way, so changes in the child don't affect the parent. Suppose that you create a new process (type sh to start a new shell as the second process). Then go to some directory other than the one you were using, like /tmp, by typing cd /tmp. Then type pwd to make sure that you are in /tmp. Leave the new shell by typing exit and type pwd back in the old shell to prove that you're back in the original directory.

This example proves that cd can't be a normal command executed in its own process. If it were,

the new directory would apply only to that process; as soon as the process was finished, you would be back in the shell with the directory unchanged.

The authors of the various shells finessed this problem using what's technically known as a *kludge.* (Something that works but that you're not proud of, it rhymes with "huge," not with "fudge.") The kludge checks especially for the cd command and handles it itself in the shell. The exit and logout commands also are handled in the shell for the same reason.

Here's the example where you may run into this: If you make a shell script (see Chapter 15) that contains a cd command, the cd affects only subsequent commands in that script. After your shell script is done running, you find yourself back in the original directory as though the cd had never occurred. Although it's possible to write a script that does change the directory, it's so complicated that even wizards shrink from the task.

belonging to a particular user. To see all the processes that you started, type the following incantation:

```
ps -aux | grep tracy
```

Replace Tracy's name with your own user name. This redirects the output of the ps command to the grep command (described in Chapter 8), which throws away all the lines except those that contain your user name.

Starting Background Processes

Starting a background command is simplicity itself. You can run any program you want in the background; when you type the command, stick a space and an ampersand (&) at the end of the line just before you press Enter.

Suppose you want to use troff to print a file (even though we warned you not to). This is bound to take a long time, for example, so typing the ampersand to run it in the background is wise:

```
troff a_really_large_file &
```

The shell starts the command and immediately comes back to ask you for another command. It prints a number, which is the *process ID* (or PID) assigned to the command you just started. (Some shells print a small number, which they call the *job number,* and a larger number, which is the PID.) If you know the PID, you can check up on your background program with the ps command. If you get tired of waiting for the background process, you can get rid of it with the kill command and the PID (see Chapter 24).

You can start as many programs simultaneously as you want in this way. In practice, you rarely want more than three or four because only one computer is switching back and forth among the various programs; the more simultaneous things you do, the slower each one runs.

When your background program finishes, the C, Korn, BASH, and SVR4 Bourne shells tell you that it's finished; older versions of the Bourne shell say nothing.

If you know that a program is going to take a long time (a program that crunches for a long time to produce a report, for example), you can use the nice command with that program. The nice command tells the program to run in a nice way so that it gets a smaller share of the computer than it would otherwise. The niced program takes longer to run, but other programs run faster, which is usually a good trade-off if the niced program was going to take a long time anyway. To use it, you just type nice followed by the command to run:

```
nice genreport Tuesday.raw &
```

You almost always use nice to run programs in the background because it would take an inexplicably saintly user to want to slow down a program he was going to sit and wait for.

If you want to wait for background programs to finish, the wait command waits for you until they're all finished. If you get impatient, you can interrupt wait with Ctrl-C (or Del, depending on your system); these keystrokes interrupt only the wait and leave the background processes unmolested.

The Magic of Job Control

Quite a while ago (in about 1979), people (actually, our pal Bill) noticed that, many times, you run a program, realize that it's going to take longer than you thought, and decide that you want to switch it to a background program. At the time, the only choices you had were to wait or to kill the program and start it over by using an & to run it in the background. Job control lets you change your mind after you start a program.

The job-control business requires cooperation from your shell. In SVR4, BSD, and Linux, all three shells handle job control. In some earlier versions of UNIX, only the C shell, or sometimes the C shell and Korn shell, handle job control.

Suppose that you start a big, slow program by typing the following line:

```
bigslowprogram somefile anotherfile
```

The program runs in the foreground because you didn't use an ampersand (&). Then you realize that you have better things to do than wait, so you press Ctrl-Z. The shell should respond with the message Stopped. (If it doesn't, you don't have a job-control shell. Sorry. Skip the rest of this chapter.) At this point, your program is in limbo. You can do three things to it:

- ✔ You can continue it in the foreground as though nothing had happened, by typing fg (which stands for *f*oreground).

- ✔ You can stick it in the background by typing bg (for *b*ackground), which makes the program act as though you started it with an & in the first place.

- ✔ You can kill it if you decide that you shouldn't have run it at all. This method is slightly more complicated; details follow.

Take this job and . . .

UNIX calls every background program you start a *job*. A job can consist of several processes (which, as you know, are running programs). To print a list of all your files in all your directories with titles, for example, you can type this line:

```
ls -lR | pr -h "My files" | lp &
```

This command lists the files with ls, adds titles with pr, and sends the mess to the printer with lp, all in the background. Although you use three different programs and three separate processes, UNIX considers it one job because each program needs the other two in order to get work done.

Every regular command (those you issue without an &) is also a job, although, until you use Ctrl-Z to stop it, that's not a very interesting piece of information. You can use the jobs command to see which jobs are active. Here's a typical response to the jobs command:

```
[1]    - Stopped (signal)      elm
[2]    + Stopped          vi somefile
```

This list shows two jobs, both of which have been stopped with Ctrl-Z. One is elm, the mail-reading program; the other is the vi editor. (The difference between Stopped (signal) and plain Stopped is interesting only to programmers, so we don't discuss it much.) One job is considered the *current job* — the one preceded by a plus sign (+); it's the one most recently started or stopped. The rest are regular background jobs and can be stopped or running.

. . . *Stick it in the background*

You can tell any stopped job to continue in the background with the bg command. A plain bg continues the current job (the one marked by a plus sign) in the background. To tell UNIX to continue some other job, you must identify the job. You identify a job by typing a percent sign (%) followed either by the job number reported by jobs or by enough of the command to uniquely identify it. In this case, the elm job can be called %1, %elm, or %e because no other job used a command starting with an *e*. As a special case, %% refers to the current job. Some other % combinations are available, but no one uses them. Typing bg %e, for example, continues the elm job in the background.

. . . *Run it in a window in the foreground*

To put a process in the foreground, where it runs normally and can use the terminal, you use the fg command. Continuing a job in the foreground is such a common thing that you can use a shortcut: You just type the percent sign and the job identifier. Typing %1 or %e, for example, continues the elm job in the foreground; %v or %% continues the vi editor in the foreground.

. . . *Shove it*

To get rid of a stopped or background job, use the kill command with the job identifier or (if it's easier, for some reason) the PID. You can get rid of the vi editor job by typing this line:

```
kill %v
```

Do windows and job control mix?

If you use a GUI system like Motif, you can run lots of programs in lots of windows; is there any need for this Ctrl-Z nonsense? By and large, the answer is no; it's much easier to pop up three windows to run three programs than it is to flip the programs around in one window. (Chapter 12 shows you how to pop up new windows.)

Even if you use a GUI, it doesn't hurt to learn about job control. It's not hard to use, and someday you may be stuck in a single window (such as when you use telnet to access another system) or be banished to a regular non-X terminal; then you will appreciate what job control has to offer.

Typically, you start a job, realize that it will take longer than you want to wait, press Ctrl-Z to stop it, and then type bg to continue that process in the background.

Alternatively, you interrupt a program by pressing Ctrl-Z, run a second program, and when the second program is finished, type fg or %% to continue the original program.

You don't often bring in the gangster kill to turn out the lights on a program, but it's nice to know that you have friends in the underworld who can put a nasty program to sleep for good. Chapter 24 talks more about it.

Can two programs use the terminal?

Suppose that a program running in the background tries to read input from your terminal. Severe confusion can result (and did, in pre-job-control versions of UNIX) if both the background program and a foreground program — or even worse, two or three background programs — try to read at the same time. Which one gets the stuff you type? Early versions of UNIX did the worst possible thing: A gremlin inside the computer flipped a coin to decide who got each line of input. That was, to put it mildly, not very satisfactory.

With the advent of job control, UNIX enforced a new rule: Background jobs can't read from the terminal. If one of them tries, it stops, much as though you had pressed Ctrl-Z. Suppose that you try to run the ed editor in the background:

```
ed some.file &
```

UNIX responds:

```
[1]   + Stopped (tty input)    ed
```

As soon as ed started, and wanted to see whether you were typing anything it should know about, the job stopped. You can continue ed as a foreground program by typing fg or %% if you want to type something for ed. Or you can kill it (which is all that ed deserves) by typing kill %%.

Full-screen programs and job control

Programs that take over the entire screen, notably the vi and emacs editors and mail programs such as elm, treat the Ctrl-Z interrupt in a slightly different way. Just stopping the program and starting it again later isn't adequate; the screen would show the results of what you did in the meantime. To solve this problem, full-screen programs make arrangements with UNIX to be notified when you press Ctrl-Z, and again when you continue them so that they can do something appropriate, like redraw the screen when you continue. This process generally is all automatic and obvious, although people occasionally are confused when the screen is magically returned after they give the `fg` command.

Taming background terminal output

Any program, foreground or background, usually can scribble on-screen anything it wants at any time it wants. More often than not, that's OK because most programs are well behaved about not blathering when they're in the background.

In some cases, however, particularly when you use a full-screen editor, the interspersed output gets on your nerves. Fortunately, job control lets you solve this problem. You can put your terminal into *terminal output stop* mode: When a background program wants to send something to the terminal, it stops, just as it does when it wants to read something. You then have

the same alternatives to continue that program in the foreground if you want to see what it has to say or kill it if you don't. To turn on output stop mode, type this command:

```
stty tostop
```

To turn off output stop mode, type this line:

```
stty -tostop
```

The `stty` command is used to make all sorts of changes to the setup of your terminal. See the section, "Setting Up the Terminal the Way You Like It," in Chapter 28 if you want to know what else it can do.

Chapter 17

The DOS-to-UNIX Rosetta Stone

In This Chapter

▶ UNIX commands that do the same things as DOS commands you wish you could use

▶ UNIX command options that make UNIX commands act more like DOS commands

*F*or those of you who know DOS, this chapter provides a translation of your favorite DOS commands into UNIX. For those of you who have stayed far away from DOS, skip this chapter.

Much of DOS was based on UNIX, so some commands act the same in both systems, like `mkdir` to make a directory. Other commands are basically the same but have subtle differences that can trip you up. `cd` (or CD), for example, changes directories in both DOS and UNIX, but, if you don't specify the directory to change to, DOS and UNIX take you to two different places. Other commands are similar but have different names, like UNIX's `ls` and DOS's DIR. Some DOS commands have absolutely no counterparts in UNIX (thank heavens), like the notorious RECOVER command, found in early versions of DOS.

For each commonly used DOS command, we explain how to get UNIX to do the same thing, more or less. Unless we indicate otherwise, we're talking about DOS 6.2. To make clear which commands are DOS and which are UNIX, we capitalize the DOS commands and keep the UNIX commands in the `special font` you have become used to. (DOS doesn't care whether you type commands in capital or small letters. As you know, UNIX does care, and most of its commands are spelled with small letters.)

The Most Important Differences

Slashes! You know how you finally learned to type backslashes (\) in your DOS filenames? It's time to flip them around because UNIX uses regular slashes (/). This takes months of getting used to, but there's no way around it.

On the other hand, it surely is nice that filenames can be longer in UNIX than they can in DOS. You're not limited to eight little characters with a three-letter extension. Go nuts with your filenames; name your next file this way:

```
terrific.file.name.possible.only.in.UNIX
```

(Most UNIX systems permit long filenames, although older ones limit you to 14 characters. They all let you use as many dots as you want in the name.)

Although we are talking about filenames, remember that even though DOS doesn't care about capitalization, UNIX does. In UNIX, capital and small letters are considered to be different letters, so don't mix them up.

ATTRIB

The DOS ATTRIB command lets you change the *attributes* of files, such as whether they are hidden or read-only or need to be backed up (archived).

ATTRIB +H

The DOS ATTRIB +H command makes a file *hidden* so that it doesn't show up on directory listings. To do this in UNIX, rename the file with a filename that begins with a period. A file named .secret, for example, does not appear on ls listings. To ask for a listing of all files, including hidden files, you can type ls -a.

ATTRIB -H

The DOS ATTRIB -H command "unhides" files; the thing you do in UNIX is rename files so that they don't begin with periods. Watch out, though: Some hidden files must stay hidden in order to work. The .login and .profile files, for example (your shell executes one of these every time you log in) don't work if you rename them to anything else.

ATTRIB +R and ATTRIB -R

The DOS ATTRIB +R and ATTRIB -R commands control whether a file is *read-only*. In UNIX, every file is owned by someone; the owner can control who can read it (r), change it (w), and, for a program, run it (x). Chapter 5 discusses this stuff in more detail.

To set permissions for a file you own so that no one (not even you) can change it (equivalent to DOS's read-only attribute), type this line:

```
chmod ugo-w filename
```

To set permissions so that only you can change the file, type the following:

```
chmod go-w filename
chmod u+w filename
```

In all these commands, of course, use the name of the file rather than *filename*.

BACKUP, MSBACKUP, and RESTORE

In DOS, the BACKUP and MSBACKUP commands store stuff on floppy disks in a specialized backup format, and RESTORE gets your stuff back. In most cases, your UNIX system administrator handles backups. If this is not true for you, programs called `tar` (for *tape archive*), `cpio` (for *copy in* or out), and `pax` (for *portable archive exchange*) save and restore UNIX files to and from tapes and floppies. If you need to do your own backups, get an expert to write a script that does the backup; the details of controlling disks and floppies vary wildly among versions of UNIX. Chapter 23 talks about making and using backups.

CHDIR, or CD

The DOS CHDIR or CD command changes directories — that is, it makes another directory the working directory. It works in pretty much the same way as the UNIX `cd` command, except when you type the command by itself. If you don't tell the DOS CD command where you want to move, it doesn't move anywhere. Instead, it tells you where you are now. The UNIX equivalent is the `pwd` command, which tells you where in your directory structure you are.

The UNIX `cd` command moves you back to your home directory if you don't type a directory name. (See Chapter 6.)

CHKDSK

The DOS CHKDSK command checks the current disk for logical problems. Then it tells you how much space on the disk is used and how much is free.

On UNIX, unless you are the system administrator, you should try not to think about the possibility of your disk having logical problems. To find out how much space is free on your disk, type `df`.

DOS batch files and UNIX shell scripts

If you have used batch files in DOS, you can use similar things, called *shell scripts,* in UNIX. In case you don't know, a DOS *batch file* is a text file that contains a series of DOS commands, one per line. Amazingly, a UNIX shell script is a text file that contains a series of UNIX commands, one per line. In DOS, batch files have names that end with the .BAT extension. In UNIX, you can name a shell script anything you want. See Chapter 15 for some hints about writing shell scripts.

In DOS, if you have a batch file named AUTOEXEC.BAT in the root directory of the disk

(continued)

(continued)

you load DOS from, DOS runs that batch file automatically whenever you start DOS (whenever you start or restart the computer). UNIX has a similar shell script.

If you're using the Bourne, Korn, or BASH shell and have a file called .profile in your home directory, this file is executed automatically whenever you log in. The C shell equivalent file is .login. You can edit these files with a text editor. Your system administrator probably has already given you a .profile or .login file full of stuff for your local environment. Don't take anything out without consulting your system ad-

ministrator. If you want to add commands, add them at the end of the file.

The DOS CONFIG.SYS file contains information about your hardware and software configuration. When you turn on your computer, after it loads DOS but before it runs the AUTOEXEC.BAT file, the system looks in this file to configure DOS for your system.

UNIX configuration is entirely different and, in most cases, is not your problem. In most cases, UNIX systems automatically adapt themselves to whatever hardware is attached to the computer.

This command shows the free space on all disks (see the section, "Ignoring NFS," in Chapter 20), so you have to figure out which disk is yours by looking for the one that matches the beginning of your home directory name (the one that pwd displays).

You can also type du to find out how much space your files use. The du command (for *disk usage*) reports the amount of space used by the files in each directory and subdirectory. (If a directory has subdirectories, the space used in the subdirectories is included in the amount for the directory.)

COPY and XCOPY

The DOS COPY and XCOPY commands copy files (no kidding). The UNIX cp command works in almost the same way (see Chapter 5). In DOS, you can omit the directory you are copying to if you want to copy to the current directory. In UNIX, you can't do this. Instead, you have to type a period (.) to indicate that you want to copy to the working directory.

In DOS you type the following line, for example, to copy the LETTER.WP file from the \DOCS directory to the current directory:

```
COPY \DOCS\LETTER.WP
```

In UNIX, you type this line to do the same thing:

```
cp /docs/letter.wp .
```

The period at the end of the line tells UNIX to copy the file to the working directory.

The DOS XCOPY command, unlike COPY, can copy more than just the current directory. The /S option tells XCOPY to copy all subdirectories of the current directory, too.

In most versions of UNIX, you can use the `-r` option with the `cp` command to do the same thing (see Chapter 5):

```
cp -r /usr/margy/* .
```

With this command, UNIX copies to the working directory not only all the files in /usr/margy but also all the subdirectories. If any subdirectories are in /usr/margy, UNIX creates corresponding subdirectories in the working directory and then copies the files that are in them. This is a great way to make a backup copy of all the files in your home directory, including any subdirectories. (**Note:** Hidden files won't be copied.)

DATE and TIME

The DOS DATE and TIME commands display the date and time and let you change them. In UNIX, type `date`. The `date` command displays both the date and time. You shouldn't need to change them. If you do, talk to your system administrator.

DEBUG

The DOS DEBUG command lets you, among other things, edit files that contain programs. You can look at their contents as characters (ASCII) or numbers (hexadecimal, no less). You have to be kind of nuts to try this. The `ed`, `vi`, and `emacs` programs let you edit files, if you must (see Chapter 13). If you really want to look at the bits in a file, the `od` command (for *octal display*) lets you display a file in octal, hex, decimal, ASCII, and about 45 other formats.

DEL and ERASE

The DOS DEL and ERASE commands delete files. The UNIX `rm` command works in the same way (see Chapter 5). In both systems, *be careful!* The `rm` command doesn't ask you for confirmation if you try to delete all the files in a directory, so be even more careful. The `rm` command does ask for confirmation if you try to delete a file that is protected so that you can't write to it. If you really want to delete a protected file, type y when UNIX asks for confirmation.

DIR

Everyone's favorite DOS command is DIR: It lists the files in a directory. It is similar to the UNIX `ls` command, but the options are different (see Chapter 5). To get a UNIX listing that looks like the regular DOS DIR file list, type `ls  -l`. This command shows the size, date, and owner of every file in the directory.

DIR /W

The DOS DIR /W command displays just the filenames in several columns across the screen. UNIX can do this, too; indeed, most versions of UNIX automatically display listings in columns. If your version of UNIX doesn't, try this approach: `ls  -x`.

DIR /P

DIR /P pauses after filling up the screen with a directory listing so that you have time to read the filenames. The UNIX equivalent redirects the output of `ls` to the `more` command, which does the pausing (see Chapters 5 and 7):

```
ls | more
```

DIR /O

DIR usually lists the files in any old order (actually, it's the order in which they occur in DOS's internal recordkeeping system, which is more or less the order in which the files were made). The /O option sorts them in alphabetical order. The UNIX `ls` command sorts them this way automatically.

DIR /S

The /S option tells the DOS DIR command to include all the files in any subdirectories of the current directory. The UNIX equivalent is `ls  -R`.

DISKCOPY and DISKCOMP

The DOS DISKCOPY and DISKCOMP commands copy and compare (respectively) a floppy disk. Because UNIX almost never uses floppy disks, most versions don't have equivalent commands.

DOSKEY

DOSKEY is a cool little DOS command, available since DOS 5, that lets you give the same command without retyping it. In UNIX, doing this depends on which shell you use. See Chapter 2 for descriptions of the Big Four shells and which one you are using (you may even have written it down on your Cheat Sheet card in the front of the book).

If you use the BASH shell (bash), press the up-arrow key or Ctrl-P (for *previous*) and then Enter to repeat the last command.

If you are using the C shell (csh), type !!.

If you use the Korn shell (ksh), type r.

If you use the Bourne shell (sh), you are out of luck. (Sorry!)

EDIT and EDLIN

EDLIN is the yucky old DOS line editor that nobody uses if there is any alternative (it's gone in DOS 6); EDIT is the DOS editor (added in DOS 5). To edit files in UNIX, use ed, vi, emacs, or pico (see Chapter 13).

FIND

If you think that the UNIX equivalent to the DOS FIND command is the find command, you are sadly mistaken. Far too easy. The DOS FIND command examines a file and looks for the characters you specify. It's like a weaker version of the UNIX grep command (see Chapter 8 for how to use grep). (We're sure that you remember that the UNIX find command looks in directories for a filename you specify!)

FORMAT

The DOS FORMAT command prepares a floppy disk for use, by erasing anything that was on it. Although many UNIX systems don't even use floppy disks, the ones that do usually have a format command that formats a floppy. Ask an expert for help.

HELP

The DOS HELP command displays some help text about the command you specify. In UNIX, use the man command (see Chapter 27). To get help about the ls command, for example, type:

```
man ls
```

Or if that flies off the screen too fast to read, try

```
man ls | more
```

Some UNIX systems even have a `help` program. Try typing `help` to see whether yours does. Most `help` programs show you a little menu that lets you choose what to get help about. One choice is usually quit, so press q to leave.

MEM

MEM tells you how much of your computer's memory is free and how much is being used (that's RAM memory, not space-on-the-disk memory). All current UNIX systems have virtual memory, so the amount in use isn't your problem.

MKDIR, or MD

The DOS MKDIR or MD command makes a new directory, just like the UNIX `mkdir` command does (see Chapter 6).

MORE

DOS has filters just like UNIX! The DOS MORE filter acts almost the same as the UNIX `more` filter (see Chapter 7). In DOS, however, you can't type this line to see a file one screen at a time, as you can in UNIX:

```
more filename
```

With DOS, you must stick a < after the MORE, like this: `MORE < filename`.

PATH

The DOS PATH command tells DOS which directories to look in when it has trouble finding the program you want to run. In UNIX, you use a shell variable to contain this information. We were hoping not to have to tell you that there were such things as *shell variables,* but there's one anyway.

In UNIX, the shell variable called `PATH` contains a list of the directories UNIX searches whenever you ask it to run a program. Your system administrator probably set it up for you, and you probably don't need to change it.

To see the current value of the `PATH` variable in the Bourne, Korn, or BASH shell, type

```
echo $PATH
```

To see it in the C shell, type this:

```
echo $path
```

This line is the UNIX equivalent of typing just PATH in DOS.

Changing your path (that is, adding a directory to the path) is kind of a pain. If you really need to do so, see Chapter 15.

PROMPT

The DOS PROMPT command changes the prompt from the ever-unpopular C:\> to something more helpful. You can do this in UNIX too, but you should get a UNIX wizard or your system administrator to help you change the prompt permanently rather than just until you log out.

We like our prompts to contain the current working directory so that we have an idea where we are. If you are working on a network, it can be nice to see also the name of the computer you are using. Ask your local wizard for his or her opinion: People who use UNIX heavily always have strong opinions about what type of prompt is best.

It no longer is considered particularly funny to change your prompt to something like "Yes, master?" or "I wait to do your bidding, all-powerful one!" If you ask a UNIX expert to help you do this, he or she will be highly unimpressed.

RENAME, or REN

The DOS RENAME command renames a file. In UNIX, you use the mv command (see Chapter 5). RENAME can't move a file to a different directory at the same time, but mv can.

REPLACE

The REPLACE command is new; it copies a file from one directory to another and updates older copies. It has several options to control the way copying proceeds. Consider this DOS command:

```
REPLACE A:NEWFILE.DOC C:\ /S
```

It searches all the directories on drive C for files named NEWFILE.DOC. If it finds any, it replaces them with the NEWFILE.DOC file on the floppy disk in drive A.

To do the same thing in UNIX, you have to use the find command (see Chapter 8). If you have a file called newfile.doc in the current directory and you want to update any file by that name in your home directory and all subdirectories (/usr/you, for example, if your user name is you), type something like this:

```
find /usr/you -name newfile.doc -exec cp /newfile.doc {} \;
```

This wild and crazy command tells find to start its search in /usr/you and look for files with the name newfile.doc; if it finds any matches, find will execute the UNIX command cp /newfile.doc and replace the {} with the place where it found the file. This is a bit confusing, but you probably never have used the DOS REPLACE command, either.

RMDIR, or RD

The DOS RMDIR, or RD, command removes a directory. In DOS, before you can remove a directory, you first must delete all the files and subdirectories in it so that it is empty. The UNIX rmdir command works in the same way (see Chapter 6). If you don't want to delete everything in the directory beforehand, however, you can use the rm command to delete, in one devastating stroke, both the directory and everything it contains:

```
rm -r directoryname
```

The -r option (which stands for *recursive*) tells rm to delete all files and subdirectories (and subdirectories of subdirectories, and so on) of the directory you name.

You can delete lots of important files in a hurry with this command. Watch out! To make it safer, you can tell UNIX to ask before deleting each file, by adding the -i option:

```
rm -ir directoryname
```

In UNIX, you can't abbreviate the rmdir command as rd. UNIX ignores you if you try this stunt. The rmdir command is dangerous enough, UNIX figures, that you should have to do a little typing if you want to use it.

SET

The DOS SET command sets or displays the contents of DOS environment variables. UNIX has environment variables, also called shell variables; we've tried not to talk about them in this book.

To display the contents of a UNIX shell variable, type this line (use the actual name of the variable):

```
echo $VARIABLENAME
```

Most shell variable names are capitalized, for no particular reason. To set an environment variable in the Bourne, Korn, or BASH shell, type this line:

```
VARIABLENAME=whatever
```

In the C shell, type this line:

```
set VARIABLENAME whatever
```

The PATH shell variable, for example, contains the list of directories UNIX searches whenever you want to run a program. To see it, type this line in the Bourne, Korn, or BASH shell:

```
echo $PATH
```

To see it in the C shell, type:

```
echo $path
```

To change it (a bad idea, actually), type this line in the Bourne, Korn, or BASH shell:

```
PATH=/bin:/etc:/usr/you:
export PATH
```

Or in the C shell:

```
set path=(/bin /etc /usr/you)
```

You can see why you should not change this variable unless you know the list of directories that contain programs on your system.

For more information on variables, see *MORE UNIX For Dummies,* which has a whole chapter about them.

SORT

The DOS SORT command works in almost the same way as the UNIX sort command (see Chapter 7). In UNIX, however, you don't need a < before the filename if you are sorting a file. In DOS, you type this line: SORT < filename.

In UNIX, you just type this line:

```
sort filename
```

UNDELETE and UNFORMAT

The DOS UNDELETE command (added in DOS 5) undeletes files you erased accidentally — under certain circumstances, anyway. UNFORMAT tries to reverse the process of formatting a disk. UNIX doesn't come with any commands like these unless you have the Norton Utilities for UNIX, in which case you undelete files with the nue command. See Chapter 23 for what to do if you accidentally delete a file.

VER

The DOS VER command tells you which version of DOS you are using. To find out which UNIX version and shell you are using, see Chapter 2.

Part V

The World Outside the UNIX Biosphere

The 5th Wave   **By Rich Tennant**

"C'MON BRICKMAN, YOU KNOW AS WELL AS I DO THAT 'NOSE-SCANNING' IS OUR BEST DEFENSE AGAINST UNAUTHORIZED ACCESS TO PERSONAL FILES."

In this part...

Most computers that run UNIX are connected to other computers. Many are parts of networks, many have telephone connections to UNIX computers in other places, and many are connected to the Internet. This part talks about how to send messages and share files with other people on your computer, other people on your local area network, and other computers out there on the Internet.

Chapter 18

Who's Out There?

● ●

In This Chapter

▶ Find out who else is using your computer

▶ Communicate with them

● ●

*F*rom the beginning, UNIX was designed as a multi-user system. In the early years of UNIX computing, it was considered greedy to keep to yourself an entire PDP-11/45 (a 1972 vintage minicomputer about the speed of a PC AT but the size of a trash compactor). It was also kind of expensive. These days, the cost argument is much less compelling — unless your computer is a Cray supercomputer or the like — but UNIX remains multiuser partly because it always was and partly because multiuser systems make it easier to share programs and data.

Even if you have your own workstation but are attached to a network, your machine is potentially multiuser because other people can log in to your machine over the *net* (as we technoids call a network). (On the other hand, you can log in to their machines too. See Chapters 20 and 21 for details.)

Of course, in this day and age, all anyone ever talks about is the Internet. If your computer is attached to the Internet, there are literally millions of computers that you can talk to.

In this chapter, you see how to nose around and find out who's on your system and on other systems on the network. Then you can look into getting in touch with them. If you are the only person who ever uses your computer and you don't have a network or a phone line (your computer is all alone in the world), skip this chapter and the following three.

Finding Out Who's on Your Computer

There are two main commands you can use to find out who's using your machine: who and finger. The simple way is just to type who.

The typical response is something like this:

```
root        console     Dec 29 20:16
john1       vt01        Dec 21 15:19
john1       ttyp2       Jan 6 16:36
john1       ttyp1       Jan 6 17:20
john1       ttyp0       Jan 6 16:36
```

You see the user, the terminal, and the login time. User john1 is logged in four times because he has a bunch of X terminal windows, each of which counts as a login session. The exact output from who varies from one version of UNIX to another, but it always contains at least this much. You can also type who am i, and UNIX prints just the line for the terminal (or terminal window) in which you typed the command.

A considerably more informative program is finger. The finger command produces a more useful report than who does:

```
Login   Name              TTY Idle   When         Office
root    0000-Admin(0000)  co 1:11    Tue 20:16
john1   John R. Levine    vt 1:11    Mon 15:19    x3712
john1   John R. Levine    p2 1:11    Wed 16:36    x3712
john1   John R. Levine    p1         Wed 17:20    x3712
john1   John R. Levine    p0         Wed 16:36    x3712
```

Although finger reports the same stuff as who does, it also looks up the user's real name (if it's in the user password file) and tells how long the terminal has been idle (how long it's been since the user last typed something). If the system administrator enters the information, it also usually gives an office phone number, room number, or other handy info about where the user works.

You can also use finger to ask about a specific user, and UNIX looks up some extra info about that user. Here, we used it to look up one of the authors:

```
finger john1
```

UNIX returned this information:

```
Login name: johnl                In real life: John R. Levine
Directory: /usr/johnl            Shell: /bin/sh
On since Dec 21 15:19:45 on vt01 1 hour 27 minutes Idle Time
Project: Working on "UNIX for Dummies, 2nd Ed."
Plan:
Write many books, become famous.
```

The Project and Plan lines are the contents of files called `.project` and `.plan` in the login directory. (Yes, the filenames start with periods.) It has become customary to put a clever remark in your `.plan` file, but please don't overdo it. If the user is logged in on more than one terminal or terminal window, `finger` gives a full report for each terminal. The `finger johnl` command we gave, in fact, reported five — one for each login — but we edited it to save paper.

Finding Out Who's on Other Computers

If your machine is on a network, you can use `rwho` and `finger` to find about other machines. You type the system name you want to check up on after an @ (at sign). (Chapter 19 has more information about system names.) We can check a nearby system, for example:

```
finger @spdcc
```

The `spdcc` machine turns out to be not very busy:

```
[spdcc.com]
Login    Name                  TTY Idle    When        Office
uucp     Uucp Daemon           02          Wed 20:13
johnl    John R. Levine        03          Wed 20:44   Rm 418
dyer     Steve Dyer            p0   1      Wed 08:13
```

You can also ask about an individual by putting that user's name in front of the @:

```
finger johnl@spdcc
```

This command gives the same sort of report as a local `finger` does:

```
[spdcc.com]
Login name: johnl            In real life: John R. Levine
Directory: /var/users/johnl  Shell: /bin/csh
On since Jan 6 9:22:45 on tty02    2 minutes Idle Time
Plan:
no plan
```

If you're on the Internet, you can — in principle — finger any machine on the Net. Because there's no rule that says machines must answer when you call, in many cases you get a "connection refused" response or even no response.

Some systems, particularly main network machines at universities, have set up `finger` to return user-directory information. If you ask who's at MIT

```
finger @mit.edu
```

you get an introduction to its on-line directory:

```
[mit.edu]
Student data loaded as of Dec 15, Staff data loaded as of Dec
        19. Notify the Registrar or Personnel as appro-
        priate to change your information. This service
        is maintained by Distributed Computing and Net-
        work Services.

Send Comments regarding this service to mitdir@mit.edu. Use
        finger help@mit.edu for some instructions.
```

You can try to finger a particular individual at MIT too:

```
finger chomsky@mit.edu
```

Now you can see the public data on that individual:

```
[mit.edu]
... There was 1 match to your request.
      name: Chomsky, Noam A
     email: CHOMSKY@ATHENA.MIT.EDU
     phone: (617) 555-7819
   address: 20D-219
department: Linguistics & Philos
     title: Institute Professor (on Leave, Year)
     alias: N-chomsky
```

You can engage in wholesale nosiness by using `rwho`; this command attempts to compile a list of all the people using all the machines in the local network.

Chatting with People on Your Computer

After you have figured out who is on your computer, you may want to send them a message. There are two general schools of message sending. The first is the real-time school, in which the message appears on the other user's screen while you wait, presumably because it's an extremely urgent message. The write and talk commands let you do that. Excessive use of real-time messages is a good way to make enemies quickly because you interrupt people's work all over the place. Be sparing in your blather.

The second school is electronic mail, or e-mail, in which you send a message that the other user looks at when it's convenient. E-mail is a large topic on its own that we're saving for Chapter 19.

Real-time terminal communication has been likened to talking to someone on the moon because it's so slow; it's limited by the speed at which people type. Here on Earth, most of us have phones; the most sensible thing to do is send a one-line message asking the other user to call you.

The simpler real-time communications command is write. If someone writes to you, you see something like the following on your screen:

```
Message from john1 on iecc (ttyp1) [ Wed Jan 6 20:28:42 ] ...
Please call me at extension 8649
<EOT>
```

Usually the message appears in the middle of an editor session and scrambles the file on your screen. You will be relieved to know that the scrambling is limited to the screen — the editor has no idea that someone is writing to you; the file is OK.

In either vi or emacs, you can tell the editor to redraw what's supposed to be on-screen by pressing Ctrl-L (if you're in input mode in vi, press Esc first).

To write to a user, use the write command and give the name of the user you want to talk to:

```
write john1
```

After you press Enter, write tells you absolutely nothing, which means that it is waiting for your message. Type the message, which can be as many lines long as you want. When you are done, press Ctrl-D (the general end-of-input character) or the interrupt character, usually Ctrl-C or Delete. write copies every line to the other user's screen as you press Enter, so reading a long message sent by way of the `write` command is sort of like reading a poem on old Burma-Shave signs as you drive by each one.

You want to send an important message, for example, to your friend Joe, so you type these lines:

```
write joe
Yo, Joe, turn on your radio. WBUR is rebroadcasting
Terry Gross's interview with Nancy Reagan!
```

You press Enter at the end of each line. After the last line, you press Ctrl-D.

I'm talking — where are you?

Sometimes `write` tells you the user is logged in on several logical terminals:

```
johnl is logged on more than one place.
You are connected to "vt01".
Other locations are:
ttyp1
ttyp0
ttyp2
```

The `write` command is pretty dumb. If the user you are writing to is logged in on more than one terminal — or more typically, is using many windows in X — `write` picks one of them at random and writes there. You can be virtually certain that the window or terminal that `write` chooses is not the one the user is looking at. To maximize the chances of the user seeing your message, use the `finger` command to figure out which terminal is the most active (the one with the lowest idle time) and write to that window. Remember the results of the `finger` command, for example, from a few pages back:

```
Login   Name              TTY Idle   When        Office
root    0000-Admin(0000)  co 1:11    Tue 20:16
johnl   John R. Levine    vt 1:11    Mon 15:19
johnl   John R. Levine    p2 1:11    Wed 16:36
johnl   John R. Levine    p1         Wed 17:20
johnl   John R. Levine    p0         Wed 16:36
```

The best candidates to send a message to are `ttyp1` and `ttyp0`. (The `finger` command cuts out the `tty` from terminal names.)

To write to a specific terminal, give the terminal name after the user name:

```
write john1 ttyp1
```

If you are writing back to a user who just wrote to you, you should use the terminal name that was sent in his write message (such as ttyp1).

Can we talk?

You can have a somewhat spiffier conversation with the talk command, which allows simultaneous two-way typing. You use it the same way you use write, by giving a user name and optionally a terminal name, like this:

```
talk margy
```

The other user sees something like this:

```
Message from Talk_Daemon@iecc at 20:47 ...
talk: connection requested by john1@IECC
talk: respond with: talk john1@IECC
```

If someone tries to talk to you, and you're interested in responding, type the talk command it suggests. If you're in the middle of a text editor or other program, you must exit to the shell first.

While talk is running, it splits your screen and arranges things so that what you type appears in the top half and what the other user types appears in the bottom half. Unlike write, talk immediately passes what you type — without waiting for an Enter — which means that you can see all the other user's typing mistakes and vice versa. When you get tired of talk, exit by pressing Ctrl-D.

Chatting with People on Other Computers

The talk command is designed to talk to users on other computers. If the other computer is a long way away, typing rather than talking can make sense. As the Internet stretches around the world, you may find yourself "talking" with someone for whom English is not a native language. In that case, typing can be faster than trying to understand someone with a strong accent across a noisy phone connection.

Computers have names too, which are usually called *machine names* (more on this in Chapters 20 and 21). To talk to someone on another computer, give `talk` the user name and machine name:

```
talk johnl@iecc.mycorp.com
```

After you're connected, talk works just like talking to a local user, except sometimes it can take several seconds for characters to get from one machine to another on an intercontinental link.

Reading the Writing on the Wall

For the truly megalomaniacal among you, a program called `wall` blats what you type to every single terminal and window on your entire computer. You use it much like `write`:

```
wall
Free pizza in the upstairs conference room in 5 minutes!
```

As with write, you tell wall that you're finished by pressing Ctrl-D. Be sparing in your use of `wall` unless you want a bunch of new enemies.

Note that `wall` affects only the people who use your computer, not everyone on your network.

Chapter 19
Automating Your Office Gossip

● ●

In This Chapter

▶ What is e-mail?

▶ What are e-mail addresses?

▶ Where is your mailbox?

▶ How to use the `mail` program

▶ How to use the `elm` program

▶ How to use the `pine` program

▶ How to organize your mail into neat piles

● ●

*E*lectronic mail (or e-mail) is the high-tech way to automate interoffice chatter, gossip, and innuendo. Using e-mail, you can quickly and efficiently circulate memos and other written information to your coworkers, including directions to the beer bash this Saturday and quotes from the latest Dave Barry column. You can even send and receive e-mail from people outside your organization, if you and they use networked computers.

If your organization uses e-mail, you probably already have some. In fact, there may be vitally important but unread mail waiting in your mailbox at this very moment. Probably not, but who knows? You can tell whether unread messages are in your mailbox because UNIX displays this message when you log in:

```
You have mail.
```

What You Need in Order to Use E-Mail

A UNIX system handles e-mail for users on that system. To exchange e-mail with the outside world, your computer must be on a network — or at least have a phone line and a modem. You definitely don't want to know how to set up a mail network or make connections to other computers; if your computer doesn't already have e-mail, it's time to talk to a UNIX wizard.

In the great tradition of UNIX standardization, there are about 14 different mail sending and receiving programs. (Fortunately, they can all exchange mail with each other.) To find out whether your computer can do e-mail, try using the simple `mail` program to see whether you have any mail waiting. Just type `mail`.

UNIX says `No mail` if no mail is waiting, or it blats a copy of the first unread message on your screen. In the latter case, if you don't want to read your mail right now, press x (for e*x*it) and press Enter to get out. We talk more about reading your mail later in this chapter.

Addressing the Mail

E-mail, like regular mail (which is usually referred to by e-mail advocates as *snail mail*), needs an address, usually called a *net address* or *e-mail address.* To send mail to a person, you send it to his user name (see Chapter 1 for information about logging in with a user name). If the other user uses a different computer than the one you use, the mail system has to know which computer the other person is on — and the address gets more complicated.

Sending mail to people on your computer

For people who use the very same computer you do (that is, you both use terminals connected to the same computer running UNIX), the mail address is just their user name. If you enter `georgew` for your user name, that's your mail address, too. Make sure that you don't use capital letters in the mail address unless the user name uses capital letters.

Sending mail to people on other computers

You can send mail to people who use other computers if your computer is connected to their computer on a network. For people who use other computers, you send mail by telling the mail system which computer they use.

Computers have names too, you know. They sometimes have boring names that indicate what they're used for, like `marketing` or `corpacctg`. Sometimes all the computers in an organization are named according to a more interesting scheme, like naming them all after fish, spices, or cartoon characters. It's traditional in UNIX networks to give the computers tasteful yet memorable names. At one company where we worked, we named the computers haddock, cod, and flounder. The next company used basil, chervil, dill, fennel, and ginger. At Internet for Dummies Central, they're called chico, astrud, xuxa, tom, and ivan, after some of our favorite Brazilian singers.

When writing to someone on another computer on your network, include the computer name in the mail address by using an at sign (@) to indicate where they are "at." If Nancy, for example, has the user name nancyb and uses a computer named ginger, her mail address is nancyb@ginger.

A skillful system administrator can automatically note which computer each user in an organization uses. With luck, you can merely send mail by user name, and the system automagically figures out which computer to send it to.

 If you have trouble with addresses, the easiest way to send a message is to wait until someone sends a message to you and then reply to it. All mail programs have a command (usually r) that replies to a message. Messages almost always have return addresses, and the r command lets you send a message without typing an address.

Sending mail to people "out there"

If your computer network has phone connections to the outside world, you can probably also send mail to people out in the wide world of The Net: the invisible network of UNIX and other computers that extends worldwide. Check with your system administrator or other e-mail users to find out if your organization is "on the net" (connected to the outside world).

To do this, you need a net address for the person you want to send mail to. Type it exactly the way she wrote it. Internet addresses tend to look like this:

```
ellenz@persimmon.woofity.com
```

The part in front of the @ is the person's user name. The rest of the address is the name of the computer and other information about where the computer is, usually the name of the company. The computer name, company name, and so on are connected by periods. The last three letters frequently tell you what kind of organization it is: com is for companies, and edu is for educational institutions. Sometimes the parts of the address spell out the city, state, and country where the computer is located. It's all very well organized, really.

When you are typing net addresses, keep these points in mind:

✔ Be sure not to type any spaces in the middle of the address. There are no spaces in user names or computer names or on either side of the @ or a period.

✔ Don't capitalize anything unnecessarily. Check the capitalization of the user name and computer name. Most addresses are entirely in small letters.

✔ Don't forget the periods that separate the parts of an Internet address.

If your computer is on the Internet and you want to try out network mail, send a message to the authors of this book, at `unix@dummies.com`, and tell us what you think of the book. Our computer will send you back an automatic reply, and we'll read your message, too. (If you can get that address right, you're already halfway to being a mail wizard.)

It's dead, Jim

If you get an address wrong, you will usually get the message back within a few minutes (for mail on your own computer or your own network) or a few days (for mail that has bounced around the net). The dead letter usually has all kinds of cryptic automated error messages in it, but the gist is clear: The message didn't get delivered. Check the address and try again. Generally, the safest way to address a message is to reply to someone else's message.

Sending Stuff Other Than Text

These days, e-mail is such a widespread thing that you may want to send things other than plain old short text messages. For example, we e-mailed to our long-suffering editor most of this book as ZIP files containing Microsoft Word documents. Most mail programs now have commands for attaching files to e-mail messages, or at least for including text files in messages.

If you want to send a text file by e-mail, include the file as part of your message. However, UNIX e-mail was designed for sending text, not programs, graphics, or formatted word-processing files. Luckily, several ways of cheating have been developed so that the e-mail system doesn't realize that e-mail messages contain stuff other than text. The two most widely used methods are

✔ Uuencoding, which involves using a uuencoding program to convert the file to text and a uudecoding program to convert the text back to the original file. We describe uuencoding a bit in Chapter 15.

✔ MIME (*M*ultipurpose *I*nternet *M*ail *E*xtensions), which is much easier to use than uuencoding; many newer mail programs handle it automagically.

Sending mail to people who use on-line services

You can send mail to people who don't use UNIX. By using the net, you can usually send mail to anyone who uses CompuServe, MCI Mail, and other services.

To send mail to a CompuServe user, do this:

1. Find out his or her CompuServe user ID. It's a nine- or ten-digit number with a comma near the middle, such as 71234,5678. Most CompuServe user IDs begin with a 7, for reasons we don't claim to understand. Probably because of its mystical significance.

2. For purposes of sending mail from UNIX, replace the comma in the CompuServe user ID with a period, as in 71234.5678. Because net addresses aren't allowed to have commas, you have to do this.

3. Tack @compuserve.com to the end of the number and—voilà!—you have the person's net address, like this:

71234.5678@compuserve.com

To send mail to an MCI Mail user, you do more or less the same thing as for a CompuServe user:

1. Find out the MCI Mail account number. Your friend may not know it and may have to look on his or her MCI Mail bill to find out what it is

(MCI Mail is usually addressed by name rather than by number). The account number is a seven-digit number that looks like a phone number, like this: 123-4567.

2. Take out the hyphen and tack @mcimail.com to the end of the number. Voilà! You have the person's net address:

1234567@mcimail.com

MCI Mail can also accept real names with periods between the parts:

Richard.M.Nixon@mcimail.com

For users of DELPHI, the address is the user name followed by @delphi.com, as in

service@delphi.com

For users of AT&T Mail, the address is the user name followed by @attmail.com:

rallen@attmail.com

For users of America Online, the address is the user name followed by @aol.com:

ab2873@aol.com

For users of Prodigy, use the Prodigy user name followed by @prodigy.com, as in

XYZ666Q@prodigy.com

When we describe mail programs, we'll tell you whether they work with MIME. All UNIX mail programs work with uuencoding, because *you* have to do the work.

Before sending a file using a uuencoded or MIME attachment, you may want to send a plain, old, unattached e-mail to the intended recipient, asking whether they use uuencoding or MIME.

A Mailbox with Cardinals and Pheasants on It

To receive mail, you need a mailbox. (Not one of those tasteful roadside mailboxes, in this case. It's an invisible mailbox made up entirely of electronic data.) Your system administrator can make (or already has made) one for you if your organization uses e-mail. The mailbox comes in the form of a directory called `/usr/mail/yourusername`; it contains your unread mail and any mail you choose to leave lying around. You may also have a directory called `mail` or `Mail` (some systems capitalize it, some don't — sigh) in your home directory that you can use to sort your mail into piles and keep for historical reference.

To read the mail in your mailbox and send mail, you use a program such as `mail` or `elm` or `pine`. If you use Motif, you can use a fancy X Windows mail program like `xmail`.

Playing Postman Pat with `mail`

The basic `mail` program comes with every brand of UNIX and is an acceptable way to read and send mail. Not great, but acceptable. It can't deal with MIME attachments, if you're wondering.

Take a letter

Assuming that you want to send mail to your friend Nancy B., you can send a message with the `mail` program by typing this line:

```
mail nancyb
```

Some versions of `mail` prompt you to enter a subject line for the message; others respond by doing absolutely nothing. You can tell that something is afoot because you don't see a UNIX shell prompt such as $ or % anymore. The `mail` program is waiting for you to type the message. So type something, as many lines long as you want. Press Enter when the line reaches the right end of the screen (or window) to make it easier to read. Otherwise, your line wraps around to another line, and UNIX may put the line break in the middle of a word.

When you finish typing the message, type a period on a line by itself to tell the `mail` program that you are finished. The `mail` program confirms that it has sent the message by doing absolutely nothing except displaying a UNIX prompt. (Some particularly ancient versions of `mail` don't understand the dot, so you have to tell it that you are finished by pressing Ctrl-D.)

Because the mail program is so helpful, you may want to consider using a better program, like elm or pine. If you have to use mail, send yourself a test message to make sure that it is working. System V computers usually have a really old and awful mail program called mail and a somewhat better one called Mail. (These guys really had a lot of fun thinking up names for these programs.) If you can use Mail rather than mail, do so, because it's more likely to work the way it's supposed to. (Often, mail doesn't even understand Internet mail addresses.)

What's in my mailbox?

To read your mail, reply to letters, and do other mail-related stuff, type mail. The mail program starts by showing you your unread mail. Some versions print the first unread message or show a list of incoming messages. Then the program displays a prompt:

?

The mail program understands many commands and is ready for you to type one.

If it hasn't already shown you a list of messages, press h to tell mail to show you a listing of the messages in your mailbox (if there are any).

Figure 19-1 shows what you might see when you start the mail program. The little > shows you which message mail is working with (the *current message*).

```
3 letters found in /usr/mail/margy, 0 scheduled for deletion, 0 newly arrived
     >    3      283     tonias      Wed Dec 20 11:51:57 1995
          2      365     jordany     Wed Dec 20 11:51:45 1995
          1     1738     john1       Tue Dec 19 23:58:50 1995
     ?
```

Figure 19-1: What you might see when you start the mail program.

Talking to mail

The mail program understands lots of commands, including these:

- ✔ Press Enter to see the current message (the one the > points to).
- ✔ To move to a different message, type the message number (the first thing on the line in the list of headers).

- Press d to delete the current message (usually after you have read it).
- Press u to undelete a message you didn't want to delete.
- Press m and type *mailaddress* to send (mail) a new message. (Use a real user name or mail address rather than *mailaddress*.)
- Press r to reply to the current message.
- Press z to see more message headers if there are too many to fit on-screen.
- Press p to print the current message.
- Press q to quit the mail program.
- Press ? for further help.

What does it say? What does it say?

To read a message, type its message number (the number at the beginning of the line). To read the current message (the one with the >), just press Enter. The mail program displays the message — or the first screen of it, if it is a long message.

TIP

What's all this junk at the beginning of the message?

An e-mail message has a *header* that the mail program (mail, elm, pine, or whatever) creates automatically. The header consists of the following pieces:

- The To address (the person to receive the mail)
- The From address (the return address)
- The Cc addresses (the addresses to send copies to)
- The Bcc address (the addresses to send blind copies to)
- The subject

- Optional information you rarely use, such as expiration date, priority, which mailer mailed the message, and sometimes (for incoming messages) the arcane route that the message took to get to you

Don't worry if the header looks like gobbledygook — it is. On incoming mail, there can be all sorts of extra glop in the header that reports on which systems have passed it along, which program was used to send the mail, and lots of other useless stuff.

You can specify Cc addresses, subject, and other information for messages you send.

When you finish reading the message, you can do several things with it:

- Delete it (press d).
- Reply to it (press r). Then type a message. End the message by typing . (a period) on a line by itself.
- Save it (see the next section).

If you don't make any other arrangements, messages you have read are saved in a file called mbox, which can get pretty big if you don't edit it now and then.

Saving your letters for posterity

You can save a message in a text file to edit later or include in a word-processing document. To save the current message (the one you are reading or have just finished reading), type this line:

```
s filename
```

Replace *filename* with the name of the text file you want to create. If the text file already exists, mail adds the current message to the end of the file; you can save a series of messages to a single text file in this way.

Run that by me again

To print a message (on-screen, not on the printer), press p. You'll want to do this when looking at a list of messages and you want to see a message's contents. If you want to see a message other than the current one, put the message number (shown in the list of headers) after the p, as in p 5.

Bye, mail

To quit mail, press q. You see the UNIX prompt.

Playing Postman Pat with elm

The elm mail-reading program is a heck of a lot easier to use than is either version of the mail program. The elm program even tells you what is going on once in a while. It also helps you organize your mail into folders if you plan to save your messages.

To read, send, or peruse mail that you left lying around the last time, type elm. The elm program displays a list of your mail messages (see Figure 19-2).

```
Mailbox is '/usr/mail/margy' with 3 messages [ELM 2.3 PL11]
     1    Dec 20 John R. Levine     (49)    a few troff hints
0    2    Dec 21 Jordan M. Young    (12)    Bye, bye, Brazil!
N    3    Dec 21 Meg Young          (10)    Hi, cutie
```

Figure 19-2: A list of mail messages in elm.

This display is called the *mail index*. The first letter in each line tells which messages are new (N), old and already read (blank), old and unread (O), and deleted (D). The listing also shows the date the mail was received, who sent it, the number of lines in the message, and the subject. Below the index are instructions, including the one-letter commands used to read and send mail.

✔ Use the ↑ and ↓ (or press j and k) to highlight the message you want to read, reply to, delete, or whatever.

✔ Press Enter to read the highlighted message.

✔ Press d to delete a message.

✔ Press u to undelete a message you didn't want to delete.

✔ Press m to send a message.

✔ Press r to reply to a message.

✔ Press f to forward a message to someone else.

✔ Press > or s to save the message in a folder or text file.

✔ Press p to print the message.

✔ Press q to quit the elm program.

✔ Press ? for more help.

Just put a stamp on it

To use elm to send mail, press m. The program asks for the address, the subject of the message, and addresses to send copies to. Then it runs a text editor, usually vi. (You can arrange for elm to run another editor if you loathe vi as much as we do — see the upcoming tip.) Use the editor to type the text of the message. When you finish, save the message and exit from the editor. (If you are forced to use vi, press Escape and type ZZ to save the message and exit from vi.)

Tell the world!

Then elm gives you a chance to edit the message (perhaps to add a P.S.), fool with the header (useful if you decide that your message is so fascinating it should be sent to a wider audience), forget the whole thing, or send the message off.

Press h to edit the header for the message. elm displays all the components of the header, including the addressee and the subject line. You can change most of them or add names of people to receive copies of the message (Cc's).

To change each of these things, press the letter shown before the parenthesis. For example, to add Cc's, press c. elm asks for the list of addresses to send copies to. Enter the addresses, separated by at least one space, and press Enter. If elm recognizes the address, it displays the person's actual name in parentheses after the address. Otherwise, it shows just the address you typed.

When you are done fooling with the header, press Enter to indicate that you are done. elm asks what to do with the message:

```
And now: s
Choose e)dit message, !)shell, h)eaders, c)opy file, s)end, or f)orget.
```

Press s to send it. You can also press e to go back and edit some more, h to change the headers (To, Cc, Bcc, and Subject, for example), and some less useful choices that you don't have to worry about.

You can change the editor elm uses for writing and editing mail messages. (Thank goodness, because otherwise you might have to use vi!) When you are using elm and looking at the mail index, do the following:

1. **Press** o **to look at the** elm **options.**

2. **Press** e **to change the editor you use.**

3. **Type the name of the editor you usually use to edit text files (we like** emacs **and** pico**).**

4. **Press** > **to save this change.**

5. **Finally, press** i **to see the mail index again.**

Old friends say hello

To read a message, highlight its line in the mail index and press Enter. The elm program displays the message — or the first screen of it, if it is a long message.

When you finish reading the message, you can do several things with it:

- ✔ Delete it (press d).
- ✔ Forward it (press f and tell elm the address to forward it to).
- ✔ Reply to it (press r).
- ✔ Save it. To leave it hanging around in your mailbox, press the spacebar to leave the current message and go to the next message, or press i to leave the current message and return to the mail index. In either case, the message remains unaltered. Alternatively, you can save the message in a folder or text file (see the following sections).

Saving your mail for a rainy day

If you like to save mail messages, you can save them with elm in folders, one folder per topic or one folder per sender. You can have lots of folders — each one is just a text file in your Mail directory (note the initial capital letter).

To save a message to a folder, either highlight the message in the mail index or display the message. Then press > or s. The elm program asks for the name of the folder you want to save the message to. For some reason, folder names begin with = (an equal sign). The elm program suggests a folder with the name of the person who sent the message, assuming that you want to save messages organized by sender. But you can type any name you want (no space, and no funny characters other than the = at the beginning).

To see the messages in a folder, return to the mail index and press c to change folders. Type the name of the folder you want to use (or press ? to see a list of your folders). Be sure to type the = at the beginning of the folder name. You see a list of messages just like the mail index of your original mailbox.

All the same commands work in a folder that work in the your regular mailbox. For example, once you highlight a message, you can read it by pressing Enter, forward it by pressing f, or delete it by pressing d.

To return to your regular mailbox, press c again and type ! when elm asks for the name of the folder (don't ask us why).

Mail for word processors

You can also save a message in a text file so that you can edit it later or include it in a word-processing document. Use the > or s command to move the message, but, rather than type a folder name (which always begins with a =), type a filename (like *message.text*). The elm program creates the file in your home directory and puts the message there. If the file already exists, elm adds the message to the end of the existing file so that you can save a series of messages to a single text file.

Taking it with you

To print a message on the printer, highlight the message in the mail index or display the message. Then press p to print it. (This only works if the printer is attached to the UNIX system, not if you're dialed in from a PC with a printer on it. Sorry.)

Attaching stuff using elm

Unfortunately, most versions of elm can't attach files to e-mail messages using the popular MIME system we described earlier in this chapter. Bummer, but there it is.

If you want to send a text file, just include it in your e-mail message. The emacs command to include another file in a message is Ctrl-X I (just plain I).

If you want to send a file that contains something other than text, you can do it with uuencoding. Here's how:

1. **Create a uuencoded version of the file you want to send, by typing this command:**

   ```
   uuencode file-to-send new-name > temp
   ```

   In this command, replace *file-to-send* with the file you want to uuencode, *new-name* with the name that you want the file to have when it is uudecoded, and *temp* with any temporary filename (*junk* is another perennial favorite).

2. **Run elm and compose a new message. Address it as usual.**

3. **At the beginning of the message, explain that you are sending a uuencoded message.**

4. **At the end of the message, include the file you created in Step 1 (which is called *temp*, or whatever you typed in place of *temp*). If you use emacs as your editor, press Ctrl-X I to include the file.**

5. **Send the message.**

Dealing with uuencoded stuff

If you receive a message that contains a uuencoded file, tell elm to run the message through the uudecoder, by typing:

```
|uudecode
```

That's a vertical bar and the name of the command uudecode. The original file should be reconstituted.

So what's the new file called? Look on the *begin* line of the uu-incoming file (or the original e-mail message that contained the file) — it shows the length of the file in bytes and the name the uudecoded file will have.

Netiquette

E-mail has been around long enough for an etiquette style to have sprung up around it, just as with real mail. Here are some tips:

✔ Be polite. The written word tends to sound stronger and more dogmatic than speech; sarcasm and little jokes don't always work.

✔ Don't write anything when you are annoyed. If you get a message that you find totally obnoxious, *don't answer it right away!* You will be sorry if you do, because you will overreact and look just as obnoxious yourself. How do we know this? We used to do it, too. All e-mailers do at first, until they learn not to take e-mail too seriously. The exchange of needlessly obnoxious messages is so common that it has a name: *flaming.* Don't do it.

✔ Be brief.

✔ Be sure to sign your messages. The header shows where a message comes from, but your recipient may not remember who you are from your cryptic e-mail address.

✔ Use normal punctuation and capitalization. That is, DON'T CAPITALIZE EVERYTHING. It looks as though you are shouting, and that's not polite (see first tip in this list).

✔ Watch out for acronyms. E-mail is full of them, and you had better know what the common ones mean. A list of acronyms is at the end of this sidebar.

✔ Don't assume that e-mail is private. Any recipient of your mail can easily forward it to other people. Some mail addresses are really mailing lists that redistribute messages to many other people. And glitches in the mail system may send your messages to various electronic dead-letter offices. In one famous case, a mistaken mail address sent a message to tens of thousands of readers. It started "Darling, at last we have a way to send messages that is completely private...."

✔ If you need to indicate emotion, use *emoticons,* little pictures made up of characters to look like faces. If you see : -), for example, just look at it sideways: You see a little smiley face that usually means whatever you just read was a joke. (You get a sad face if you use the other parenthesis for the mouth.) Some people — particularly those who use CompuServe — type <grin> or <g> or <smile>. (An opposing viewpoint says that if you need one of those emotion things, it's a better idea to rewrite your message to make what you mean clearer.)

Here's a list of common e-mail acronyms:

BTW	By The Way
IMHO	In My Humble Opinion
IOW	In Other Words
PITA	Pain In The A**
PMFJI	Pardon Me For Jumping In
ROF,L	Rolling On Floor, Laughing
RSN	Real Soon Now (ha!)
RTFM	Read the Manual (that is, look it up yourself)
TIA	Thanks In Advance

Playing Postman Pat with pine

The pine program was originally a cut-down version of elm intended for novice users, which makes it even easier to use than elm, even though now it's gotten a lot more powerful than elm ever was. It has lots of nice menus to remind you of what to do next, and it even uses pico, a simple editor, for composing mail.

To run pine, just type pine. You see a display like the one in Figure 19-3.

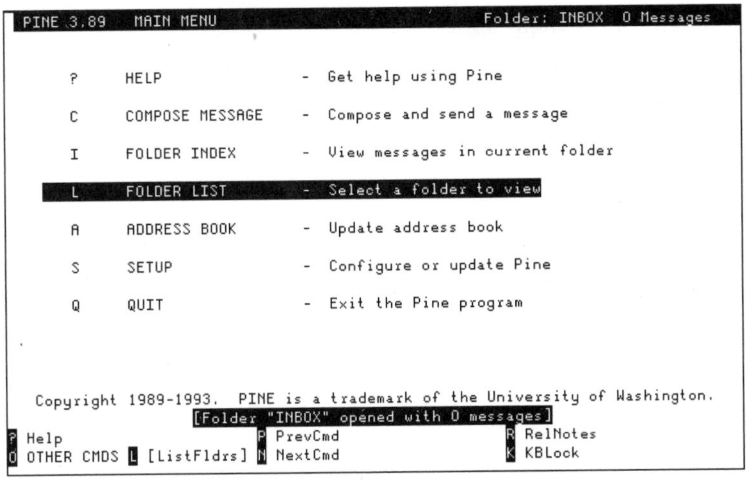

```
PINE 3.89   MAIN MENU                              Folder: INBOX   0 Messages


        ?    HELP              - Get help using Pine

        C    COMPOSE MESSAGE   - Compose and send a message

        I    FOLDER INDEX      - View messages in current folder

        L    FOLDER LIST       - Select a folder to view

        A    ADDRESS BOOK      - Update address book

        S    SETUP             - Configure or update Pine

        Q    QUIT              - Exit the Pine program



     Copyright 1989-1993.  PINE is a trademark of the University of Washington.
                    [Folder "INBOX" opened with 0 messages]
 P Help                        P PrevCmd              R RelNotes
 O OTHER CMDS L [ListFldrs] N NextCmd                 K KBLock
```

Figure 19-3: pine's menu, listing the most popular commands.

This is pine's *main menu*, with a list of its favorite commands. Like elm, pine uses one-letter commands. Notice that one command is highlighted — you can also choose commands by pressing the up- and down-arrow keys to move the highlight and then pressing Enter.

The commands you are most likely to use are the following:

  ✔ Press c to compose (write a new message).

  ✔ Press i to see a list of your messages.

  ✔ Press q to exit from pine.

  ✔ Press ? for lots of helpful on-line help.

Into the postbox

To use pine to send mail, press c. The pine program runs pico, a nice simple editor that we describe in more detail in Chapter 13. Rather than starting with a blank file, you see the headers ready for you to fill in — To, Cc, Attchmnt (for attaching files to a message), and Subject. Use pico to type the header information and the text of your message. Then press Ctrl-X to leave pico. When you do so, pine sends the message and displays the main menu again.

If you decide not to send the message after all, you can press Ctrl-C to cancel it.

I'm pining for some mail

To read your mail, press i to see the index of messages (Figure 19-4). The messages are numbered, with codes (N for new messages you haven't read, D for messages you have deleted, and A for messages you have answered) in the left margin. One of the messages is highlighted.

```
  PINE 3.89   FOLDER INDEX                 Folder: INBOX  Message 1 of 3 NEW

+ N 1    Apr  6 Margy Levine Young      (695) How about lunch?
+ N 2    Apr  6 To: John R Levine       (474) Trying out some software!
+ N 3    Apr  6 Margy Levine Young      (710) It's budget time again...

















P Help        M Main Menu  P PrevMsg   - PrevPage   D Delete     R Reply
O OTHER CMDS  V [ViewMsg]  N NextMsg   Spc NextPage  U Undelete   F Forward
```

Figure 19-4: A list of your messages, in pine.

To read a message, move the highlight to it, using the up- and down-arrow keys or p (for *previous*) and n (for *next*). Then press v to view the message.

When you are looking at a message, here are some things you can do:

- ✔ Forward the message to someone else by pressing f. Then pine lets you start composing a message, with the text of the original message included in the text of this message.

- ✔ Reply to the person who sent the message by pressing r; pine automatically addresses the message to the person who sent the original one.

- ✔ Delete the message by pressing d. The message doesn't disappear right away, but it is marked with a D on the list of messages. When you exit from pine, your deleted messages really get deleted. (If you change your mind, you can undelete a message by pressing u.)

- ✔ Move on to the next message by pressing n. Or move back to the preceding one by pressing p.

- ✔ Return to pine's main menu by pressing m.

Send this file, too

The pine program can handle MIME attachments with great ease and flair — there's nothing to it. To attach a file in pine, press Ctrl-J while you are composing the message. When pine prompts you for the filename, type it and press Enter. That's all it takes!

Chapter 20

My Files Are Where?

*I*f your UNIX system is attached to a network, in all likelihood some or all of your files are stored on a machine far away from where you are. If your system isn't networked — or if it has only slow telephone network connections — you can skip this chapter.

Quite a few different schemes let computers use files on other machines. They are named mostly with TLAs (*three-letter acronyms*) such as AFS, RFS, and NFS. This chapter talks mostly about NFS because that's the most commonly used scheme, even though, in many ways, it works the worst. If you didn't like the C shell or the vi editor, you won't like NFS either; it also was written by Bill, the big guy with the strong opinions.

You'll Never Find Your Stuff

The NFS (*Network File System*) program lets you treat files on another computer in more or less the same way you treat files on your own computer. There are several reasons you might want to use NFS, and they are discussed in this chapter.

Share!

The most common reason for using NFS is that you have a bunch of similar computers scattered around, all running more or less the same programs. Rather than load every program on every computer, the system administrator loads one copy of everything on one computer (the *server*) so that all the other computers (the *clients*) can share the programs. This arrangement saves disk space and makes the administrator's job much easier — because when a program is updated on the server, everyone gets the updated version immediately. The alternative is to update dozens of different machines over the network or even to run around to all of them with floppies or tapes in hand.

One backup for all, and all for one backup

Centralizing the files on a server makes backup and administration easier. It's much easier to administer one disk of 4,000 megabytes than to administer 10 disks of 400 megabytes apiece. It's also easier to back up everything because everything is all in one place rather than spread around on a dozen machines.

I think I'll work here today

Another use of NFS is to make a bunch of workstations function as a shared time-sharing system. It is reasonably straightforward to set up a bunch of workstations so that you can sit down at any one of them, log in, and use the same set of files regardless of where on the network they physically reside. This capability is a great convenience. Also, by using programs like `rlogin` (discussed in the next chapter), you can log in to another machine on the network and work from that machine (which is handy if the other machine is faster than yours or has some special feature you want to use).

A penny saved is a network used

In an extreme case, a system can have diskless workstations that use NFS for all disk needs. For a while, diskless workstations were popular because one big disk on a server was cheaper than several little disks on every workstation. They're less popular now; it turns out that sending every bit of disk action over the network is painfully slow. It helps a lot if you have a small local disk for scratch space; besides, little disks aren't very expensive these days. People also noted that the largest program they used on their workstation was the X Windows server program; they could instead use X terminals, which are cheaper than diskless workstations and get just as good performance at a lower cost.

Talking with "the other computer"

A final use of NFS is in *heterogeneous networks,* a fancy term for networks with different kinds of computers. NFS is available for all sorts of computers from PCs to mainframes. It's common to run a version of NFS on PCs to let PC users use files physically located on UNIX or other systems. *Gateways* connect NFS to AppleTalk for the benefit of Macintosh users, as well as to NFS versions for all non-UNIX workstations, such as DEC VAX workstations running VMS.

The original version of NFS was written for Sun workstations, so NFS still works better on UNIX than it does on other systems. File formats vary a little from one computer to the next, which makes things — in classic computer style — not quite as convenient as you want them to be. On DOS machines, for example, text files are stored with two characters at the end of every line, carriage return (Ctrl-M) and line feed (Ctrl-J); UNIX text files use just line-feed characters. The practical effect is that DOS editors and word processors treat UNIX files peculiarly, often treating the entire document as one enormous paragraph with hard carriage returns where the line-feed characters were; UNIX editors handle DOS files acceptably, but they show the carriage-return character at the end of every line as the ugly sequence ^M.

When we were writing this book, John frequently plugged his Windows laptop into his home Ethernet (yep, he has one, held up by duct tape), fired up the NFS server on his laptop, and all of the files on his laptop's disk became available to his UNIX box. Then he could type a `cp -R` command on his UNIX box to copy all of the files on his laptop to his UNIX box. Poof! Instant backup.

Ignoring NFS

Except when NFS screws up, you don't have to worry about using it. Your system administrator did all the hard work when she installed it.

Files passed over the network act almost exactly like those on the local machine; in most cases, you can treat them the same. The primary difference is that access to files through NFS is about twice as slow as access to files on a local machine. This problem usually isn't a big one because, for most of the stuff you do, the machine doesn't spend much time waiting for the disk anyway.

When you do something *really* big and slow (like repaginating a 500-page document), it might be worth it to see whether you can log in to the machine on which the files reside and run the program there.

Where are those files, anyway?

NFS works by mounting remote directories. *Mounting* means pretending that a directory on another disk or even on another computer is actually part of the directory system on your disk. This means that files that are stored in lots of different places can appear to be nicely organized into one tree-structure directory.

Whenever UNIX sees the name of a directory, /stars/elvis, for example, it checks for any names in the directory that are *mount points,* directories where one disk is logically attached to another.

Your system might have the directory /stars mounted from some other machine, for example, and then the directory elvis and all the files in it reside on the other machine.

This ain't the local Mounties

There are two kinds of directories you can mount:

- **Local directories.** These directories are on disks on your own machine. Being able to mount local directories is useful if your computer has several disk drives, and you want them to appear connected.

- **Remote directories.** These directories are mounted by NFS and are on disks on some other computer.

For example, your computer might have two disks, /dev/sd0a and /dev/sd1b. Your /usr directory, which contains your home directory — and maybe some other people's directories too — might be on /dev/sd0a, while other files you use, for budgeting, are in /budget on /dev/sd1b. It is more convenient for /usr to be a subdirectory of the same / (root) directory as /budget so that you can use the cd command to move between them.

Disk free, as free as the . . .

The easiest way to tell which files are where is with the df (*Disk Free* space) command. It prints the amount of free space on every disk and tells you where the disks are. Here's a typical piece of df output:

```
Filesystem        kbytes    used     avail    capacity   Mounted on
/dev/sd0a         30383     6587     20758    24%        /
/dev/sd0g         157658    124254   17639    88%        /usr
/dev/sd0h         364378    261795   66146    80%        /home
/dev/sd3a         15671     1030     13074    7%         /tmp
/dev/sd3g         1175742   758508   299660   72%        /mnt
server-sys:/usr/spool/mail
                  300481    190865   79567    71%        /var/spool/mail
server-sys:/usr/lib/news
                  300481    190865   79567    71%        /usr/lib/news
server-sys:/usr/spool/news
                  298068    243877   24384    91%        /var/spool/news
```

In this example, the directory / resides on a local disk (a disk on your own computer) named /dev/sd0a, /usr resides on /dev/sd0g, /home resides on /dev/sd0h, and so forth. (We won't go into disk names other than to say that anything in /dev is on the local machine.) The directory /var/spool/mail is really the directory /usr/spool/mail on machine server-sys, /usr/lib/news is really /usr/lib/news on machine server-sys, and so forth.

Some of the local directory names are the same as the remote machine's directory names — and some aren't. This can, and often does, cause considerable confusion; unfortunately, it's usually unavoidable. A system administrator with any sense will at least mount each directory with a consistent name wherever it's mounted so that /var/documents/bigproject is the same no matter which computer you're working on.

A database known as NIS (Network Information System) makes it easier to keep the naming process straight. It's discussed later in this chapter, but in general, don't worry about it unless your system administrator messes up.

What NFS cannot do

NFS sounds great so far. Files can be, here, there, and anywhere, and it all works automagically! Works great, right? Almost.

The problem is that NFS is not very reliable. In particular, occasionally it just doesn't work. Data sometimes gets lost. This flaw in NFS is in its design; recent versions have largely but not entirely alleviated this problem. If you want to know what the problem is, read the sidebar, "Why NFS is out of state" (even if you do, it won't help).

I refuse to update these files

NFS is particularly bad at handling simultaneous updates — that is, when different computers update the same file at the same time. Some locking features are supposed to enable different computers to take turns updating stuff, but the locks don't work very well.

The most common instance of simultaneous update is in databases. NFS just isn't appropriate for databases. Fortunately, any database worth anything has its own provisions for remote-access and locking, so in practice, it's not a problem.

The place where simultaneous updates can be an issue is when you have a directory full of files that several people update (such as log files that people add notes to as things happen). If you do this in the obvious way with NFS, sooner or later (probably sooner), data disappears into the void. You can circumvent this problem relatively easily by always running the program that does the logging on the same computer, probably by using the rsh command described in Chapter 21.

Mommy, NFS won't share

The other thing NFS cannot do is handle devices, such as tapes, printers, and terminals. Most systems that have a tape drive hook up the tape drive as a file called something like /dev/tape; that makes it easy to back up stuff by running a backup program and telling it to write the backup to /dev/tape. If your machine doesn't have a tape drive, and the one in the next office does, you might think that the obvious way to make a backup is to mount the other machine's /dev/tape with NFS and tell the backup program to use the remote tape. That doesn't work.

Why NFS is out of state

We discuss the technical theology of remote file access here. Still reading? Geez, what a glutton for punishment.

There are two general ways to handle communication between server (the machine with the files) and client (the machine that wants to use them). One approach is known as *stateless*, and the other (for lack of a better word) is called *stateful*.

The stateful approach is more straightforward. The two machines have a conversation, the gist of which runs something like this:

"I want to read a file called `/usr/elvis/current-whereabouts`."

"Very good, sir — an excellent choice."

"Can I have the first piece of that file I just asked about?"

"Certainly, sir. It's so-and-so."

"Thank you so much. May I have the next piece?"

"My pleasure. It's such-and-such."

The only problem here occurs if one machine crashes during the conversation. When it comes back, the server has no recollection of what it was talking about, the conversation cannot be reestablished easily, and all sorts of special recovery schemes are necessary to get things back in sync. ("Beg pardon, old boy, I've had a spot of amnesia. Can you remind me what we were chatting about?")

Back when Bill was writing NFS, he didn't feel like writing all that recovery code (it's difficult to write, and boring, to boot) so he made NFS stateless. This decision gave NFS a severe case of amnesia on the part of all the servers. Rather than keep track of which client is asking for which file, NFS couldn't care less. The NFS servers don't have the faintest idea who their clients are and forget everything about a client from one request to the next. The conversation goes more like this:

"I want to read `/usr/elvis/current-whereabouts`."

"It's all the same to me. On my disk, it's file number 86345."

"Send me the first piece of file 86345."

"Well, OK, if you insist. It's so-and-so."

"Send me the second piece of file 86345."

"Who the heck are you? Hardly matters — I wouldn't remember, even if you told me. Anyway, the answer is such-and-such."

The advantage here is that, if the server crashes, when it comes back up it can pick up where it left off. Because it didn't know anything about its clients anyway, it doesn't forget anything. The disadvantage is that it's difficult to determine whether a request got lost or, because of network glitchery, got handled twice. In a stateful setup, it's easy to tell: Every message has a number. If messages 106 and 108 arrive without 107 between them, you know that something got lost. Stateless messages don't have numbers (it wouldn't matter if they did, because the stateless server doesn't remember the number from one message to the next), so there's no way to tell whether a message got lost. In practice, if a client doesn't get an answer to a request within a few seconds, it repeats the request because NFS requests are supposed to be *idempotent* (this 25-cent word means that it doesn't hurt if the server does them more than once).

Most requests are indeed idempotent (it doesn't matter whether you write the same stuff to the same part of a file twice in a row) — but not all of them are. If the request was something like

(continued)

(continued)

"delete the furble file," and the server in fact received the request but lost the response, the second time that the client sends the request, the server complains that the file is not there and sends back an error (even though, from the client's point of view, the file was there when it asked to delete it). Are you confused yet? We certainly are.

There are more complex sequences of repeated and lost messages that can cause the contents of a file to be thrown away by mistake. (No, we don't go into detail — we know that you have already stopped reading this part.) Fortunately, such sequences are rare, although they have been known to happen.

If you are wondering why NFS doesn't handle tapes, printers, and the like, it's because even Bill couldn't figure out how to make an idempotent printer — one in which printing a page twice was the same thing as printing it once. Perhaps he could have used transparent ink.

Why doesn't it work? It just doesn't. NFS doesn't do tapes — or printers or anything else, except disks. To make the backup, you must do things the other way: Run the backup program on the machine with the tape drive and get to your files through NFS. Most system administrators and all wizards are painfully aware of the limitations of NFS and can help you make tapes on other people's machines if that's what you need to do.

NFS and System Crashes

What happens if you're working with NFS, your files are stored on a server, and the server crashes? The answer is, you wait. Eventually, when the server comes back, you continue from where you left off. If it's a severe crash, you may wait a long time. In one extreme case (so we have heard), a program on an NFS client system waited more than six months while the server crashed, was dismantled, and shipped back to the manufacturer and then was refurbished, shipped back, reloaded from tape, and rebooted — at which point the client program continued. You probably won't be so patient.

The worst practical problem is that, if a program stalls while it is waiting for a dead NFS server, there is no way to stop or kill the program, short of rebooting your UNIX computer.

Recent versions of NFS have features called soft and hard mounts (not as indecent as they sound, but close) that make it possible to stop a program that has stalled while waiting for a dead server. The problem is that if a server is merely slow and not dead (and believe us, a server loaded with hundreds of clients can be impressively slow), a client may assume that the server is dead and stop a program. Had the client been a little more patient, the server would have responded, and the program could have completed its task.

TECHNICAL STUFF

What's in a name?

One of the trickiest problems in networked computing is giving consistent names to everything. If user `melvin` has internal user number `1234` and home directory `/usr/drones/melvin` on one computer in a network, he probably should also have the same internal number and same home directory on all the other computers in the network. With this type of an arrangement, no matter which computer he logs in to, he can access the correct files. Similarly, every machine on the network has a name that must be known consistently by all the other machines, NFS directories should be mounted using the same names on all machines, and so forth.

In a network with more than two or three machines, keeping the naming information complete and up-to-date can be a major challenge for a system administrator. User names and users' directory names are in a file called `/etc/passwd`, the machine names are in `/etc/hosts`, NFS directory names are in `/etc/fstab`, and four or five other files should be kept consistent among machines.

Originally, the administrator had to update all those files by hand. (You can't just share them through NFS because it turns out that the system needs some of the information in those files to start NFS.) When a new user was added, all the `/etc/passwd` files had to be updated, and so forth. It was, to put it mildly, a pain.

An answer to this confusion is *NIS*, the *N*etwork *I*nformation *S*ystem. NIS keeps nearly all of the name information in a central database on one or two machines called the NIS servers. (The NIS servers can also be NFS servers, although they don't have to be.) Every machine's copy of `/etc/passwd`, `/etc/hosts`, and so on contains just enough information to get NFS and NIS started; thereafter, all the user names, machine names, NFS directory names, and so forth come from NIS. To add a new user, the administrator has to update only the central NIS database; all the machines on the network then can retrieve from NIS the new user name, number, home directory, and any other relevant information.

It is a pain for the administrator to get NIS set up in the first place, but, after it's set up, it works well. Some administrators resist using it because they don't want to go to the trouble of setting it up. On a network of more than two or three machines, however, NIS is well worth the trouble.

NIS was originally called Yellow Pages, but the British phone company owns the exclusive trademark rights for that term in Britain, so the name was changed to NIS (a trademark no one else wanted). Some people still call it Yellow Pages, and some commands that control NIS databases still begin with the letters `yp`.

What Other File Systems Do I Have to Contend With?

Although NFS is the most widely used network file facility, you may run into some others. Many of these systems can coexist; it is common to have a single machine running both NFS and RFS or both NFS and AFS. Here are other file facilities you may run across:

✔ RFS (Remote File Sharing) is an NFS competitor that originally was written at AT&T. (NFS is originally from Sun Microsystems.) RFS avoids NFS's reliability problems and flakiness, but works only on UNIX System V systems — not BSD, DOS, Macs, or anything else. If your entire network runs System V, your administrator may use RFS rather than NFS (and you can ignore all the rude things we said about NFS).

✔ AFS (Andrew File System), written at Carnegie Mellon University, is designed to support thousands of clients that share more or less the same set of files. Unlike NFS and RFS, AFS works reasonably well over long-distance network links to enable machines thousands of physical miles apart to share files.

✔ Novell NetWare, the most common network for DOS PCs, also works on UNIX systems, generally with one or two UNIX systems as servers and zillions of PCs as clients. Now that Novell owns the company that supports UNIX System V, you can get Novell UNIXWare on UNIX systems.

Chapter 21

Stealing Computer Time and Files — Network Bandits

*I*f your computer is on a network, sooner or later you have to use computers other than your own. You can do lots of things over a network; the most widely used are remote login and file transfer.

Many UNIX systems are attached to the Big Mazooma of networks, the Internet, which hooks together several million computers around the world. Most of the UNIX network software was originally written at Berkeley specifically for use on the Internet, so all of these commands work just fine on the Internet. The only difference you may notice is that while you can refer to computers on your own network with simple names like pumpkin, to talk to computers on the Internet you have to give their true names, which can be long and tedious, like iecc.cambridge.ma.us (the name our computer used to have.)

Remote login is no more than logging in to some other computer from your own. While you're logged in to the other computer, whatever you type is passed to the other computer; whatever responses the other computer makes are passed back to you. In the great UNIX tradition of never leaving well enough alone, there are two slightly different remote-login programs: telnet and rlogin. A variant of rlogin called rsh lets you do commands one at a time on other computers.

A *file transfer* copies files from one system to another. You can copy files from other systems to your system, and from your system to others. There are two different — how did you know that? — file-transfer programs: ftp (which is widely used on the Internet) and rcp.

Logging In, Logging Out

Telnetting (in English, you can verb any word you want) involves no more than typing `telnet` and the name of the computer you want to log in to:

```
telnet pumpkin
```

UNIX tells you that it is making the connection and then gives the login prompt:

```
Trying...
Connected to pumpkin.bigcorp.com.
Escape character is '^]'. SunOS UNIX (pumpkin.bigcorp.com)
login:
```

At the login prompt, you type your user name and then your password. After the other computer connects, you log in exactly as though you were sitting at the other computer. In the following example, we typed `john1` as our user name and then gave our secret password:

```
login: john1
Password:
Last login: Thu Jan 7 23:03:58 from squash
SunOS Release 4.1.2 (PUMPKIN) #3: Fri Oct 16 00:20:44 EDT
1992 Please confirm (or change) your terminal type.
TERM = (ansi)
```

If the other computer asks what type of terminal you're using, give the answer appropriate to the terminal you're using. (If you're using an X terminal window, it's `xterm`. Try `VT-100`, `ANSI`, or `TTY` if you're using a dumb terminal or PC.)

The normal way to leave `telnet` is to log out from the other computer by typing `logout`. UNIX gives you the following message to tell you that the other computer has hung up the phone, so to speak:

```
Bye Bye
Connection closed by foreign host.
```

Sometimes the other computer is recalcitrant and doesn't want to let you go. Remember, you're in control. To force your way out, you first must get the attention of the `telnet` program: press Ctrl-] (that's a right square bracket). A few versions of `telnet` use a different escape character to get `telnet`'s attention (it tells you which character when you first connect to the other system). After you get `telnet`'s attention, type `quit` to tell `telnet` to wrap things up and return to the shell.

Telnetting is widely used on the Internet — in fact, we wrote a whole chapter about it in *MORE UNIX For Dummies.* You can `telnet` to lots of computers over the Internet, including the card catalog systems of lots of libraries — great when you are looking for a book.

The Lazy Man's Remote Login

The `telnet` command is general. You can use it to log in to all sorts of machines — whether or not they're running UNIX. If you want to log in to another UNIX system, the `rlogin` command is usually more convenient because it automates more of the process. You use `rlogin` in much the same way you use `telnet`:

```
rlogin pumpkin
```

UNIX responds with the following:

```
Last login: Fri Jan 8 14:30:28 from squash
SunOS Release 4.1.2 (PUMPKIN) #3: Fri Oct 16 00:20:44 EDT
Please confirm (or change) your terminal type.
TERM = (vt100)
```

Hey! It didn't ask for the user name or password. What happened? You frequently have a setup in which a bunch of machines use the same set of user names. (We mention this in Chapter 20. There's even a database called NIS that helps keep all the names consistent across all the machines.) In that case, after you log in to one machine, all the others can safely assume that, if you log in to one of them, you will use the same user name to log in to others.

The `rlogin` command also passes along the terminal type you're using, so even if the other system asks you to enter your terminal type, it always guesses correctly if you don't tell it explicitly.

If the remote system doesn't recognize your user name, it asks you to type a user name and password, just like `telnet` does.

One place where `rlogin` is quite different from `telnet` is in how you escape from a recalcitrant remote system: You type ~. (a tilde followed by a period) on a line by itself. What you have to press is Enter (or Return), tilde, period, Enter.

TECHNICAL STUFF

Dialing out

Another command that acts sort of like `telnet` is `cu` (for *call UNIX*). It activates a simple "terminal emulator" program that calls out over the phone. Despite its name, `cu` can call *any* system with a modem compatible with the one on your computer. The program is useful for calling on-line services like MCI Mail and CompuServe.

Your system administrator has to set up the list of system names and phone numbers that `cu` uses.

After they are set up, you call out by simply typing the following line:

```
cu systemname
```

You escape from `cu` and hang up the phone in the same way you escape from `rlogin`: by typing `~.` (a tilde followed by a period on a line by themselves).

One Command at a Time

Sometimes `rlogin` is overkill for what you want to do — you just want to run one command at a time. In this type of situation, the `rsh` command (for *remote shell*) does the trick:

```
rsh pumpkin lpq
```

You give `rsh` the name of the system you want to use and the command you want to run on that system. This example runs the command `lpq` on system `pumpkin` (remember that `lpq` asks what's waiting for the printer on `pumpkin`).

The `rsh` command uses the same user-name strategy that `rlogin` does, so if you can use `rlogin` to access a system and not give a user name or a password, you can use `rsh` also. But because `rsh` doesn't handle the terminal very cleverly, you can't use full-screen commands like `vi` and `emacs`. You can use `ed`, however. Wow.

An old program, also called `rsh`, sometimes conflicts with the `rsh` we're talking about here. The old `rsh` is the *restricted shell*, a version of the Bourne shell that's of no use to you. If you type `rsh pumpkin`, and UNIX responds with `pumpkin: pumpkin: cannot open`, or displays a $ and sits there, you have the old `rsh`. If UNIX displays the $, type `exit` to make it go away. If you have the old `rsh`, what we're calling `rsh` is probably called `remsh` or `rshell`, so try these commands instead.

Blatting Files Across the Network

Although `telnet` and `rlogin` may be the next best thing to being there, sometimes there's no place like your home machine. If you want to use files that are on another machine, often the easiest thing to do is to copy them back to your own machine. There are two programs to do this: `rcp` and `ftp`. We discuss `rcp` first because it's much simpler to use. However, the other program (`ftp`) is much more widely used, including the famous Internet *anonymous FTP*.

The sweet-and-simple file-transfer program

The idea behind `rcp` is that it works just like `cp` (the standard copy command), but it also works on remote files that you own or that you at least have access to. To refer to a file on another UNIX machine, type the machine name and a colon before the filename. To copy a file named `mydata` from the machine named `pumpkin` and call it `pumpkindata`, you type the following:

```
rcp pumpkin:mydata pumpkindata
```

To copy it the other way (from a file called `pumpkindata` on your machine to a file called `mydata` on a machine called `pumpkin`), you type this line:

```
rcp pumpkindata pumpkin:mydata
```

The `rcp` program uses the same user-name rules as do `rlogin` and `rsh`. If your user name on the other system is different from that on your own system, type the user name and an @ sign before the machine name:

```
rcp steph@pumpkin:mydata pumpkindata
```

If you want to copy files in another user's directory (`tracy`, for example) on the other system, place the user's name *after* a ~ (a tilde) *before* the filename. To copy one of Tracy's files, type

```
rcp pumpkin:~tracy/somefile tracyfile
```

To copy an entire directory at a time, you can use the `-r` (for *recursive*) flag to tell `rcp` to copy the entire contents of a directory:

```
rcp -r pumpkin:projectdir .
```

This command says to copy the directory `projectdir` on machine `pumpkin` into the current directory (the period is the nickname for the current directory) on the local machine.

You can combine all this notation in an illegible festival of punctuation:

```
rcp -r steph@pumpkin:~tracy/projectdir tracy-project
```

Translation: Go to machine `pumpkin`, where my user name is `steph`, and get from user `tracy` a directory called `projectdir` and copy it to a directory on this machine called `tracy-project`. Whew!

In the finest UNIX tradition, `rcp` is extremely taciturn: It says nothing unless something goes wrong. If you are copying a lot of files over a network, it can take a while (a couple of minutes), so you may have to be more patient than usual while waiting for it to do its work. It is done when you see the UNIX prompt.

If you copied stuff *to* another machine and want to see whether it worked, use `rsh` to give an `ls` command to see which files are on the other machine:

```
rcp -r projectdir pumpkin:squashproject
rsh pumpkin ls -l squashproject
```

Although `rcp` is pretty reliable (if it didn't complain, the copy almost certainly worked), it never hurts to be sure.

The `rcp` command works only for copying a file to or from another UNIX machine. If you want to copy files to or from some other type of system, try `ftp`, described in the next section.

The he-man's file-transfer program

Sometimes `rcp` isn't studly enough to satisfy your file-transfer needs, particularly if you want to copy to or from a non-UNIX machine or if you want to retrieve files from a public file archive on a machine on which you don't have a personal account. Instead, you can use the FTP (File Transfer Protocol) system which is widely used on computers all over the Internet. Thousands of files are available free for the asking using FTP.

When you need more file-transfer power, you run the `ftp` program and give it the name of the machine to which you want to connect, like this:

```
ftp pumpkin
```

(We're giving this pumpkin machine a workout!) The ftp program responds by giving a login prompt similar to the one telnet does:

```
Connected to pumpkin.spdcc.com.
220 pumpkin.spdcc.com FTP server (SunOS 4.1) ready.
Name (pumpkin:john1):
```

You always have to log in. The ftp program suggests that you use your own user name (as good a guess as any). Press Enter, if the user name it suggests is the one you want to use, or type the user name you do want to use and press Enter. It then asks for your password (the same one you use when you log in):

```
331 Password required for john1.
Password:
230 User john1 logged in.
```

If you don't have a user name on the machine you're trying to access, you may still be able to use ftp. See the section, "Anonymous FTP," for details.

After you're logged in with ftp, you can use lots and lots of commands — far more than we have any intention of explaining. But, first things first; to leave ftp, type quit:

The program probably responds politely:

```
221 Goodbye.
```

If ftp is in the middle of a long transfer, and you decide that it's not worth waiting for, press Ctrl-C or whatever your interrupt character is (it's the Delete key in some places) to get back to ftp. Then you can either quit or try another command. When the network connection is slow, it can take the better part of a minute to stop a transfer. Pressing Ctrl-C over and over is a good way to pass the time while you wait. Perhaps a nice bossa nova beat is appropriate.

Listing remote directories

An ftp command that you use a lot is dir; it lists the directory on the remote machine by using ls (or an equivalent program if the remote machine is not running UNIX).

```
ftp> dir
```

The result of the dir command is that your basic ls -l report is displayed (see Chapter 5) with some junk from ftp that tells you what it's doing (see Figure 21-1).

```
200 PORT command successful.
150 ASCII data connection for /bin/ls (140.186.80.3,1398) (0 bytes).
total 52
-rwxr-xr-x    1 johnl      staff          1066 Oct 21 16:23      .login
-rwxr-xr-x    1 johnl      staff           283 Feb 14  1990      .logout
-rw-rw-rw-    1 johnl      staff             2 Jul 31 00:03      .msgsrc
-rw-------    1 johnl      staff          1282 Jan 27  1992      .netrc
-rw-r--r--    1 johnl      group           100 Jan  6 20:50      .plan
-rwxr-xr-x    1 johnl      staff           232 Feb 14  1990      .profile
-rw-r--r--    1 johnl      group            57 Jan  8 14:31      .rhosts
drwxr-xr-x    2 johnl      staff           512 Jul 14 16:07      News
drwxr-xr-x    2 johnl      staff           512 Dec 22 18:15      bin
drwx------    2 johnl   ·   group           512 Jan  8 14:28      mail
226 ASCII Transfer complete.
1454 bytes received in 1.1 seconds (1.3 Kbytes/s)
```

Figure 21-1: An example of the result of typing the `dir` command in `ftp`.

The `ftp` command is the opposite of `rcp`, chattiness-wise. You just can't shut it up; it insists on telling you all about what it's doing.

Copying files to and from the other system

To use `ftp` to retrieve files from the remote system, use the `get` command:

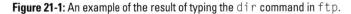

```
ftp> get .plan pumpkin-plan
```

You give `get` the name of the file on the other machine and the name of the file you want it to make on your machine. If both names are the same (they usually are), you can omit the second name. The `ftp` program gives the usual chatty report as it copies the file:

```
200 PORT command successful.
150 ASCII data connection for .plan (140.186.80.3,1403) (100 bytes).
226 ASCII Transfer complete.
local: pumpkin-plan remote: .plan
102 bytes received in 0.051 seconds (2 Kbytes/s)
```

To copy files to the remote system, use `put`, which is much like `get`:

```
ftp> put letter-to-fred
```

The `ftp` program gives the same sort of output:

```
200 PORT command successful.
150 ASCII data connection for ltr-to-fred (140.6.80.3,2702).
226 ASCII Transfer complete.
local: ltr-to-fred remote: ltr-to-fred
2831 bytes sent in 0.067 seconds (41 Kbytes/s)
```

You can provide a second filename if you want to call the file something else on the other system.

`ftp` normally doesn't say anything between the time it starts to copy a file and the time it finishes. If you copy a large file over a slow network connection, it can be hard to tell the difference between a slow connection and a dead connection. If you'd like some reassurance, type the `hash` command before you use `get` or `put`. That tells `ftp` to print a hash mark (#) every time it has copied another thousand characters. **Warning:** Watching a line of ###### crawl across the screen is really boring.

Changing directories

If the files you want are in some other directory on the remote system, `ftp` has a `cd` command that works just like the regular shell `cd` command, except that it is effective on only the remote machine. You can change the current directory on your local machine using `lcd`.

To change the remote directory, type:

```
ftp> cd mail
```

Of course, `ftp`, voluble as ever, tells you that the command worked:

```
250 CWD command successful.
```

If you're not sure which directory you're in, `ftp` also has a `pwd` command that works like you expect it to:

```
ftp> pwd
```

You get the obvious response:

```
257 "/mnt/users/johnl/mail" is current directory.
```

Copying lots of files

If you want to use ftp to copy a bunch of files, typing all those get and put commands can be mighty tedious. You can copy a group of files with mget and mput. The mget command gets many files; mput puts many files. You list all the files you want to put or get on one line (you can even use * and ? wildcards). The files are copied with the names they already have. (It's possible to change the names as you copy them, but the method is so arcane that even most wizards don't use it.) Each command asks, before it copies each file, whether you want to copy that particular file. Press y if you want to copy and n if not.

Suppose that you want to copy some files from the remote system's current directory to your current directory. To have ftp interactively let you select the files you want to copy, type this:

```
ftp> mget *
```

For every file you tell ftp to copy, it gives the usual report (see Figure 21-2).

```
mget budget? y
200 PORT command successful.
150 ASCII data connection for budget (140.186.80.3,2752) (14657 bytes).
226 ASCII Transfer complete.
local: budget remote: budget
14750 bytes received in 0.27 seconds (53 Kbytes/s)
mget budgerigar? n
mget letter-to-fred? n
mget saved-messages? y
200 PORT command successful.
150 ASCII data connection for saved-messages (140.186.80.3,2754) (0 bytes).
226 ASCII Transfer complete.
```

Figure 21-2: Using the mget command to get a buncha files.

To copy most of the files in a directory, the easiest thing to do is to type mget * or mput * and then pick the files you want as ftp asks the questions.

To shut ftp up so that it doesn't ask questions (a method more in line with the UNIX "you asked for it, you got it" philosophy), type the command prompt on a line by itself before you give the mget or mput command. Then ftp copies all the files you asked for without stopping. Be sure that you type the command correctly; this is a good way to generate a lot of useless network traffic.

FTPing files that don't contain text

Normally, ftp assumes that the files you're copying contain plain ASCII text. If the remote machine isn't running UNIX, ftp usually automatically adjusts the file contents as they come or go to account for the various ways that other computers store text files.

As often as not, the files you're transferring don't contain text. They can be programs, or databases, or word processor files. (Even though word processor documents contain mostly text, they also contain nonprinting glop to specify page sizes, fonts, and the like.) Before you copy anything that doesn't contain text, give the binary command to tell ftp not to mess with the files and to copy them verbatim:

```
ftp> binary
```

As you expected, ftp can't help itself; it says:

```
20 0 Type set to I.
```

(If you care, I stands for *I*mage. But you probably don't.) You can use binary mode to copy text files from one UNIX system to another because ftp doesn't need to make any adjustments to text files between UNIX systems.

If you're copying large files (longer than 20,000 characters or so), you can save time if you first compress them (see Chapter 14), copy the compressed versions, and then uncompress them on the other machine. The time it takes to compress and uncompress can be considerably less than the time you save using ftp on the smaller compressed versions. When you retrieve files from a public archive, they're almost always in a compressed form to save disk space and transfer time, so you should read up on compressing anyway.

Leaving the world of FTP

To stop talking to ftp (and to shut it up for good), type quit. You see the nice, plain UNIX prompt — a welcome relief after all that chatter.

Anonymous FTP

If your computer is on the Internet, there are thousands — maybe tens of thousands — of machines from which you can ftp files by using anonymous ftp. Available material ranges from scanned images of girls in bathing suits (all G-rated, so let's not be tasteless here) to transcripts of Supreme Court decisions. These machines let anyone use ftp and the user name anonymous to log in. You can usually use any password you want, but convention says that you use your full network e-mail address, including the @ and machine name (see Chapter 19 if you don't know what it is).

One large `ftp` repository is run by UUNET, a nonprofit service that handles enormous amounts of e-mail and net news for UNIX systems. Their repository is on a machine called `ftp.uu.net`, so here's what it looks like when you log in:

```
ftp ftp.uu.net
Connected to ftp.uu.net.
220 ftp.UU.NET FTP server (Version 6.34 Thu Oct 22 14:32:01 EDT 1992) ready.
Name (ftp.uu.net:johnl): anonymous
331 Guest login ok, send e-mail address as password.
Password: type your e-mail address here
230-
230-                    Welcome to the UUNET archive.
230-      A service of UUNET Technologies Inc, Falls Church, Virginia
```

After you log in, use lots of `cd` and `dir` commands to find out what's available. Most directories contain files called README that you can retrieve to see an explanation of what the directory contains. In many cases (not in UUNET, however), all the interesting files are in a directory called `pub`; type `cd pub` if the first directory you see doesn't look promising.

Most `ftp` archives are run informally by individuals at schools and companies; when you log in, they ask you to limit the amount you retrieve or the times of day you retrieve stuff. Please honor these requests, or the archives will simply go away.

FTP's greatest hits

If you're able to do anonymous FTP on the Internet, here are a few sites with interesting stuff. For more details and more sites, see our books *MORE UNIX For Dummies* (which has two chapters on FTPing and what to do with the stuff you find), *The Internet For Dummies, MORE Internet For Dummies,* and *Internet Secrets,* all published by IDG Books. (Collect them all!)

Frequently Asked Questions (rtfm.mit.edu)

Usenet is a huge networked bulletin board with discussions in upwards of 10,000 topic areas. In many of those topic areas, volunteers compile answers to Frequently Asked Questions (FAQs), and all of those FAQs are archived together, providing a treasure trove of useful and useless information. Look in directories /pub/usenet-by-group and /pub/usenet-by-hierarchy.

RTFM is very popular, and you may have trouble getting in at peak hours. (RTFM is a standard Internet abbreviation for Read The Manual.)

The Senate (`ftp.senate.gov`)

That's the U.S. Senate in Washington, D.C., where you can find a growing archive of info about Senate activities and individual senators.

The Wiretap (`wiretap.spies.com`)

The ominously named Internet Wiretap is in fact an archive of text documents from around the world. To avoid copyright problems, it's heavy on government documents and on texts written long enough ago that the copyright has lapsed. There are quite a few actual books. We like *Anne of Green Gables* and *The Wizard of Oz*.

Software

A tremendous amount of freeware and shareware software is available via anonymous FTP. When you read about interesting new Internet programs, stay alert for the addresses of FTP servers from which the programs can be transferred.

URLs for FTPing

Yikes! Another three-letter-acronym (TLA), for Uniform Resource Locator. URLs are ways of naming Internet resources, and we talk about them a bunch in *The Internet For Dummies*. The way you describe a file that you can get over the Internet using the `ftp` program is like this:

```
ftp://hostname/pathname
```

For example, if you see this URL

```
ftp://rtfm.mit.edu/pub/net/
    internet.txt
```

that means to FTP to `rtfm.mit.edu`, move to the `/pub/net` directory, and get the `internet.txt` file.

Part VI
Help!

In this part...

The point of this book is to help you when things go wrong. That's what makes it so different from "good news" books that talk only about how everything works in a perfect world. This part contains lists of things that can go wrong and error messages you might see, and things you can do about them.

Chapter 22

Disaster Relief

● ●

In This Chapter

▶ My computer won't turn on

▶ My mouse is acting glitchy

▶ The network is gone

▶ These aren't my files!

▶ It's not listening!

▶ I give up . . . .

● ●

*T*here is always the tiny, infinitesimal chance that you may run into some kind of problem with your computer. It can be something major (like losing the funniest interoffice memo you've seen in years) or minor (like accidentally deleting the analysis you have spent two months creating).

Some computer problems you can fix; some you can't. It's similar to cars: You can pump gas yourself and maybe change the oil, but when it's time to rebuild the engine, call for help. (We do, anyway.) This chapter describes some problems you may run into, with suggestions for what to do.

My Computer Won't Turn On

You come in to the office one morning, flip the switch on your computer, and nothing happens. No friendly whir, nothing on-screen. Uh-oh. Lots of things could have happened, so check these possibilities:

✔ **Is the computer plugged in?** It sounds stupid, but we have had computer problems when the people who clean the office bumped vacuum cleaners into the outlet that our equipment was plugged in to. If you're using a terminal or X terminal, this applies to the terminal and the computer.

✔ **Check the switch.** If the computer is plugged into a power strip that has its own on-off switch, people have been known to turn off the switch inadvertently with their toes.

✔ **Is the computer still attached?** Are the cables that connect the computer, keyboard, screen, and whatever else still connected? If your terminal is connected to a network, is the network cable firmly attached to the computer? Try wiggling it a little even if it looks OK.

✔ **Is there power in the rest of the office?** Plug a lamp into the same outlet as the computer and make sure that it turns on. (True story: "Hello, help desk? My computer won't turn on." "Is it plugged in correctly?" "I can't tell. The power failed and none of the lights work.")

✔ **Is the picture on the screen turned off?** The computer can be on, and the screen can even be on, but the picture on the screen can be dimmed. Fool with the brightness knob (remember where the knob was positioned when you started fiddling with it).

✔ **Does your computer have a screen-blanker program?** Press a key (we like to press the Shift key because it has no other effect on the computer) to make sure that a screen-blanker program didn't black out your screen as a favor to you. Moving the mouse a little also unblanks the screen.

If it's not a power problem, it's probably not something you can fix yourself. Call your system administrator for help. Some component may have burned out. Stay calm — this does *not* mean that the files stored on your disk are gone. They are probably fine; disks remember data perfectly well with the power off.

My Mouse Is Acting Glitchy

If you have a computer with a male mouse, dust or crumbs inside it can prevent the ball from rolling smoothly. Most mice with balls have a way to remove the ball for cleaning, usually by turning a plastic ring that surrounds the opening for the ball, or by sliding the ring to the front or side. (We won't begin to suggest appropriate names for that ring.) Turn the mouse over so that the ball falls into your hand and not on the floor, gently wipe off the grit, and snap it all back together. Female mice appreciate it if you occasionally wipe off the mouse pad with a tissue. Also, look at the bottom of your female mouse; if it's on and working, you should be able to see a little, red lamp.

The Network Is Gone

You can't print on the printer down the hall and you can't run certain programs. The problem may be that your computer is not communicating properly with the network to which it is normally attached.

Most network problems are not for the faint of heart. One thing you can try is to check the cables in the back of your computer. Is the network cable firmly attached to the computer? Try wiggling it a little even if it looks OK. (See Chapter 9 for more details.) Otherwise, it's time to call in the experts.

These Aren't My Files!

Normally, when you log in, you start working in your home directory. If you type cd, you return to the home directory from whichever directory you may have roamed to.

If cd doesn't get you back home, you may not be who you think you are. Try typing whoami or who am i. If someone else's user name appears, your computer thinks that that's who you are! A coworker may have logged in to your computer to do some work for a moment.

You then have two options:

✔ Send some malicious e-mail; it appears as though your coworker sent it. Delete all her files that look important, and then log out and pretend that nothing happened.

✔ Log out without fouling anything up — type logout — and then log in as yourself. Maybe you have to type exit or just press Ctrl-D. At any rate, when you see the login screen, log in as yourself.

Most courses in business ethics tell you that option 2 is preferred by all but the slimiest of bottom-feeding MBAs, but the urge to send goofy e-mail is sometimes irresistible. Remember: You might be caught.

It's Not Listening!

The computer is on, you are working away, and suddenly it doesn't respond to anything you type. It's the Abominable Frozen Computer.

The computer is probably fine — it's a program that has frozen up. Here are some things to try to get the program's attention:

✔ Press Esc a bunch of times.

✔ Press Ctrl-C a bunch of times.

✔ Press Ctrl-D a bunch of times.

✔ Press Ctrl-S and Ctrl-Q a bunch of times. (You never know what will work.)

 ✔ If you are running Motif, or another X Windows-based system, see whether you can use the mouse to select another window or whether you can type a command or two in a shell window. If you can, you can probably arrange to murder the frozen program and start it up again.

 ✔ If your window system is completely stuck, you can usually murder the window system, start it over again, and not have to restart your computer.

If your computer is on a network or has more than one terminal, you can ask a computer guru to kill the program. If you're feeling brave, you can kill it yourself. When you kill a program, you lose any work you were doing in that program since the last time you saved data to the disk.

Tell the wizard what happened (in order), which programs were running, and what you did. She will probably kill the process (see Chapter 24). If you have a number of processes running, she may kill one after another until your computer feels better.

I Give Up . . . .

Sometimes discretion is the better part of valor (whatever that means). If you need to call for help, be sure to do the following:

 ✔ **Don't turn off the computer.** Unless flames are coming out of the screen and threatening to engulf your entire office, this is not a good idea. Even then, you might be better off waiting for it to trip the circuit breaker than facing your wizard, who will surely ask, "Did you turn if off?"

 ✔ **Know the symptoms.** Be ready to tell someone what happened and which actions you took to fix the problem.

 ✔ **Know what has changed recently.** Did you install new software? Did you run something you have never run before? New things are always suspicious. A claim of "I didn't change anything" does not endear you to your wizard. Something, somewhere, *must* have changed.

 ✔ If you call for help by phone, **call from within reach of the computer.** Your savior may want you to try a few maneuvers at the keyboard.

Chapter 23

The Case of the Missing Files

Sooner or later, you will delete a file by mistake. Scratch that *later*. Sooner than you think, you will delete a file by mistake. In far too many cases, you are out of luck, but there are a few things you can do to avoid disaster.

How You Clobber Files

Contrary to the usual image of UNIX users being radically technical and without a creative bone in their bodies, we submit that typical UNIX users are immensely creative. They can come up with a zillion inventive ways to avoid the computer altogether and, when forced to sit down to stare the computer in the face, can come up with a dozen more inventive reasons for why things went wrong. There are lots of ways you can make files disappear (either intentionally or accidentally). The following sections list the four main ways you can trash files — although you can probably come up with a dozen new and creative ways to do the vanishing act with files.

Clobbering files with rm

Because disks are not infinitely large, sooner or later you have to get rid of some files. (Some wag once said that the only thing standard among UNIX systems is the message-of-the-day reminding users to delete unneeded files.)

The normal way to get rid of files is the rm (for *remove*) command. Until (notice that we didn't say *unless*) you screw up, rm removes only what you want it to. Recall that you tell rm the names of the files you want to remove, like this:

```
rm thisfile thatfile somedir/anotherfile
```

You can remove more than one file at a time, and you can specify files in other directories (rm removes just the file and not the directory).

This method is usually pretty safe. The tricky part comes when you use wildcards. If you use a word processor that leaves backup files with names ending in .bak, for example, you can get rid of all of them with this command:

```
rm *.bak
```

That's no problem — unless you put in an extra space (**Don't type this line!**):

```
rm * .bak
```

Note that there is a little, tiny space between the asterisk and the dot. In response to this command, UNIX says this:

```
rm: .bak non-existent
```

Uh-oh. UNIX decided you wanted to delete two things: * and .bak. Because the asterisk wildcard matches every single filename in the working directory, every single filename in the working directory is deleted. Then UNIX tries to delete a file called .bak, which isn't there. Bad move.

At this point, we recommend that you panic, gnash your teeth, and throw Nerf balls at the computer. After you calm down a little, read the rest of this chapter for some possible ways to get your files back.

You can also make less destructive but still aggravating mistakes when you forget which files you have. Suppose that you have files called section01, section02, and so on up to section19. You want to get rid of all of them and type this line:

```
rm sec*
```

Now suppose that you forgot you also have a file called second.version that you want to keep. Oops. Bye-bye, second.version.

The obvious solution is to delete things one at a time. But, unless you are an extremely fast and steady typist, that's not very practical. In the following sections, we make some suggestions about that, too.

Clobbering files with cp, mv, *and* ln

Are you feeling paranoid yet, as though every time you press the R and M keys you're going to blow away a year's worth of work? Wait — it gets worse.

The cp, mv, and ln commands can also clobber files by mistake. If you use one of these programs to copy, rename, or link a file, and there is already a file by the new name, the existing file gets clobbered. Suppose that you type this line:

```
mv elbow armpit
```

If you already had a file called armpit — blam! — it's gone! The same thing happens if you copy or link. (Copying is a *little* different; see the upcoming sidebar if you care.) Here's an example of the most annoying case of blasting away good files with trash when you use the copy command:

```
cp important.file.save important.file
```

As a responsible and paranoid computer user, you want to save a copy of an important file before you make some changes. But your fingers work a little faster than your brain, and you get the two names switched (left-handed users are particularly prone to getting names sdrawkcab), and — blam! (again) — you've just copied an obsolete saved version over the current version. Fortunately, you can arrange your file-saving habits to make this kind of mistake harmless, or at least mostly harmless.

Creaming files using redirection

A third popular way to blow valuable files away is by using redirection. If you redirect the output of a command to a file that already exists — whammo! — UNIX blows away the existing file and replaces it with your redirected output. For example, you type

```
ls -al > dirlist
```

However, you already have a file named dirlist. Well, it's gone now, replaced with the new list.

Several of the UNIX shells can be persuaded to take pity on you, and not to let you clobber files by mistake. In so-called *noclobber* mode, if you redirect output to a file that already exists, it won't do it, printing an error message instead.

TECHNICAL STUFF

Links, copies, moves, truncation, and other details about file destruction

Clobber-wise, copying files works a little differently from moving and linking files. More often than not, the practical difference is unimportant, although in a few cases, it can be worth knowing about.

The cp command does one thing as it clobbers a file; mv and ln do another. The difference is noticeable only if additional names or links were created for that file with ln. (See Chapter 8 for how to create links, or additional names, for files using the ln command.)

Clobbering a file with cp: Suppose that you have two files, first and second. You give second an additional name by using this ln command:

```
ln second extra.name
```

Now suppose that you accidentally (who knows why) type cp first second (remember that you already have a file called second). What happens to the file named second? The cp command replaces the current contents of second with a copy of first. That is, it replaces the text (or whatever) that second contains with whatever first contains. This change affects the file named extra.name too, because this is another name for the file second. If you use cat or a text editor to look at second or extra.name, you see a copy of first. The original contents of second and extra.name are gone with the wind.

Clobbering a file with mv **or** ln: "So what?" you ask, to cut to the heart of the matter. Here's the interesting part (interesting to us, anyway). If you had used mv or ln rather than cp, the second file would not be gone. The mv and ln commands

don't fool with the contents of the file — they just change what filename is connected with what contents. Suppose that you type this line:

```
mv first second
```

The mv command disconnects the name second from its current contents. The contents are still linked to the name extra.name, so that file is still safe and sound. The mv command then connects the name second to the contents of first, and finally disconnects the name first from the file. Now there is no file called first.

As a result, the contents of the second file are not clobbered (you can use the other name for the file to see them). The ln command works the same way as mv to disconnect filenames and not touch the contents of files.

The message here is that if you have just fouled up an mv or ln command, you may still have hope of retrieving the old file (if it had other links).

Clobbering files with soft links: To add more confusion, the story is a little different if you use soft links rather than regular hard links. (See Chapter 8 to learn how soft links can link files from different file systems.) Because soft links are just aliases for the true filename, if you do something to the original file, all the links refer to the changed file because it has the same name. On the other hand, if you use cp to change one of the links, the cp command replaces the contents of the original file; mv and ln affect just the link.

Confused? The moral is the same with soft links: After a botched mv or ln, you may still be able to find the original file if it had another name. It can't hurt to look.

If you use the BASH shell, you can give this command:

```
noclobber=1
```

If you use the C shell, you can give this incantation:

```
set noclobber
```

Better yet, get a UNIX wizard to help you include it in your .cshrc (for the C shell) or .profile (for BASH) file so that the command is given automagically every time you start the shell. By the way, if you really *do* want to clobber a file, delete the old version with rm first.

When you redirect output into a file, you can tell UNIX to add the output to the end of an existing file. Instead of typing one >, type two, like this:

```
ls -al >> dirlist
```

Wrecking files with text editors

The fourth way that you're likely to smash files is in a botched editor session. The problem usually comes up after you have been editing a file for a while and realize that you have completely screwed up; the changes you have made are not what you want, so you decide to leave the editor. On the way out, however, you write the botched changes to the disk and wreck the original file. A similar problem occurs when you use an editor to look at a file; although you may not intend to change anything, you may make some inadvertent changes. (This can easily happen in emacs, where pretty much anything you type goes straight into the file.) If not careful, you can write the changes to the disk by mistake.

If you use vi, you can avoid the accidental-clobber problem by typing view rather than vi. The view editor is the same as the vi editor (vi and view are links to the same program); view works the same as vi except that it doesn't let you write changes to the file. Keep it in mind.

Some versions of emacs can mark files as read-only so that you can't make changes to the files, but the methods of doing this aren't entirely standardized. In GNU Emacs, you press Ctrl-X Ctrl-R in a file window, and Emacs puts an inscrutable %% on the status line at the bottom of the screen. To be even more careful, you can use Ctrl-X Ctrl-R to open a file read-only in the first place.

GNU Emacs is usually set up so that it saves the old contents of a changed file in a file with the name of the original file with a tilde (~) added. If your smashed file is called MyNovel, the unsmashed version is MyNovel~.

Ways to Try to Get Files Back

Well, now you've done it; you've clobbered something important, and you really, *really* want it back. Let's see what we can do.

If you're used to other systems, like DOS, in which you can magically "unerase" stuff, we're sorry to tell you that UNIX doesn't let you do that. If it's gone, it's gone. (A version of the Norton Utilities that includes an unerase command is available for some versions of UNIX, but it isn't widely used.)

Copies, copies, everywhere

Maybe you have stashed away in a different directory other copies of the file you deleted. For our important files, we stick copies in a directory called save. Also, sometimes you can reconstruct the information from a different form. If you clobber a word processor file, for example, you may have a backup version (the .bak files mentioned earlier in this chapter) that's pretty close to the current version; you might have printed the deleted file to a file (rather than directly to the printer) and can edit the print file into document form.

If you share your computer with other people or use a network, see whether someone else has a copy. It's a rare file that really exists in only one place.

Call in the backup squad

It's really gone, huh? Now it's time for the final line of defense: backups. You *do* have backups, don't you?

We interrupt this chapter for a stern lecture: *Always make backups.* If your system administrator is on the ball, tape backups are made automatically every night; all you have to do is go to the administrator, with chocolate-chip cookies in hand, and ask very politely for some help getting your valuable file back from the previous night's backups. If no backups exist, it's fair to jump up and down and scream that someone had better get on the ball.

Seriously, backups are a standard part of any administrator's job, by making the backups personally or by overseeing operators who do the backing up. (After the procedures are set up, making backup tapes is so simple that you can practically train your dog to do it. One reason that it sometimes doesn't get done is that backing up is boring.)

If your system administrator doesn't make backups, you better learn how to do it. If you have a tape unit on your machine, the procedure is usually as follows:

1. **Put a tape in the tape unit and flip the latch to seat the tape firmly.**

2. **Give a command to copy files to the tape, usually the `tar` (*t*ape *ar*chive) or `pax` (*p*ortable *a*rchive e*x*change) program; on Sun workstations, the program is `bar` (*b*ackup *ar*chive).**

   The exact things you say to the `tar` program vary from one system to another, mostly because of the peculiarities of different tape units. You can't use the regular `cp` command because tapes aren't logically organized the same way disks are. This can take a while, an hour for a largish disk.

3. **Take the tape out of the tape unit.**

4. **Write the current date on the label so that you know that it is a current backup.**

   (The sensibly paranoid alternate several tapes, in case one of them goes bad. We describe this subject in more detail in the next sidebar.)

5. **Put the tape back in its box and put the box back on the shelf.**

Why you need backups

Making backups is a pain. But the question isn't *whether* you will lose data, it's *when*. Here are some events that have sent us heading for the backup tapes:

- ✔ The obvious one: We deleted a file by mistake.

- ✔ Just as we were saving a file, the power failed and scrambled both the old and new versions of the file. Yikes!

- ✔ One day, while working on the insides of the computer (one of us is a closet nerd), we accidentally dropped a screwdriver on the disk controller. Exciting sparks came out and fried the controller card that attaches the disk to the rest of the computer. We got a new controller card and found that, although the disk was physically fine, the new controller wasn't quite compatible with the old one, and we had to reformat the disk and restore everything from tape.

- ✔ We remembered hearing that we should absolutely, positively run a "disk-head parking" program before moving our hard disk, so we ran one. Unfortunately, it was a version that was incompatible with our hard disk, so it parked the disk head right off the edge of the disk, way out past what you might call the Long-Term Parking Area. We could hear the disk head banging on the side of the hard disk as it tried to get back on. Rats!

- ✔ Back in the good old days, computers weighed about 15,000 pounds, and you needed a fork lift to move one. Now they weigh about 25 pounds, which means that if the cleaning people bump into one with a vacuum cleaner, they can knock it over with a clunk that can put an unreadable ding into the disk. Oops — sorry, lady.

You probably have horror stories of your own, but they all have the same moral: Make those backups!

The usual way to back stuff up on Linux is to use `tar`. To back up to tape, type

```
tar cvf /dev/rft0 *
```

The `cvf` means Create, Verbose Report, to File, and `/dev/rft0` is the name of the tape unit. The `*` means to back up all of the files in your directory; if you have a lot, you can list specific files and directories instead.

Some systems don't have tapes; they have floppy disks. Floppies are a major pain for backup use for two reasons: You need a stack of them, and you must format them first.

Before you can use a floppy disk, you must format it, which means that the computer writes some bookkeeping junk on it to mark where to put the data and, in the process, checks to be sure that no bad spots are on the floppy. Fortunately, you only have to do this one time per disk. Formatting disks is easy but tedious, and of course (sing along with us as we say this), it varies from one system to another. You stick the blank disk in the computer, type the formatting command, and UNIX does it. If you're stuck with floppy backups, ask your administrator for help setting up the procedure and, while you're feeding all the disks into the drive, consider getting a tape drive.

If you back up to floppies, type this to Linux:

```
tar cvMf /dev/fd0 *
```

The M means Multiple disks, since you can't put much stuff on one disk. Linux will tell you when to swap disks. Be sure to write the backup date and the disk number on each disk, so they don't get out of order.

If you have a lot of files, copying everything to tape can take a while (an hour or so). You might want to do the backup over lunch. Or do what we do and have your administrator arrange to run the `tar` program automatically every night at about 3 a.m. We leave a tape in the tape unit every night; when we come back the next morning, the backup's been done, and we take the tape out and put it away. The `tar` command creates a report that is e-mailed to us so that we can check to see whether the tape was written correctly.

Getting stuff back from a tape is somewhat trickier because you want to restore just the files you clobbered. Ask for help — at least the first time. Generally speaking, you put the tape in the drive the same way you did to make the backup and then type a `tar` or `pax` command similar to one of these:

```
tar xvf /dev/tape somedir/clobberedfile
pax -rv -f /dev/tape somedir/clobberedfile
```

In the `tar` command, `xvf` stands for eXtract Verbosely From; in the `pax` command `-rv -f` similarly means Read Verbosely From. Either way, it's followed by the name of your tape drive (often, /dev/tape, except on Linux where it's usually /dev/rft0) and the name of the file to look for. The tape spins as tar or pax runs down the tape looking for the file you want. When the tape finds the file, it reads the file onto the disk, reports that it did so, and stops. If you clobbered a bunch of files, you can use wildcards, like this:

```
tar xvf /dev/tape "somedir/*"
pax -rv -f /dev/tape "somedir/*"
```

TIP

Backup strategies

The obvious way to do tape backups is to copy the entire contents of the disk to a tape every night. But here are a couple reasons that suggest that might not be the best approach:

✔ The disk might contain too much stuff to fit on a tape. Tape and disk manufacturers continually battle to see who can outstrip the other. The battle is pretty evenly matched — as we write, they're both in the 8 gigabyte (8,000 megabyte) range, although many people are still using 150MB tapes, which are smaller than most disks on UNIX systems.

✔ You might not notice for a day or two that you clobbered something important, so a scheme that gives you a few days' grace to get your data back would be nice.

✔ Murphy's Law says that the system will fail as it's writing a backup tape, so you better not depend on one tape.

The best scheme is a combination of rotating and incremental backups. With *rotating backups,* a set of tapes is used in rotation; five tapes, for example, one written every Monday, one every Tuesday, and so on. Because each tape is written only once a week, if you delete a file by mistake on Tuesday, for example, the file is still on the Monday tape until the following Monday. You then have nearly a week to realize that it's gone and get it back. The number of tapes you use depends on your budget and your paranoia. Some people use

as few as two, some as many as seven. (We use four because we bought a four-pack of tapes.)

With *incremental backups,* you back up only what's changed. Generally, you do a full backup of everything on the disk at infrequent intervals — once a month, for example. This process may take five or six tapes, but because you do it only once a month, it's not that bad a job. For the daily incremental backup, you back up only what has changed since the last full backup (it should fit on a single tape). Any given file then is either on the full backup (if it hasn't changed in a long time) or on the current backup, so there are only two places to look.

If you have a large tape budget, you may want to have two sets of tapes you use alternately for full backups, in case your system fails while it is writing the full backups. Sometimes, full backups are stored off-site in a bank vault or other safe place, but there's a trade-off: the security of the vault versus the inconvenience of going to the bank when you need to recover a file. If you're really paranoid, you can have two full backups, one off-site and one on.

Your system administrator should handle all of this, of course. It's useful to understand at least the rudiments of backup theory, however, so that, when the administrator hands you several different tapes that might contain your file, you will understand why.

You have to quote the wildcards because the files to match are on the tape, where tar or pax can find them, not on the disk where the shell (which normally handles wildcards) can find them.

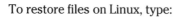

To restore files on Linux, type:

```
tar xvf /dev/rft0 "somedir/*" # if it's on tape
tar xvMf /dev/fd0 "somedir/*" # if it's on floppies
```

If you want to see what files are on the tape, but not restore any of them just now, use one of these commands:

```
tar tvf /dev/tape
pax -v -f /dev/tape
```

You should try to run the restore command from the same directory where the program that made the backup tape ran; if it's a system backup, that's probably the root directory (/).

Three Ways to Not Lose Files

Now you're probably quaking in your boots (or sandals, depending on where you live). You figure that, if you so much as touch the keyboard, you will do horrible, irreparable damage and spend the next week spinning tapes. It's not that bad. Here are some tricks to avoid deleting files by mistake.

Are you sure you wanna clobber this one?

When you delete files with rm, use the -i (for *i*nteractive) switch, like this:

```
rm -i s*
```

This line tells rm to ask you before it deletes each file, prompting you with the filename and a question mark. You answer Y if you want to delete it, and N to tell UNIX not to delete. (Remember that the question UNIX asks is, "Should I delete this?" and not "Do you want to keep this?")

The main problem with -i is it can get tedious when you want to delete a lot of files. When you do that, you probably use wildcards. To be safe, check that the wildcards refer to the files you think they do. To make that check, use the ls command with the same wildcard. If you want to delete all the files that start with *section,* for example, and you think that you can get away with typing only *sec* and an asterisk, you had better check what *sec** refers to.

```
ls sec*
```

UNIX responds with an appropriate list:

```
second.version   section04   section08   section12   section16
section01        section05   section09   section13   section17
section02        section06   section10   section14   section18
section03        section07   section11   section15   section19
```

Hey, look! There's second.version. You don't want to delete that; looks like you will have to type out section* to get the correct files in this case.

Idiot-proofing save files

The best way to make temporary backup copies of files is to make a directory called save and put all saved copies of files there, as shown in this example:

```
mkdir save
cp important.file save
```

These commands tell UNIX to make a directory called save and then to make a copy of important.file to save/important.file. If you reverse the order of the names, nothing happens. Suppose that you type this line instead:

```
cp save important.file
```

UNIX makes this observation:

```
cp : <save> directory
```

UNIX is saying that you can copy a file to a directory but that you can't copy a directory to a file. As a result, it doesn't copy anything. To copy a file back from the save directory, you have to use its full name: save/important.file.

A variation on this is a two-step delete. Suppose that you have a bunch of files you want to get rid of but there are some good files mixed in the same directory. Make a directory called trash and then use mv to move to the trash directory the files you plan to delete:

```
mkdir trash
mv thisfile thatfile these* trash
mv otherfile somefile trash
```

Then use the `ls` command to check the contents of `trash`. If there's something in that directory you want, move it back to the current directory:

```
mv trash/these.are.still.good .
```

(The dot at the end there means to put the file back in the current directory.) After you're sure that there's nothing but trash in `trash`, you can use `rm` with the `-r` option:

```
rm -r trash
```

This line tells `rm` to get rid of `trash` and everything in it.

Don't write on that!

Another thing you can do to avoid damage to important files is to make them read-only. When you make files read-only, you prevent `cp` and text editors from changing them. You can still delete them, although `rm`, `mv`, and `ln` ask before doing so. The `chmod` command changes the "mode" of a file (as explained in the section, "If Mom says no, go ask Dad," in Chapter 5). Here's how to use `chmod` to make a file read-only:

```
chmod -w crucial-file
```

The `-w` means *not writable*. To make changes to the file later, do another `chmod` but use `+w` instead. (This isn't inspired command syntax, but the old syntax was even worse and used octal digits.) After a file is made not writable, editors can't change it. The `vi` program and some versions of `emacs` even display a note on-screen that the file is read-only. If you try to delete it, `rm`, `mv`, or `ln` asks you in a uniquely user-hostile way whether that's really what you had in mind. Suppose that you type the following line, and `crucial-file` is a read-only file:

```
rm crucial-file
```

UNIX responds with this line:

```
crucial-file: 444 mode ?
```

The number may not be 444; it may be 440 or 400 (depending on whether your system administrator has set things up so that people can normally see the contents of other people's files). As with `rm -i`, you type Y if you want to delete the file, or N to say that you don't want to delete this valuable data.

Chapter 24
Killing Processes Softly

• •

• •

*Y*ou can almost always get rid of recalcitrant programs without rebooting. In this chapter, we talk about how to figure out which processes you have and how to make unwanted ones go away. Before reading this chapter, be sure that you've read Chapter 16, where we talk about how you can juggle processes yourself and do neat tricks like stop one program, run another one, go back to the first one, and pick up exactly where you left off.

Why Killing Is Sometimes Justified

Why kill a process? Don't even the smallest processes deserve to live? In a word, no. Sometimes a program hangs, and your computer just sits there. Or sometimes a program gets stuck in some kind of loop, and will never end. Or sometimes you give the wrong command and realize you don't want to run that program. To stop the process in which a program is running, kill the process. Suppose that you're working along, and you find that you have a program that just won't stop. Vell, ve haff vays to make eet stop. First, we discuss the normal ways to kill a process, and then we get into some serious artillery.

What Process? (Reprise)

In Chapter 16, we told you — in the section, "Are There Any Processes in the House?" — how to use the ps command to see what processes are running. If you are too weak from struggling with UNIX to turn back to Chapter 16, just type the ps command to see a list of your processes. Note the PID (process ID) of the process that you want to kill. You can identify which process needs to be offed, because ps shows you the command line that started each process.

50 Ways to Kill Your Process

The usual way to get rid of a process is to press the *interrupt character,* which is usually Ctrl-C, although sometimes it's Del or Delete. In most cases, the rogue program gives up peaceably and you end up back in the shell. Sometimes, though, the program arranges to handle Ctrl-C itself. If you use the ed editor (if you're a masochist) and you press Ctrl-C, for example, ed returns to command mode rather than give up and throw away any work you have done. To exit ed, you have to use the q command.

If the interrupt character doesn't work, you can up the ante and use the *quit character,* generally Ctrl-\ (a reverse slash or backslash — not the regular forward slash). The quit character not only kills the program but also saves the dead body of the process (this description is awfully morbid, but we didn't invent these terms) in a file called, for arcane historical reasons, core. The shell then gives this requiem:

```
Quit (core dumped)
```

This message tells you that the process is dead and that its body has been put on ice with the filename core. (You don't always get a core file, depending on warts not worth detailing here, but the Quit message means your process is definitely deceased.)

Most programs that catch Ctrl-C give up under the greater onslaught of Ctrl-\. If the program you were running is one written locally, your system administrator may appreciate it if you save the core file because it includes clues about what was going wrong when you killed the program. Otherwise, delete any core files with rm because they're a waste of space.

It is possible for a program to immunize itself to Ctrl-\ (ed, for example, just ignores it), so the next possibility is the *stop character* (always Ctrl-Z). The stop character doesn't kill the program, it just puts it to sleep and returns you to the shell. (See Chapter 16 for more information about what Ctrl-Z really does and how it can be useful even with programs you like.) After you're back in the shell, you can apply the stronger medicine described in the next section.

For Ctrl-Z to work, your shell must do some of the work. Many versions of the Bourne shell aren't up to it and ignore Ctrl-Z. The C, BASH, and Korn shells are Ctrl-Z-aware.

Dirty Deeds, Done Dirt Cheap

No more Mister Nice Guy: It's time for merciless slaughter. If you were successful in the previous section at putting the process to sleep with Ctrl-Z, go ahead and kill it with the procedure in this section.

All the following techniques require that you have a terminal or window in which you can type some commands to do the dirty deeds. If Ctrl-Z didn't work to put the process to sleep, you may not have a shell prompt at which to type the requisite commands. Here are other places you can use to type the commands to kill the process:

- ✔ If you're running X Windows, any window other than the one with the stuck program will do.

- ✔ Otherwise, you may have to find another terminal attached to your computer or go to another computer on the network and use telnet or rlogin to get into your computer.

- ✔ If there's no other terminal or window and no other way into the machine, you're out of luck and probably will have to reboot. Before you reboot, check with your system administrator, who may know some other tricks.

Here is a simple two-step procedure for murdering a rogue process:

1. **Find out the rogue process's true name.**

2. **Utter the true name in an appropriate spell to murder it.**

The true name of a process is its PID, one of the things that ps reports. First, do a ps command to find out the PID of your victim. To find out the PID, do this:

1. **If you pressed Ctrl-Z to put the rogue process to sleep, and you are using the same terminal to kill it utterly, type a plain** ps.

2. **Otherwise, you may have to use a different terminal to kill the process, because the amok process has taken over your own terminal. In this case, you have to tell ps which user's processes you want to see.**

If you use Linux, type

```
ps -u username
```

Replace *username* with your own login name, so that you see the processes that you are running.

If you use System V, type

```
ps -fu username
```

If you use BSD, type

```
ps -a
```

Suppose that you saw the following listing after typing ps -fu john1, which lists all the processes for user john1 (the listing is shortened to save space):

```
UID    PID   PPID  C  STIME  TTY      TIME COMMAND
john1  24806 24799 0  Jan 18  ?       0:39 xclock
```

The PID of the process you want to kill is 24806. You kill it by using the kill command:

```
kill 24806
```

The normal kind of kill sends a request to a process: "Please, nice Mr. Process, would you be so kind as to croak?" This method usually works, but occasionally a program won't take the hint. Another kind of kill, the ominously named Number-Nine kill, offers the victim no choice:

```
kill -9 24806
```

If you stopped a particularly uncooperative program with Ctrl-Z, a regular kill may provoke it to retaliate by trying to take over your terminal (something the shell fortunately prevents). Here's a true-life transcript of our attempts to murder our old text editor pal, ed. First we pressed Ctrl-Z, which put it to sleep. Then we tried a regular kill; when ed tried to strike back, we did a Number Nine. Sayonara, Bud.

```
% ed badfile
?badfile
Ctrl-Z
Stopped
% ps
   PID TTY       TIME COMMAND
 12746 ttyp1     0:00 ed
 12747 ttyp1     0:00 ps
 11643 ttyp1     0:02 -csh
% kill 12746
?
[1] + Stopped (tty input)    ed badfile
% kill -9 12746
[1]    Killed               ed badfile
```

When X Goes Bad

If you're using X Windows in any of its multiple guises (particularly Motif) and are especially unlucky, X itself may freeze the entire screen. If you can get into your computer through another terminal or a network, you can get rid of X Windows itself; this makes all the programs using X go away so that you have to log in all over again. The trick is to figure out which program is X Windows. Here's an edited `ps` report from a System V system:

```
UID    PID    PPID   C  STIME   TTY    TIME COMMAND
john1  24788  19593  0  Jan 18  vt01   0:00 /usr/bin/X11/xinit
john1  24789  24788  5  Jan 18  ptmx   38:10 Xgp :0
```

In this case, X is called `Xgp` because the particular computer happened to have a graphics processor running the screen.

Here's the equivalent from a Sun workstation:

```
PID TT STAT   TIME COMMAND
224 co IW     0:00 /bin/sh /usr/openwin/bin/openwin
228 co IW     0:00 /usr/openwin/bin/xinit — /usr/openwin/bin/xnews :0
229 co S  149:23 /usr/openwin/bin/xnews :0 -auth /usr/john1/.xnews
```

There are two easy ways to know which process is X:

- ✔ The command line has the strange code `:0`, which turns out to be X-ese for "the screen right there on the computer."

- ✔ The amount of computer time used (in the `TIME` column) is large because X is, computationally speaking, a pig.

After you figure out which process is X, you can give it the old Number-Nine kill and probably be able to log back in.

If you're using an X terminal, the Number-Nine kill doesn't apply because X itself runs in the terminal and not in the main computer. In this case, you kill X by restarting the X terminal. In the worst case, you turn the terminal off and back on, although your system administrator can probably tell you an easier way.

Resuscitating a terminal

If you blow away a program that reads a character at a time from your terminal, such as `vi` or `emacs`, the dead process leaves your terminal in a rather peculiar state that makes it hard to get any work done. This three-step method usually brings the terminal back:

1. Press Ctrl-J. The shell may complain about strangely named nonexistent commands. Ignore its whining.

2. Type `stty`, a space, and `sane` (as opposed to the insane state your terminal is in). Press Enter. You may not see anything on-screen. Remain calm.

3. Press Ctrl-J again. This should put your terminal back in a usable state. For more about the mysterious `stty` command, see Chapter 28.

Chapter 25

My Computer Says It Hates Me

• •

In This Chapter

▶ Lots of error messages

▶ What they mean

▶ What to do about them

• •

*Y*ou type a command. UNIX says something incomprehensible. What does it mean? And what should you do? Look in this chapter for the error message. We tell you what it means and what you can do to fix the problem. Most error messages start with the name of the command you tried to use. If you want to use the cp command to copy a file, for example, but you spell the name of the file wrong, cp can't find a file with the name you typed. So UNIX says something like this:

```
cp: No such file or directory
```

At the beginning of the line is the name of the command that failed to work. After the colon comes the UNIX error message — UNIX's attempt to explain the problem.

This chapter contains the most common error messages, in alphabetical order. In some of the explanations, we refer to *arguments,* not because we feel argumentative, but because it is the technical name for the information you type on the command line after the command. Suppose that you type this line:

```
cp letter.to.santa save
```

The command is cp, letter.to.santa is the first argument, and save is the second argument. You can have lots of arguments: The number depends on the command you use (cp requires two). Type a space between arguments.

There are also things called *options,* which tell the command how you want it to work. Options always start with a hyphen (-). Suppose that you type this line:

```
ls -l
```

The -l tells the ls command how you want to display the files. Options don't count as arguments. For example, if you type this line:

```
ls -l *
```

the -l is an option, and * is the first (not the second) argument. Nitpicky stuff, huh? But if UNIX complains about a particular argument or option, it is handy to know exactly which item it doesn't like.

Arg list too long

Meaning: The list of arguments is too long.

Probable cause: When you type a wildcard character as part of a filename or pathname, UNIX replaces it with the list of filenames and then calls the command. If you go wild with the asterisks, the result is a very long list. The list can be more than 5,000 characters long, so it is unlikely that you typed too long a list of filenames unless you are an unusually fast typist.

Example: In the root directory (/), you type this line:

```
ls */*
```

If a lot of files are in the root directory and its subdirectories, */* turns into a really long list.

Solution: Check the wildcards you used in the command and use fewer of them. Newer versions of UNIX allow much longer argument lists than older ones did; if you're using a modern system like Linux or BSD/OS and get this message, something strange is probably going on.

Broken pipe

Meaning: You are running two programs connected by a pipe (|), and the program at the receiving end of the pipe exited before it received all of its data.

Probable cause: You get this error occasionally when you use a pipe (|) to redirect the output of a program into the more program and then press q to cancel the more program before you see all the output. The program has no place to put its output because you canceled the more program, so you get this error. In this case, the error is harmless.

Example: You type this line:

```
furgle | more
```

The furgle program (whatever it is) gives you screen after screen of boring information. You press q to cancel the more program, but the furgle program gives you the error message.

Solution: Nothing to do — it's not really an error!

Cannot access

See the message No such file or directory.

Cross-device link

See the message Different file system.

Device or resource busy

Meaning: A device, such as a terminal or printer, is in use by another program.

Probable cause: You may see this message when you try to use cu to access a terminal that's already in use by another program or user (see Chapter 21).

Solution: Wait until the other user finishes.

Different file system

Meaning: You are using the ln command to create a link to a file in a different file system (a different disk or a disk on a different computer).

Probable cause: If your system can't do soft links (see Chapter 7), you can't create a link from one file system to another. The file you want to link to is probably in a different file system from the directory in which you want to make the link (usually the working directory).

Solution: Use the df command to find out which disks your computer has and which directories are on which disks. (See Chapter 20 to figure out what file systems you are dealing with.)

If your version of UNIX can't do soft links, you are out of luck. The only solution may be to make a copy of the file rather than to create a link to it.

File exists

Meaning: A file already exists by that name.

Probable cause: When UNIX expected the name of the file you wanted to create, you typed the name of a file that already exists.

Solution: This message is rarely seen because most UNIX commands blow away an existing file when they want to create a new one by the same name.

File table overflow

Meaning: The system is way too busy and can't juggle as many files simultaneously as all the users have asked it to.

Probable cause: The system isn't configured right or someone is doing way too much work.

Solution: Complain to the system administrator.

File too large

Meaning: You are trying to make a file that is too big.

Probable cause: There is a maximum file size set by your system administrator. Maximum file sizes prevent a messed-up program from making a file that uses up the entire disk by mistake. It is unlikely that you really want to make a file this big. Usually it happens when you use >> to add a copy of a file to itself, so you end up copying the file over and over until it passes the preset size limit.

Solution: Check the command and make sure that you are saying what you mean. If you are sure that you want to make a really big file, talk your system administrator into upping your file-size limit.

Illegal option

Meaning: You type an option that doesn't work with the command.

Probable cause: You type a hyphen in front of a filename or you type the wrong option.

Example: You type this line:

```
ls -j
```

There is no -j option for the ls command, so you get an error message. Frequently, after the illegal option message, UNIX also prints a line about usage, which is its cryptic way of reminding you about which options *do* work with the command. (*See also* Usage.)

Solution: Check your typing. Look up the command in this book to make sure that you know which option you want. Or use the man command to display an exhaustive (and exhausting) list of every option the command might possibly understand.

Insufficient arguments

Meaning: You left out some information.

Probable cause: The command you are using needs more arguments than the ones you typed. UNIX may also print a usage message in its attempt to tell you which arguments you should have typed. (*See also* Usage.)

Example: The cp command needs two arguments: The first one tells UNIX what to copy from, and the second one tells it what to copy to. You can't leave out either one.

Solution: Check your typing. If it is a command that you don't use very often, check to make sure that you have the correct arguments and options.

I/O error

Meaning: *I/O* is computerese for *i*nput and *o*utput. This message means that UNIX has some physical problem reading or writing information on a disk, tape, screen, or wherever your information lives.

Probable cause: Broken disk drive.

Solution: Tell your system administrator; you may have big trouble ahead.

Is a directory

Meaning: You typed the name of a directory when UNIX wanted a filename.

Probable cause: The command you typed is trying to do something to a directory rather than to a file. You can't, for example, change a directory by editing it.

Note that emacs has a special mode for "editing" directories (called dired mode). But emacs has its own special way to create, rename, and delete files.

Solution: Make sure that you type a filename, not the name of a directory, when you mean to work on a file.

Login incorrect

Meaning: You are trying to log in and didn't enter a correct user name or corresponding password.

Probable cause: Two possibilities exist: One is that you typed your password wrong, and the other is that you typed your user name wrong.

Solution: Type very slowly and deliberately, especially when you type your password and can't see what you are doing. If you have trouble remembering your password, use the passwd command to change it to something more memorable (see Chapter 2).

No process can be found

See the message No such process.

No such file or directory

Meaning: UNIX can't find a file or directory with the name you typed.

Probable cause: You spelled a filename or pathname wrong. This happens to most of us at least ten times a day. If you typed a pathname, you may have misspelled any of the directory names it contains. You may also have capitalized something incorrectly.

Solution: Check your spelling and capitalization. Use the ls command to see how the file and directory names are spelled and whether any letters are capitalized. For pathnames, check to see whether it should begin with a slash (which means that it is an absolute pathname which describes the path from the root directory) or not (which means that it is a relative pathname which describes the path from the current working directory). See Chapter 5 for more information about pathnames.

No such process

Meaning: UNIX can't find the process you are referring to.

Probable cause: You have given a command that deals with processes, probably a `kill` command to stop a runaway process. (See Chapter 24 for what a process is and why you may want to kill the poor thing.)

Solution: The process may already have gone away, in which case there's no problem. You may have mistyped the PID, the number that specifies which process to do in. Check your typing and use the `ps` command to check the PID.

No more processes

Meaning: Your system can't create any more new processes.

Probable cause: This message appears when you tell UNIX to create a new process, and UNIX can't. This message may appear if the system doesn't have any more space for creating the process needed to run a command. Occasionally you get this message on very busy systems when you try to run something, or if you start dozens of background processes.

Solution: Wait a minute and try the command again. If you start lots of background processes, get rid of some of them. If you see this message very often, complain to your system administrator.

No space left on device

Meaning: The disk is full.

Probable cause: Either your files take up too much space or someone else's do.

Solution: Delete something to make space. If you don't think you can delete anything or you don't have any large files, talk to your system administrator. She has probably already gotten the same message and is checking to see who is taking up all the space.

Not a directory

Meaning: UNIX needed the name of a directory, but you typed a filename or the name of something else.

Probable cause: Either you spelled a directory name wrong or forgot to create a new directory.

Solution: If you are referring to a new directory you planned to make, make it first by using the mkdir command. If you are referring to an existing directory, get the spelling right. Use the ls command to see how the directory name is spelled.

Not enough space

Meaning: The system has no more space in memory (not on disk).

Probable cause: Things are much too busy in your system. You probably caught UNIX when it was in the middle of getting itself organized.

Solution: Wait a minute and try the command again. If you see this message very often, complain to your system administrator.

Permission denied

Meaning: You don't have permission to do whatever the last command you issued tried to do.

Probable cause: You are trying to change, move, or delete a file you don't own.

Solution: Use the ls -l command to find out who owns the file and what its permissions are (see Chapter 5 for information about permissions). If you think that you ought to be able to mess with the file, make your own copy of it or talk to the owner of the file or your system administrator.

RE error

Meaning: You are using the grep program and it doesn't understand what you are searching for. (*RE* stands for *regular expression*, the technoid name for the patterns that grep uses.)

Probable cause: You probably have to use backslashes before a character that is a wildcard in grep.

Example: You type this line:

```
grep '[x' myfile
```

Solution: Put a backslash before any character that has a special wildcard meaning in grep (grep wildcards include periods, asterisks, square brackets, dollar signs, and carets). If you are searching for text that contains special characters, put single quotation marks around the text to match.

Read-only file system

Meaning: You are trying to change a file that UNIX is not allowed to change.

Probable cause: Some disks, particularly NFS remote disks, are read-only, so you can't create, delete, or change files on them. It doesn't matter what the permissions are for the individual files: The entire file system can't be changed.

Solution: Talk to your system administrator. Or make a copy of the file you want to change and change the copy.

Too many links

Meaning: You are trying to make so many links to a file that you have exceeded the maximum number of links to a file.

Probable cause: The maximum number of links to a file is 1,000. (You must be a heck of a typist to get this message.) Because the parent directory is linked to each of its subdirectories, you also get this message if you try to make more than 1,000 subdirectories in one directory.

Solution: Stop making links.

Usage

Meaning: UNIX doesn't like the number or types of arguments that you typed after the command. It is telling you (in its own cryptic way) the correct way to use the command.

Probable cause: UNIX usually displays this message with another, more specific message. Check out the other message to see the real problem. The usage message is UNIX's reminder about how to use the command. After usage you see the command, followed by the options and arguments you can use with the command. Unfortunately, there's no clue about what the options do.

Example: You type this line:

```
kill abc
```

UNIX responds with this:

```
usage: kill [ -signo ] pid
```

This line means that the correct way to use the kill command is to type kill, a space, (optionally) the type of signal you want to send to the process, another space, and then the process ID. Not that this advice is entirely clear from the message!

Solution: Check your typing, as always. Make sure that spaces are present between things on the line (between filenames or between a filename and an option, for example). If you don't use this command very often, check to make sure that you have the correct arguments (filenames and so on) and options (things that begin with a dash, like the -l in ls -l). Look up the command in this book or consult the UNIX manual page about it.

444 mode? (or another three-digit number)

Meaning: You told UNIX to delete a file that you don't have permission to change.

Probable cause: You are using rm, mv, or ln to remove or replace a read-only protected file or a file that belongs to someone else. (See Chapter 5 for information about permissions.) Rather than refuse outright to do what you asked, UNIX asks you whether you really want to do this.

Example: You used the chmod command to make a really important file read-only. Then you decided to delete it by typing this line:

```
rm important.file
```

The `444 mode?` message is UNIX asking whether you really want to delete it, even though the file is read-only.

Solution: The question mark at the end of this message indicates that UNIX is asking you a question. By divine intuition, you are supposed to guess that UNIX is asking whether you want to go ahead and do the command anyway. Press Y to go ahead and do the command; press N to cancel it (for this file, anyway).

Part VII
The Part of Tens

The 5th Wave   By Rich Tennant

"OOPS, I FORGOT TO LOG OFF AGAIN."

In this part...

There's a lot of stuff in UNIX — much more than we try to stuff into this book. The real, official manuals for a UNIX system take up about three feet of shelf space. (For economical reasons, all the pages in those manuals are blank because no one ever reads them, but if you don't tell, neither will we.)

In this part, we try to organize some useful facts (as useful as anything about UNIX is going to be) into neat lists of ten facts apiece so that maybe they will be easier to remember.

Astute readers might notice that none of these lists contains exactly 10 items. Well, see, we were using mixed radix arithmetic (survivors of new math may remember some of this from fourth grade), so a chapter with 8 items has 10 items counting in base 8, a chapter with 12 items has 10 items counting in base 12, a chapter — what? You say that we can't bamboozle you with nonsense like that? OK, the truth is that we can't count.

So read on — there's some good stuff in here regardless of what the numbers say.

Chapter 26

Ten Common Mistakes

*H*ere are ten (or so) of the most common user mistakes we have run into. Although you will probably invent some new ones yourself, at least avoid the ones on this list.

Mistyping Commands

If you type a command that the UNIX shell doesn't understand, it says that it can't find it. The reason is that it looks high and low for a file with the name you just typed, hoping to find the program you want to run. And then it says

```
blurfle: Command not found.
```

Or perhaps it says

```
blurfle: not found
```

The exact wording varies from shell to shell (we bet you already guessed that).

> ✔ **Check your spelling (as always).** You may have typed a correctly spelled English word rather than the garbled set of letters that comprise the name of the program.

✔ **Check your capitalization.** Capital and small letters count as completely different things in filenames and, therefore, in commands. Nearly every command uses only small letters.

✔ **Change directories (maybe).** You may have given the right command, but UNIX may not know where to look for the file containing the program. If you know where the program file is, move to that directory and give the command again. If you don't know where the file is, either look for it (see Chapter 8) or give up and ask your system administrator or local wizard.

Believing That It Will Be Easy

UNIX was designed a long, long time ago in computer time (computer years are similar to dog years, except that 50 computer years equal 1 human year). Software design has made a lot of progress since 1972, and UNIX has not. If you are used to a Macintosh or a PC with Windows, or even a PC with DOS, UNIX is not going to be easy to use.

On the other hand, UNIX has a certain cachet and glamour; it takes a macho person (of either gender) to face it. You should give yourself major kudos, and maybe even one or two of those cookies you made to bribe your UNIX wizard, every time you get UNIX to do something useful.

To Press Enter, or Not to Press Enter

Depending on which program you are using, sometimes you must press Enter (or Return) after a command, and sometimes you don't. In the UNIX shell, you *always* have to press Enter or Return before UNIX performs the command. If you don't, UNIX waits forever for you to do so.

In other programs, particularly in text editors like emacs and vi, as soon as you press the command (Ctrl-K to delete a line in emacs, for example), the program does it right away. If you press Enter or Return after the command, emacs sticks a new line in your file, and vi moves down to the next line.

When you use a program you are not familiar with, hesitate a moment before pressing Enter or Return to see whether the computer might already be performing the command. If nothing is happening, press Enter or Return.

Working in the Wrong Directory

If you use separate directories to organize your files, make sure that you are in the proper directory when you begin working. Otherwise, UNIX won't find the files you want to work on.

To find out which directory you are in, type pwd.

Remember that this command stands for *print working directory*. If you are really lost, you can type whoami.

This command tells you your user name.

To move back to your home directory, type cd.

Not Keeping Backup Copies

Sooner or later, it happens. You use rm to delete a file, and UNIX deletes the wrong file, or it deletes everything in the directory. Chances are, you typed an extra space or spelled a filename wrong, but the point is — what now?

See Chapter 23 for how to proceed if you delete something important. The best approach is to keep extra copies of important files: in another directory, on a floppy disk, or on a backup tape that either you or your system administrator makes. If you haven't talked to your system administrator about backups, now is a good time to find out whether your files are backed up automatically; you can also tell him which of your directories contain files you want backed up.

Not Keeping Files Organized

Unless you do all your work on one or two files, you will run into trouble if you don't do the following:

- ✔ Make directories for the groups of files you use (see Chapter 6). Directories help you separate your files into groups of files you use together.

- ✔ Use filenames that mean something. UNIX lets you name your files with nice long names, so take advantage of it (up to a point, anyway). Filenames should tell you what's inside the file rather than make you guess.

Turning Off the Computer

It's better to leave the computer on all the time than to turn it off at the wrong time. Chapter 1 talks about this subject in detail. UNIX can get messed up if you turn off the computer without warning it that you are going to do so.

If you use UNIX from a terminal rather than directly with a workstation, it may make sense to turn off the terminal (not the computer) at night. Check with your system administrator.

Writing Your Password on a Note Next to the Computer

OK, maybe this doesn't apply if you work at home, live alone, and don't have any friends, cleaning people, or burglars. But, otherwise, you should keep your password to yourself. Not that anyone has malicious intent — let's not get paranoid — but people can get curious around computers. And you never know when an inquisitive 14-year-old will appear on the scene who knows more about UNIX than you do. If you can't remember your password, choose a new one that is more memorable. See Chapter 1 for hints.

Sending Angry Electronic Mail (Flaming)

There is something insidious about electronic mail. There you are, sitting alone in your cubicle with your computer, and you get ticked off at something, usually some stupid message sent by a coworker. Before you know it, you have composed and sent a tactless, not to say downright rude, response.

It is easy to say things in e-mail that you would never say in person, or even write in a memo. But e-mail has an off-the-cuff, spontaneous style in most organizations, and it can get you into trouble.

Sarcasm seldom works in e-mail — instead, you just sound mean. Gentle suggestions can turn into strident demands just because they appear in ugly computer type on a computer screen. There is even a special name for rude mouthing off via e-mail — *flaming*. A message full of tactless, pointless complaints is referred to as a *flame*. A series of flames between two or more people is called a *flame war*. You get the idea.

Recipients of your mail can easily forward copies of it to anyone else, so imagine that everyone in the office might read your missives. Think twice before sending e-mail containing negative remarks! Then don't send it.

Chapter 27

Ten Times More Information Than You Want about UNIX

• •

In This Chapter

▶ How to use the man command for on-line help

▶ What's on a manual page

▶ Other sources of information

• •

*Y*ou thought that UNIX was completely unhelpful. For the most part, you are absolutely right. But a standard UNIX command called man (for *man*ual) can give you on-line help.

Sound good? Well, yes and no. The information is there, but it is written in a rather nerdy style and can be difficult to decipher; of course, each part of the on-line manual is written on the assumption that you've read the other parts and know what all the commands are called. The manual is definitely worth knowing about, though, when you just can't remember the options for a command or what to type where on the command line after the command name.

Let's Hear It from the man

The man's on-line manual contains *manual pages* for every UNIX command, and other pages about internal functions that programmers use, formats for various system file types, descriptions of some of the hardware that can be attached to your UNIX system, and other odds and ends. When you type the man command, you indicate which page or pages you want.

All manual pages have a standard format. Figure 27-1 shows part of the manual page for dcheck, a program a system administrator can use to deal with people whose files take up too much space on the disk.

```
DCHECK() Diskhog DCHECK(1)
NAME
 dcheck - send mail to potential disk hogs
SYNOPSIS
 dcheck
DESCRIPTION
 dcheck is normally run from the crons procedure to check
 if users are taking up too much space. It creates a tag
 file for such users, will send them warning mail, and
 also sends mail to the system administrator about what
 it's done.
SEE ALSO
 diskhog(1).
FILES
 $DQUOTAS/hogs/$LOGNAME - tag file indicating that
 diskhog should be run
WARNINGS
 Should know about multiple file systems.
BUGS
 None.
```

Figure 27-1: Part of the man page for dcheck, a truly arcane command.

The parts of the manual page include the following:

✔ The title of the manual page is the first line. It includes the name and page number of the manual page at the left and right ends of the line. Centered on the line may be the name of the system of which the command is a part. In this example, the dcheck command is part of the diskhog system.

✔ NAME: The one-line name of the manual page. The name is usually the command or commands the page is about, as well as a brief description.

✔ SYNOPSIS: What you type when you give the command, with a terse and cryptic example of every option available. Often makes no sense until you read the description that follows. Sometimes it still makes no sense.

✔ DESCRIPTION: A few paragraphs about the command. For commands with a lot of options, the description can run for a few pages. Usually a list of the options is presented with an explanation of every one. Sometimes examples are given, although not often enough.

✔ FILES: A list of the files this command uses. The elm and mail commands, for example, use your Mail directory, the central list of mailboxes, and other files. (These files usually are set up by your system administrator and are rarely things you want to fool with yourself.) The manual pages for elm and mail mention these files.

✔ SEE ALSO: This section lists names of related manual pages, if any.

✔ WARNINGS and BUGS: If the command has known bugs or common problems, they may be listed here. Then again, they may not be.

Reading manual pages

To see a manual page, type this line:

```
man unixcommand
```

Except, of course, substitute for `unixcommand` the name of the UNIX command you are interested in. Some versions of `man` present the manual page a screen at a time. Other versions whip the page by at maximum speed, assuming that you can read 150,000 words per minute. If that happens (and you can't read that fast), use the `more` command to show you the manual page a screen at a time:

```
man unixcommand | more
```

On the other hand, if you're on a system that normally presents manual pages a screen at a time, and you want it to whip by at full speed because you just finished a speed reading course so you *can* read 150,000 words per minute (or, more likely, because your terminal is a PC and you're capturing the terminal output to a file) type this line:

```
man - unixcommand
```

Printing manual pages

You can also print the manual pages for later perusal by typing this line:

```
man unixcommand | lpr
```

Remember to use `lp` or `lpr`. Putting the manual pages in a file first, removing the information you don't want, and printing the result is probably the best tack to take. You can type this line, for example:

```
man unixcommand > filename
```

Then edit the file with a text editor (see Chapter 13) and print it (see Chapter 10). Before you print the file, however, keep in mind that the on-line manual pages are generally identical to the printed manual pages in the dusty UNIX manuals on the shelf, except that the printed manual pages are typeset so that they're easier to read. Rather than printing the on-line page, looking the information up in the paper manual is often the better route. (Bet you didn't think we would *ever* tell you to do that!)

Finding the manual page you want

If you use the `man` command, no good way exists to find out which manual pages are available. Finding the one you want can be difficult sometimes. Suppose that you type this line:

```
man ln | more
```

UNIX shows you this message:

```
man: ln not found
```

No separate manual page exists for the `ln` command. Instead, it shares a set of pages with `cp` and `mv`. You get information about `ln` by typing this line:

```
man cp | more
```

(Typical UNIX ease of use!) If `man` doesn't display anything about the command you want, try some similar commands. BSD UNIX systems have an `apropos` command that suggests manual pages relevant to a particular topic, so you can type `apropos ln` to see what it has to say.

It's a bird, it's a plane, it's xman*!*

If you use X Windows or Motif, you can use the `xman` command to look at manual pages. The nice thing about `xman` is that it displays a list of the available manual pages. When you run `xman`, up pops a little box with three buttons, one of which is labeled Manual Page. If you click on that button, a larger window then displays a manual page describing `xman`. Select Display Directory from the Options menu on that page, or press Ctrl-D as a shortcut, to see a screen of all of the manual pages it has, probably more than 100 of them. Click on the one you want to see, and `xman` switches to that page. Press Ctrl-D again to return to the directory of manual pages. Read the initial description of `xman` for other tricks you can get `xman` to do, like show you two or three different pages at a time, or search for keywords in manual-page titles.

Scanning the Networks

If your system is connected to the Internet, or you have dial-up access to an Internet provider, you can connect to Usenet, a gigantic distributed on-line bulletin board. Since most of the systems on Usenet are running on UNIX systems, you'll find a great deal of discussion about UNIX issues and questions.

We say a little about Usenet in Chapter 28 and quite a lot more about it in *MORE UNIX For Dummies* and *The Internet For Dummies, 2nd Edition,* both from IDG Books Worldwide.

Your basic UNIX news

Usenet discussions are loosely organized into about 10,000 topic areas or *newsgroups.* Some of the newsgroups that discuss UNIX topics can be found in Table 27-1.

Table 27-1	UNIX-Related Newsgroups
Group	*Description*
comp.unix.admin	UNIX system administration.
comp.unix.advocacy	Arguments about how wonderful UNIX is.
comp.unix.aix	AIX, IBM's version of UNIX.
comp.unix.amiga	UNIX on the Commodore Amiga.
comp.unix.aux	Apple's AUX for the Macintosh.
comp.unix.bsd.bsdi.misc	Discussions of BSD/OS.
comp.unix.bsd.freebsd.announce	Announcements about FreeBSD UNIX.
comp.unix.bsd.freebsd.misc	Discussions of FreeBSD.
comp.unix.bsd.misc	Various BSD versions of UNIX.
comp.unix.bsd.netbsd.announce	Announcements about NetBSD UNIX.
comp.unix.bsd.netbsd.misc	Discussions of NetBSD.
comp.unix.cray	UNIX on Cray supercomputers.
comp.unix.dos-under-unix	Running MS-DOS programs under UNIX.
comp.unix.internals	Technical internals of UNIX.
comp.unix.large	UNIX on large systems.
comp.unix.misc	Random UNIX discussions.
comp.unix.msdos	UNIX tools on MS-DOS.
comp.unix.osf.osf1	OSF/1 version of UNIX.
comp.unix.pc-clone.32bit	UNIX on 32-bit IBM PC compatibles.
comp.unix.programmer	Programming on UNIX.

(continued)

Table 27-1 *(continued)*

`comp.unix.questions`	The best place to ask questions about UNIX. Look at articles first to see whether someone has just asked the same question.
`comp.unix.shell`	UNIX shells.
`comp.unix.solaris`	Sun's Solaris version of UNIX.
`comp.unix.sys5.r3`	SVR3 version of UNIX.
`comp.unix.sys5.r4`	SVR4 version of UNIX.
`comp.unix.ultrix`	Digital's Ultrix version of UNIX.
`comp.unix.unixware`	Novell UNIXWare.
`comp.unix.user-friendly`	An oxymoron.
`comp.unix.wizards`	Technical discussions among wizards.
`comp.unix.xenix.misc`	Miscellaneous versions of XENIX.
`comp.unix.xenix.sco`	SCO XENIX, a popular UNIX for PC clones.

Just for Linux

Because Linux is so popular, it has a whole bunch of discussion groups of its own. Some of these can be found in Table 27-2.

Table 27-2	Linux-Related Newsgroups
Group	*Description*
`comp.os.linux.admin`	Linux system administration.
`comp.os.linux.advocacy`	Discussions of how great Linux is.
`comp.os.linux.announce`	Announcements of new versions of Linux.
`comp.os.linux.answers`	Answers to frequently asked questions; good place to look.
`comp.os.linux.development`	Linux system development.
`comp.os.linux.development.apps`	Development of application programs.
`comp.os.linux.development.system`	Development of underlying Linux system.
`comp.os.linux.hardware`	Making Linux work with various kinds of hardware.

comp.os.linux.help	The Linux "help line," a good place to ask questions.
comp.os.linux.misc	Linux discussions that don't fit anywhere else.
comp.os.linux.networking	Networking issues.
comp.os.linux.setup	Setting up Linux.
comp.os.linux.x	X Windows on Linux.

Other Sources of Information

Your system administrator or nearby UNIX users probably have copies of UNIX manuals lying around. The pages of some of these manuals usually look very much like the manual pages you get with man.

The advantage of the printed manual is that an index is in the front (or the back). The index is usually a permuted or KWIC index (an overly clever abbreviation for *key word in context*), which means that you can find an entry by looking under any of the words in the title except for boring ones like *the*. To find the page for the cp command (the title of the manual page is *cp, ln, mv — copy, link, or move files*), for example, you can look in the permuted index under *cp, ln, mv, copy, link, move,* or *files*.

Then again, try typing help, just to see what happens. Someone may have installed some kind of help system — you never know.

UNIX is used widely enough that a growing industry of UNIX books, magazines, user groups, and conferences has sprung up. Any of them can provide additional help and information.

Read a magazine

Several weekly or monthly magazines cover UNIX. Most of them include in their titles the name UNIX or the code phrase Open Systems (for systems that act like UNIX but haven't licensed the UNIX trademark). You probably have already thrown away mail inviting you to subscribe to some, so we won't belabor the point. The major brands of workstations (Sun, Hewlett-Packard, and IBM) also have magazines that specifically cover those product lines. Some of these magazines tend to be awfully technical, but they can have product reviews and announcements about new UNIX hardware and software packages.

If you use Linux, take a look at the *Linux Journal,* the magazine for and about Linux (P.O. Box 85867, Seattle, WA 98145 USA, phone 206-527-3385, e-mail `linux@ssc.com`). The technical level varies from totally introductory to fairly technical.

Read a book

Yeah, we know, you just read a book. We mean read *another* book. Here are a few you might like:

- Levine and Young, *MORE UNIX For Dummies,* IDG Books. (Big surprise, huh?) More on UNIX shells, script-writing languages, and using the Internet from UNIX.

- Levine and Young, *UNIX For Dummies Quick Reference,* IDG Books. (Equally big surprise.) Essential information from this book squashed down into a smaller, less expensive, pocket-sized form.

- Daniel Gilly, *UNIX in a Nutshell,* O'Reilly. A very complete UNIX reference, the one we turn to when memory fails. Comes in various editions for different versions of UNIX. Intended for more advanced users than our *UNIX For Dummies Quick Reference.*

- Welsh and Kaufman, *Running LINUX,* O'Reilly. All about installing and using Linux. Medium-technical, but quite informative.

Join a user group

Two major UNIX user groups exist. The older one is called *Usenix,* which dates back to about 1976; it is traditionally for technical users. The other is *Uniforum,* formerly */usr/group,* which is more for business users. Each one sponsors annual conferences and publishes a newsletter. Local and regional UNIX user groups exist as well; you tend to find out about these groups from notes posted on physical or electronic bulletin boards. User groups can be great sources of help because chances are pretty good that someone out there has already run into many of the same problems you have and has some ideas that might help.

Chapter 28

Ten Topics You Don't Want to Know About

This chapter covers some odds and ends that are useful but more technoid than the stuff in the rest of the book. You can get along perfectly well without them, but if you're feeling brave, they can come in handy.

Typing the Same Things When You Log In

Most users find that, every time they log in, they type the same commands to set up the computer the way they like it. You may typically change to your favorite directory, for example, change the terminal settings (see the next section), check your mail, or any of a dozen other things.

The Bourne, Korn, and BASH shells look for a file called .profile in your home directory when you log in; if the file exists, the shell executes the commands in that file. The C shell has two corresponding files: .login (which it runs when you log in) and .cshrc (which it runs every time you start a new C shell, either at login time or when you type csh).

Your system administrator probably gave you a standard .profile or .login file when your account was set up; it is definitely not a good idea to mess with stuff that's already there. You may be unable to log in and have to crawl to your system administrator and beg for help. So, don't say we didn't warn you.

The standard `.profile`, `.login`, and `.cshrc` files vary considerably (why do we even finish this sentence — you know what we're going to say) from one system to another depending on the tastes of the system administrator. These files usually perform the following tasks:

- Set up the search path that the shell uses to look for commands.
- Arrange to notify you when you have new mail.
- (Sometimes) change the shell prompt from the usual $ or % to something more informative.

If you always type the same commands when you log in, it is fairly safe to add new commands at the end of `.profile` or `.login`. If you do most of your work in the directory `bigproject`, for example, you might add the following three lines to the end of the file that your shell uses to start up your UNIX session:

```
# change to bigproject, added 3/95
cd bigproject
echo Now in directory bigproject.
```

The first line is a comment the computer ignores but is useful for humans trying to figure out who changed what. Any line that starts with a pound sign (#) is a comment. The second line is a regular `cd` command. The third line is an `echo` command that displays a note to remind you of the directory you're in.

If you use the C shell, a frequently useful command to put in `.login` is this one:

```
set ignoreeof
```

Or if you use BASH, you put this in your `.profile`:

```
ignoreeof=1
```

Normally, if you press Ctrl-D in the shell, the shell assumes that you're finished for the day and logs you out — in keeping with the traditional UNIX "you asked for it, you got it" philosophy. Many people think that you should be more explicit about your intention to log out and use `ignoreeof` to tell the shell to ignore a Ctrl-D (refer to the following section to see what `eof` has to do with Ctrl-D) and log out only when you type `exit` or `logout`.

Setting Up the Terminal the Way You Want

There are about 14 zillion different settings associated with each terminal or pseudoterminal attached to a UNIX system, any of which you can change with the `stty` command. About 13.99 zillion of the 14 zillion shouldn't be messed with, or your terminal will vanish in a puff of smoke (as far as UNIX is concerned), and you will have to log in all over again or even get your system administrator to undo the damage. You can, however, safely change a few things.

All the special characters that control the terminal, such as Backspace and Ctrl-Z, are changeable. People often find that they prefer characters other than the defaults, because they got used to something else on another system, because the placement of the keys on the keyboard makes some choices more natural than others, or because their terminal emulator is dumb about switching Backspace and Delete. The special characters that control the keyboard are listed and described in Table 28-1.

Table 28-1	Terminal-Control Characters	
Name	*Typical Character*	*Meaning*
erase	Ctrl-H	Erases (backspaces over) the previous character.
kill	Ctrl-U	Discards the line typed so far.
eof	Ctrl-D	Marks the end of input to a program.
swtch	Ctrl-Z	Pauses the current program (see Chapter 16).
intr	Ctrl-C	Interrupts or kills whichever program is running.
quit	Ctrl-\	Kills the program and writes a core file.

To tell stty to change any of these control characters, you give it the name of the special character to change and the character you want to use. If you want to use a Control (Ctrl) character, you can type a caret (^ — the thing above the number *6* on the 6 key) followed by the plain character, both enclosed in quotation marks. As a special case, ^? represents the Del or Delete key. The Tab key is represented as ^I; the Backspace key is usually ^H. To make the Delete key the erase character and Ctrl-X the kill character, for example, type

```
stty erase '^?' kill '^X'
```

If you're feeling perverse, you can set the various Control characters to whatever you want. You can make the erase character q and the intr character 3, although doing so makes it difficult to get any work done because you couldn't use *q* or *3* in anything you type.

The other thing you can change is the *terminal output stop mode,* which controls whether background jobs can display messages on your terminal. (Chapter 16 explains what this means.) To allow output from background jobs to display on your terminal, turn off output stop mode by typing the following:

```
stty -tostop
```

To prevent output from background jobs, or more exactly, to make background jobs stop and wait when they want to display something, turn on output stop mode by typing this line:

```
stty tostop
```

All these `stty` commands usually go in the `.login` or `.profile` file so that the terminal is set up the way you want every time you log in.

A Really Gross Old Network

About 20 years ago, before UNIX systems were attached to real networks, a guy named Greg whipped up a program to use regular modems over regular phone lines to transfer files between two UNIX systems, for temporary use until he got a real network hooked up. He called it *UNIX to UNIX Copy,* or `uucp`. It's sort of like the Kermit or ZMODEM software that PC users may be familiar with.

Well, 20 years later, we're still using `uucp`. Its disadvantages are that it's slow (limited by the phone) and a pain to use. Its advantages are that it comes free with every version of UNIX; all you need to use it is a $75 modem plugged into the phone line. The `uucp` program can do basically one thing: copy files between computers. But it also has a *remote execution facility* — sounds painful, doesn't it? — that lets you execute a small set of commands on other computers. In practice, 95 percent of what `uucp` does is to carry electronic mail and news between UNIX computers.

Do you copy, UNIX?

In its simplest form, you use `uucp` to copy a file from one computer to another:

```
uucp myfile fluffy!hisfile
```

This command says to take the local file called `myfile` and make a copy called `hisfile` on the machine called `fluffy`. (If you use the C shell, you have to type `\!` rather than `!` because exclamation points are special characters to the C shell.) Unless the `fluffy` machine has its disks logically set up exactly the way your machine's are set up (with the same names for home directories), you also need to specify in whose directory you want to put the copy:

```
uucp myfile fluffy!~tracy/yourfile
```

This command tells uucp to put the copy in Tracy's directory. Every machine's uucp command is set up with controls that specify which remote machines are allowed to read and write using uucp. Invariably, the controls permit limited reading and almost no writing. Usually the only place you're allowed to put an incoming file is in uucp's own directory, written this way:

```
uucp myfile fluffy!~/hisfile
```

Unlike most other modem programs, uucp doesn't copy as you wait. A background daemon makes the phone call and does the copying, and tries as many times as necessary if the phone is busy. If the copy fails, either because the file isn't there (more likely when you told it to copy from a remote machine to your own) or because you're not allowed access to the files, uucp sends you electronic mail telling you about the problem.

The uucp program doesn't need a modem; two machines in the same building can talk uucp over a simple terminal-type cable. If you have a few machines and no networking budget, this is an easy way for a system administrator to get at least a little networking going to avoid carrying around disks or tapes.

UNIX mail without the stamp

People use uucp mostly to send mail and network news (described in the following section), particularly if they don't have a direct network connection. Mail addresses for uucp are also written with exclamation points. To send uucp mail to Tracy on machine fluffy, you type the following:

```
mail fluffy!tracy
```

If you use the C shell, type \! for !. Alternatively, you can use elm or some other, better mail program. You can forward uucp mail from one machine to another. If you want to send a message to Tracy on machine fluffy, but your machine doesn't talk directly to fluffy and does talk to itchy, which in turn talks to fluffy, you can type this line:

```
mail itchy!fluffy!tracy
```

This electronic whisper-down-the-lane method often goes to extremes, and mail sometimes has to take six or seven hops to get where it's going. If your system handles a lot of mail, your system administrator probably has installed automatic routing software that figures out which route to use to get to which machines, based on uucp maps distributed on Usenet (see the following section). If this is the case, you merely type the destination-machine name and the user name, and UNIX figures out how to get it there. A lot of uucp systems are out there; the uucp routing list on our system lists more than 20,000 other machines to which it has uucp paths!

How to Read So Much Electronic Gossip That You Have No Time Left to Work

Not long after `uucp` and `uucp` mail arrived, some people in North Carolina thought that it would be neat to have a distributed bulletin-board system. People could send in messages from their local machine, the messages would be distributed to a couple of other machines, and users on all the machines could see all the messages. They figured that it would be pretty popular and there could be dozens of messages per day.

Well, they were right; it's pretty popular. Most of the machines are now connected via the Internet, although there are still plenty of dial-up links, and there are now over 100,000 machines hooked up, with sites on every continent. (We hear that there's even a machine on the Internet at the research station at the South Pole.) The system now handles about 75,000 messages totaling more than 200 megabytes (that's 200 million keystrokes) of text every day. This monster is known as *Usenet,* or sometimes *net news.*

Messages are filed in topic categories called *newsgroups,* of which there are about 10,000. Newsgroup topics range from technical discussions of computer architecture to gossip about old trains, nudism, and interminable political arguments. Reading all this stuff could take a large chunk of your workday (about 24 hours daily). Fortunately, the standard news-reading programs let you specify which groups you want to see and which ones you don't; you can identify, within groups, the topics and authors in which you are or are not interested.

There are quite a few news-reading programs, with names like `readnews` (the original, now considered old and klunky), `rn`, `trn`, `tin`, and `nn`, all of which do basically the same thing but have different ways to get around the enormous mass of messages. If your site gets news, have an experienced user show you how to use the local news-reading program.

Since the majority of computers that run net news are UNIX systems, there's quite a lot of newsgroups with discussions of UNIX topics, so Usenet can be a good way to find other people with questions and comments about UNIX. In Chapter 27, we listed some UNIX-related newsgroups.

If you get Usenet, you can probably send out your own Usenet messages. Please resist the urge to do so until you have been reading news for a few weeks so that you have an idea of what's appropriate to send and what isn't. Also, read the newsgroup called `news.announce.newusers`; it contains helpful advice for new Usenet users.

The most amazing thing about Usenet is who's in charge of it: no one. It's just a big, informal, cooperative setup. The programs most commonly used to file and transfer news were written by two guys at the University of Toronto who probably should have been working on their regular jobs instead. The various news-reading programs come from educational and commercial sites all over the world. The money to pay for the network time is, by and large, hidden in corporate telephone budgets. It's the definitive example of pioneer networking.

For more information about Usenet and other Internet services, see our *MORE UNIX For Dummies* and *The Internet For Dummies, 2nd Edition*, both from IDG Books Worldwide. The former contains details about several UNIX newsreaders.

DOS under UNIX

UNIX bigots tend to sneer at DOS machines and DOS users. There's no doubt that DOS is a pretty bad system, but there's no doubt that it also supports some pretty good software.

DOS users who switch to UNIX don't have to leave DOS behind. PC and workstation versions of UNIX have DOS-under-UNIX packages that let you run DOS in a UNIX process. If you're running an Intel 386 or 486 PC, the CPU chip has a special hardware feature called *V86 mode* that makes it possible to create a faithful emulation of a bare PC inside a UNIX process so that a regular version of DOS runs on that emulated PC.

There are several commercial V86 DOS emulators, including vp/ix, DOS Merge, and rundos, all of which work quite well. While writing this book, we used vp/ix to run the regular DOS version of Microsoft Word to do some text editing and to read and write DOS floppy disks. The emulated DOS runs nearly as fast as a separate DOS machine and has the advantage that the computer can continue to do all the other UNIX stuff and give DOS access to all your UNIX files.

If you have a non-Intel workstation, a package called SoftPC translates 386 code on-the-fly to the native code used by the workstation's CPU in a UNIX process. Again, this provides an environment in which regular DOS can run. Although the translation involves considerable overhead, workstations have become so fast that, even with the overhead, the emulated DOS machine can be as fast as a real PC.

One problem with plain DOS-under-UNIX systems is that they don't emulate the protected-mode features that Microsoft Windows needs in order to run; you can run only older, pre-3.1 versions of Windows, and Windows can't share the screen with X or Motif. Windows-under-X emulators are available on 386 and higher UNIX systems that let you run applications for Windows under X (as well as Motif because it's based on X). Windows windows can share the screen with native X and Motif applications, all running at full (not emulated) speed. Way cool.

There are a couple of commercial Windows emulators as well as a free product called Wine, discussed on Usenet in the `comp.emulators.ms-windows.wine` newsgroup.

The 5th Wave   By Rich Tennant

"IT'S NO USE, CAPTAIN. THE ONLY WAY WE'LL CRACK THIS CASE IS TO GET INTO PROF. TAMARA'S PERSONAL COMPUTER FILE, BUT NO ONE KNOWS THE PASSWORD. KILROY'S GOT A HUNCH IT STARTS WITH AN 'S', BUT HECK, THAT COULD BE ANYTHING."

Chapter 29

The UNIX Commands Come Marching Ten by Ten

●●●

*T*hroughout this book we've told you about lots of useful, interesting, fun, and sometimes dangerous commands. Here's a compendium of the most useful commands, with their most commonly used options. Stuff you have to type appears in bold. Stuff you can leave out has square brackets around it [like this].

For a more complete listing of the commands we use the most, run to your bookstore and get *UNIX For Dummies Quick Reference,* by your favorite authors (or maybe at this point, your least favorite authors).

alias

Purpose: To create an alias (nickname) for a command or show which aliases exist.

Options and arguments: If you use the C shell, the command looks like this:

```
alias [name ['command']]
```

If you use the BASH or Korn shell, it looks like this:

```
alias [name=['command']]
```

Doesn't work in the Bourne shell.

Option or
Argument ***Function***

name   Specifies the alias name.

command   Specifies the command that the name should be an alias for.

Sample: alias dir='ls -al'

Where to look: Chapter 15, section "Using an alias." To make an alias permanent, talk to a UNIX wizard about putting `alias` commands into your `.profile` or `.login` file. Or see Chapter 28, section "Typing the Same Things When You Log In"

at

Purpose: To schedule a command to run at a particular time. Great for running time-consuming commands later, such as in the middle of the night.

Options and arguments:

```
at [-m] time [date]
```

or

```
at -l
```

or

```
at -r job
```

Option or Argument	Function
-m	Sends an electronic-mail message after the command has run.
time	Indicates when you want command to run. Type the time in the format *hh:mm* followed by am or pm, or you can use a 24-hour clock. You can type midnight to run your command at night, or now + number of minutes or hours (for example, now + 6 hours).
date	Indicates date you want command to run. You type the date in the format *month date, year; month* is the name of the month (such as December or Dec, not 12), *date* is the date (25), and *year* is the four-digit year (1995). You only need the year if the date is more than twelve months in the future. (We've heard of planning ahead, but that's ridiculous!)
-l	Lists the names of commands (jobs) that you have already scheduled. Don't type anything on the command line after -l.
-r *job*	Cancels a command (job) that you previously scheduled. On the command line, type the *job* number after -r. To find out the job number, use the -l option we just described.

Sample: `at 02:00am`
`lpr long-report`
`Ctrl-D`

Where to look: Chapter 14, section "Time Is Money — Steal Some Today!"

banner

Purpose: To display text in huge, ugly letters.

Sample: `banner "Happy Birthday!"`

Where to look: Chapter 14, section "A Really Dumb Program."

bash

Purpose: To run the BASH shell, optionally running a script.

Options and arguments:

```
bash [scriptname]
```

Sample: `bash run.me`

Where to look: Chapter 2, section "Cracking the Shell."

bc

Purpose: A handy-dandy desk calculator.

Options and arguments:

```
bc [file]
```

The *file* argument specifies the name of a file full of `bc` commands. If you just want to multiply a few numbers, leave this out.

Where to look: Chapter 14, section "A Desk Calculator."

bg

Purpose: To continue a stopped job in the background. (Some older versions of the Bourne and Korn shell can't do this.)

Options and arguments:

```
bg [job]
```

The *job* argument specifies the job number that you want to run in the background. If you leave it out, UNIX assumes you mean the current job.

Where to look: Chapter 16, section ". . . Stick it in the background."

cal

Purpose: To print a calendar for a month or a year.

Options and arguments:

```
cal [month] [year]
```

Option or Argument	Function
month	Specifies the month (1 to 12) for which you want a calendar.
year	Specifies the year (1 to 9999) for which you want a calendar.

Sample: `cal 12 1996`

Where to look: Chapter 14, section "Calendar Games."

calendar

Purpose: To display appointments and reminders for today.

Where to look: Chapter 14, section "Calendar Games."

cancel

Purpose: To cancel a print job (UNIX System V only).

Options and arguments:

```
cancel requestID
```

The *requestID* argument specifies the print job you want to cancel, using the request ID number listed by the `lpstat` command (described later in this chapter).

Where to look: Chapter 10, section "Cancel the order, System V."

cat

Purpose: To display a file on-screen.

Options and arguments:

```
cat filename
```

The *filename* argument specifies the name of the file you want to see.

Sample: `cat letter.to.elvis`

Where to look: Chapter 5, section "Looking at the Guts of a File," and Chapter 7, section "The `cat` and the fiddle, er, file." Also, consider using the `more` command.

cd

Purpose: To change to another directory, that is, to change the current working directory to the directory you indicate.

Options and arguments:

```
cd [directory]
```

The *directory* argument specifies the directory to which you want to move. This directory becomes your current working directory. If you leave this out, you move to your own home directory.

Sample: `cd /usr/margy/book/u4d2`

Where to look: Chapter 6 for how to do move around UNIX's directory structure; Chapter 20 for info about changing directories that are mounted using NFS; Chapter 8 for finding lost files.

chgrp

Purpose: To change the group that has access to a file or directory (Linux and System V only).

Options and arguments:

```
chgrp newgroup filenames
```

Option or Argument	*Function*
newgroup	Specifies the name of the group that will assume ownership of the file(s).
filenames	Specifies the files to change.

Sample: `chgrp dummies chapter.20`

Where to look: Chapter 5, section "File seeks new group; can sing, dance, and do tricks."

chmod

Purpose: To change the permissions for a file.

Options and arguments:

```
chmod [-R] permissions filenames
```

Option or Argument	*Function*
-R	Tells `chmod` to change permissions on files in subdirectories, too. (Not available on older UNIXes.)
permissions	Specifies the permissions (also called the mode) to assign to the file(s). Permissions consist of a letter that tells who gets the permission (see Table 29-1), a character that indicates whether to add (+) or remove (-) the permission, and a letter that tells what kind of permission (see Table 29-2).
filenames	Specifies the file(s) to change.

Table 29-1	**Who Gets the Permission**
Code	*Who*
u	user that owns the file
g	group that owns the file
o	other (everyone else)
a	all (everybody)

Table 29-2	What Kind of Permission
Code	*What Kind*
r	read the file
w	write or edit the file
x	execute (run) the file as a program

Sample: `chmod a+x newscript`

Where to look: Chapter 5, section "If Mom says no, go ask Dad." Also, Chapter 15, section "You too can be a scriptwriter."

chown

Purpose: To change the ownership of a file (Linux and System V only).

Options and arguments:

```
chown [-R] newowner filenames
```

Option or Argument	*Function*
-R	Tells chown to change the ownership of files in subdirectories, too. (Not available on older UNIXes.)
newowner	Specifies the name of the new owner of the file (the current owner must be you, or the command won't work). Use the person's UNIX user name.
filenames	Specifies the file(s) to change.

Sample: `chown zac final.report`

Where to look: Chapter 5, section "Finding a new owner."

cmp

Purpose: To compare two files and tell you the line numbers where they differ.

Options and arguments:

```
cmp onefile anotherfile
```

Option or Argument	Function
onefile	Specifies the name of one of the files to compare.
anotherfile	Specifies the name of the other file to compare.

Sample: `cmp budget.95 budget.96`

Where to look: Chapter 14, section "Comparing Apples and Oranges."

comm

Purpose: To compare two text files, each of which is sorted in alphabetical order. The program shows you lines that are in both files versus lines that are in just one of them.

Options and arguments:

```
comm onefile anotherfile
```

Option or Argument	Function
onefile	Specifies the name of one of the files to compare.
anotherfile	Specifies the name of the other file to compare.

Sample: `comm invitation.list rsvp.list`

compress

Purpose: To shrink a file into a *compressed* file so that it takes up less space on your disk.

Options and arguments:

```
compress [-v] filenames
```

Option or Argument	Function
-v	Displays how much the file(s) compressed.
filenames	Specifies the file(s) to compress.

Sample: `compress -v letters*`

Where to look: Chapter 14, section "Squashing Your Files."

cp

Purpose: To copy one or more files.

Options and arguments:

```
cp [-i] oldfiles newfiles
```

or

```
cp [-i] [-r] oldfiles directory[/newfiles]
```

Option or Argument	*Function*
-i	Ask first, before replacing an existing file with a copied file (works only in Linux and UNIX System V Release 4).
-r	When copying a directory, copies its subdirectories too, creating new subdirectories as needed.
oldfiles	Specifies the name of the file you want to copy.
newfiles	Specifies the name to give to the new copy.
directory	Specifies the name of the directory in which you want to store a copy.

Sample: cp january.budget february.budget

Where to look: Chapter 5, section "Roger, I Copy."

csh

Purpose: To run the C shell, optionally running a script of stored commands.

Options and arguments:

```
csh [scriptname]
```

Sample: csh new.program

Where to look: Chapter 2, section "Cracking the Shell."

date

Purpose: To tell you the current date and time, taking into account your time zone and, if appropriate, daylight savings time.

Where to look: Chapter 14, "Time Is Money — Steal Some Today!"

df

Purpose: To display how much space is free on your disk.

Options and arguments:

```
df [directory]
```

The *directory* argument displays space on the file system where that directory resides.

Sample: df /usr/elvis

Where to look: Chapter 20, section "Disk free, as free as the . . ." for information on mounted directories.

diff

Purpose: To compare two files and print the lines in which the files differ.

Options and arguments:

```
diff [-b] [-i] [-w] filename1 filename2
```

or

```
diff [-b] [-i] [-w] filename1 directory1
```

or, for BSD UNIX only

```
diff [-b] [-i] [-r] [-w] directory1 directory2
```

Option or Argument	Function
-b	Treats groups of spaces (blanks) as single spaces, ignoring spacing differences.
-i	Ignores the difference between uppercase and lowercase letters. (Not available on older UNIXes.)

Option or Argument	Function
-r	When comparing two directories, tells diff to compare subdirectories too.
-w	Ignores all white space (spaces and tabs). (Not available on older UNIXes.)
filename1	Specifies one file to compare.
filename2	Specifies the other file to compare.
directory1	Specifies one directory to compare. If you tell diff to compare a file to a directory, it looks in the directory for a file of the same name and compares the two files (BSD only).
directory2	Specifies the other directory to compare. If you tell diff to compare two directories, it looks in both directories for files of the same names and compares all pairs of files with the same names. It also lists the names of files that are in one directory but not the other.

Sample: diff /usr/margy/book /usr/john/book

Where to look: Chapter 14, section "Comparing Apples and Oranges."

echo

Purpose: To echo back whatever you type on the command line after echo, expanding any wildcards using *, ?, or [ ].

Options and arguments:

```
echo [-n] stuff
```

Option or Argument	Function
-n	Don't start a new line after echoing the information (BSD only).
stuff	Specifies the information to echo.

Sample: echo "Please enter y or n, you dweeb!"

Where to Look: Chapter 15, sidebar "Your search path."

ed

Purpose: To run one of the world's ugliest line-oriented text editors.

Where to look: Chapter 13, section "Talk to Mr. ed."

elm

Purpose: To read and send e-mail.

Where to look: Chapter 19, section "Playing Postman Pat with elm."

emacs

Purpose: To run a powerful, screen-oriented text editor.

Where to look: Chapter 13, section "A novel concept in editing: emacs makes sense."

exit

Purpose: To log out. When used in a terminal window, closes the window. If exit doesn't work, try typing logout. Pressing Ctrl-D can also log you out.

Where to look: Chapter 1, section "Ciao, UNIX!" and Chapter 12, section "Getting Rid of Windows."

fg

Purpose: To continue a stopped job by running it in the foreground. (Some versions of the Bourne shell can't do this.)

Options and arguments:

```
fg [%job]
```

The *%job* argument specifies the job number that you want to run in the foreground. If you leave it out, UNIX assumes you mean the current job.

Sample: fg %2

Where to look: Chapter 16, section "The Magic of Job Control."

file

Purpose: To tell you whether something is a file, a directory, or something else entirely. If the thing is a file, the `file` command tries to guess what type of information it contains.

Options and arguments:

```
file names
```

The *names* argument specifies the directories or files that you want information about.

Sample: `file breath.of.doom`

Where to look: Chapter 14, section "What's in That File?"

find

Purpose: To find one or more files, assuming that you know their approximate filenames, and do something to them. Use this command when you can't figure out the directory where you put one or more files, but you know the filename(s). When you use the `find` command, you tell it where to start looking, usually either . (which means "right here") or / (which means "search the entire disk"). Then give the name of the file (type `-name`, a space, and the filename, possibly using wildcard characters), and then you tell `find` what to do when it finds the files, usually `-print` (to mean "display the full filenames, including the names of the directories that they are in").

Options and arguments:

```
find directories [-name filename] [-user username] [-atime +days]
    [-mtime +days] [-print] [-exec command {} \;] [-ok command {} \;]
```

Option or Argument	Function
directories	Specifies a list of directories in which you want to begin the search. The `find` command searches all the subdirectories of these directories, too. If you want to start in the current directory, just type a single period (.).

(continued)

Option or Argument	Function
-name *filename*	Specifies the name of the file(s) you want to find. If you don't know the exact name, you can use the ? and * wildcard characters. ? stands for any single character, and * stands for a group of characters. You must quote the filename if you use any wildcards.
-user *username*	Specifies the user who owns the files you want to find.
-atime +*days*	Specifies that you want only files that haven't been accessed (looked at) in at least "*days*" days. If you use a minus sign instead of the plus sign before the number of days, you get only files that were last looked at within that number of days.
-mtime +*days*	Specifies that you want only files that haven't been modified in at least "*days*" days. If you use a minus sign instead of the plus sign before the number of days, you get only files that were last changed within that number of days.
-print	Displays the names of files it finds. If you don't include this option, the `find` command may find lots of files, but it won't tell you about them.
-exec *command* {} \;	Runs the *command* each time it finds a file. When it runs the command, it substitutes the name of the file it found for the {}. Be sure to type \; at the end of the command.
-ok *command* {} \;	Works the same way as the `-exec` option, except that it asks you to confirm that you want to perform the command as it finds each file.

Sample: `find . -name brownie.recipe -print`

Where to look: Chapter 8, section "When You Know the Filename."

finger

Purpose: To list the people using your computer, with real names, not just UNIX user names.

Options and arguments:

```
finger [-s] [usernames][@computername]
```

Option or Argument	Function
-s	Specifies the short form of display, with less information about the users.
usernames	Specifies the user(s) about whom you'd like more information.
computername	Specifies the name of the computer on which to check.

Sample: `finger dougm@mitre.com`

Where to look: Chapter 18, section "Finding Out Who's on Your Computer" and "Finding Out Who's on Other Computers."

ftp

Purpose: To transfer files from one computer to another over a network.

Options and arguments:

```
ftp [-v] computername
```

Option or Argument	Function
-v	Displays lots of messages to tell you what it's doing.
computername	Specifies the computer with which you want to exchange files.

Sample: `ftp rtfm.mit.edu`

Where to look: Chapter 21, "The he-man's file-transfer program."

grep

Purpose: To find lines in one or more files that contain a particular word or phrase. There are two similar commands, `egrep` and `fgrep`, that you will probably never use.

Options and arguments:

```
grep [-i] [-l] [-v] text filenames
```

Option or Argument	Function
-i	Ignores case (uppercase and lowercase, that is) when searching.
-l	Displays only the names of the files that contain the text, not the actual lines.
-v	Specifies that you are looking for lines that *don't* contain the *text*.
text	Specifies the word or phrase to search for. If the text includes spaces or punctuation that might confuse UNIX, enclose it in quotes.
filenames	Specifies the file(s) in which to search. To search all the files in the current directory, type *.

Sample: `grep "Zac Young" *`

Where to look: Chapter 8, section "It's Bigger Than a Breadbox . . ."

gs *(ghostscript)*

Purpose: To print PostScript files, even if you don't have a PostScript printer.

Options and arguments:

```
gs [-h] [-sDEVICE=printername] filenames
```

Option or Argument	Function
-h	Displays a list of available printers.
-s	Specifies which printer to print on (replace *printername* with a name from the list you see when you give the command `gs -h`).
filenames	Names the files to print.

Sample: `gs -sDEVICE=deskjet floogle.ps`

Where to look: Chapter 10, "Seeing Ghosts."

gunzip

Purpose: To unzip gzipped files. Replaces a `.gz` file with the original file.

Options and arguments:

```
gunzip [-l] zip-file
```

Option or
Argument   ***Function***

-l   List the contents of the zip file rather than unzipping it.

-r   Recursive unzip, that is, if you give a directory name, it unzips all
              files in that directory and all of its subdirectories.

zip-file   Specifies the GNU ZIP file that contains the file(s) you want to
              unzip.

Sample: gunzip plugh.gz (Replaces plugh.gz with the uncompressed
plugh.)

Where to look: "What's GNU, zip department" in Chapter 14.

gzip

Purpose: To compress a file; replaces the original file with a GNU ZIP file with a
name ending in .gz.

Options and arguments:

```
gzip [-digit] [-r] file . . .
```

Option or
Argument   ***Function***

-digit   Controls speed and quality of compression (where digit ranges
              from 1 through 9). -1 is the fastest, -9 does the best compression.

-r   Recursive zip, that is, if you give a directory name, it zips each file
              in that directory and all of its subdirectories.

file . . .   Names files to zip. Each one is zipped separately.

Sample: gzip plugh (Replaces plugh with the compressed plugh.gz.)

Where to look: "What's GNU, zip department" in Chapter 14.

head

Purpose: To display just the first few lines of a file (usually the first ten).

Options and arguments:

```
head [-lines] filename
```

Option or Argument	Function
-lines	Specifies the number of lines to display. If you omit this option, you get ten lines.
filename	Specifies the file you want to look at.

Sample: `head hundred.page.report`

Where to look: Chapter 5, section "Looking at the Guts of a File."

history

Purpose: To list the last 20 or so commands you typed. Works only with the BASH, Korn, and C shells.

Where to look: Chapter 7, section "UNIX Is History!"

id

Purpose: To tell you your numeric user and group ID, and, on BSD, what groups you are in.

Where to look: Chapter 5, section "Rock groups, pop groups, and UNIX groups."

init

Purpose: To stop UNIX and prepare a workstation to be turned off. This command doesn't work on all workstations — check with a local expert for the correct command.

Where to look: Chapter 1, "If a train stops at a train station, what happens at a workstation?"

jobs

Purpose: To list the jobs that are running in either the foreground or the background, and the jobs that have stopped. (Some versions of the Bourne and Korn shells can't do this.) Once you've listed your jobs, you can move jobs to the foreground or the background — see `bg` and `fg`.

Where to look: Chapter 16, section "Take this job and . . ."

kill

Purpose: To cancel a job that you don't want to continue.

Options and arguments:

```
kill %job
```

or

```
kill [-9] pid
```

Option or Argument	*Function*
job	Specifies the job that you want to kill. You can use the job number listed by the jobs command, or the first few letters of the program that is running (C and Korn shells only).
-9	Tells kill to show no mercy when killing the program; kill it no matter what.
pid	Specifies the process ID of the job. You can use the ps command to find out the job's process ID. (See ps later in this chapter.)

Sample: kill %big.report

Where to look: Chapter 16, section ". . . Shove it" and Chapter 24, section "Dirty Deeds, Done Dirt Cheap."

ksh

Purpose: To run the Korn shell.

Options and arguments:

```
ksh [scriptname]
```

Sample: ksh fix.it.up

Where to look: Chapter 2, section "Cracking the Shell."

ln

Purpose: To create a link to a file so that the file has more than one name or lives in more than one directory. If you use a file all the time and are tired of moving to the directory where it lives, link the file to your home directory or to another convenient place. When you use ln, you tell it the current pathname of the file and the new filename you want in the current working directory.

Options and arguments:

```
ln [-n] [-s] existingfile newname
```

or

```
ln [-n] [-s] existingfiles directory
```

Option or Argument	Function
-n	Tells ln not to clobber existing files when creating new links — a good idea (SVR4 only).
-s	Tells ln to make a symbolic link to the file (not on older System V systems).
existingfile	Specifies the file to which you want to create a new link.
newname	Specifies the name to give to the new link.
existingfiles	Specifies the file(s) to which you want to create new link(s).
directory	Specifies the directory in which you want the new link(s).

Sample: ln /usr/katy/bin/backgammon backg

Where to look: Chapter 8, section "A File by Any Other Name."

logout

Purpose: To tell UNIX you are done using it.

Where to look: Chapter 1, "Ciao, UNIX!"

lp

Purpose: To print a file (UNIX System V only).

Options and arguments:

```
lp [-c] [-d printer] [-m] [-n copies] [-o options]
       [-P pagenumbers] [-w] filename
```

Option or Argument	*Function*
-c	Tells lp to make a copy of the file to be printed. If you edit the file between the time you give the lp command and when it is actually printed, the changes don't appear in the printout.
-d *printer*	Specifies the printer on which you want the file printed.
-m	Tells lp to send you e-mail when the file has been printed. Useful when the printer is very busy and you may have to wait your turn.
-n *copies*	Specifies the number of copies of the file to print.
-o *options*	Specifies print options, listed below.
-P *pagenumbers*	Specifies which pages to print. (That's a capital P.)
-w	Displays a message on-screen when the file has printed.
filename	Specifies the file you want to print.

Sample: lp letter.to.santa

Where to look: Chapter 10, section "Printing Stuff."

lpq

Purpose: To list the status of all the available printers (works in BSD UNIX and Linux).

Options and arguments:

```
lpq [-a] [printer]
```

Option or
Argument ***Function***

-a   Lists information about all printers.

printer   Specifies the printer you want to know about. If you don't specify
            the printer, it assumes a default, usually the printer closest to you.

Sample: `lpq laser3`

Where to look: Chapter 10, section "Cancel the order, BSD."

lpr

Purpose: To print a file (works in Linux and BSD UNIX only).

Options and arguments:

```
lpr [-Pprinter] filename
```

Option or
Argument ***Function***

-P*printer*   Specifies which printer to use.

filename   Specifies the file you want to print.

Sample: `lpr feijoada`

Where to look: Chapter 10, section "Printing Stuff."

lpstat

Purpose: To list the status of all available printers (works in UNIX System V only).

Options and arguments:

```
lpstat [-a all] [-d] [-p printers]
```

Option or
Argument ***Function***

-a all   Lists all the printers that are currently available.

-d   Lists your default printer, that is, the printer on which your files
             print unless you specify otherwise.

-p *printers* Displays the status of the printer(s) that you name.

Sample: `lpstat -a all`

Where to look: Chapter 10, section "Cancel the order, System V."

ls

Purpose: To list the files in a directory. If you don't tell it otherwise, the `ls` command lists all the files in the working directory. You can tell it the name of another directory to list, and you can specify the files you want listed by using a filename (which can include wildcards).

Options and arguments:

```
ls [-a] [-l] [-p] [-r] [-R] [-t] [-x] [pathnames]
```

Option or Argument	Function
-a	Displays all the files and subdirectories, including hidden files (files with names that begin with a dot).
-l	Displays detailed information about each file and directory, including permissions, owners, size, and when the file was last modified.
-p	Displays a slash (/) at the end of each directory name, to distinguish them from filenames (System V).
-r	Displays files in reverse order.
-R	Includes the contents of all subdirectories, too.
-t	Displays files in order of modification time.
-x	Displays the filenames in several columns across the screen (System V).
pathnames	File(s) or directory(s) to list.

Sample: `ls -al`

Where to look: Chapter 5, section "What Files Do You Have?"

mail

Purpose: To read and send e-mail. We suggest using `elm` or `pine` instead, if they are available.

Where to look: See Chapter 19.

man

Purpose: To display reference manual pages about UNIX commands.

Options and arguments:

```
man [-] [-k keywords] topic
```

Option or Argument	*Function*
-	If your UNIX system usually presents manual pages one screen at a time, this option displays them without stopping, which is useful when redirecting the output of man to a file or to the printer.
-k *keywords*	Specifies one or more keywords to search for. You will see all man pages that contain the keyword(s) in their header lines. (Not available on older UNIXes.)
topic	Specifies the topic about which you want information. Available man pages include mainly UNIX commands, with a small number of general topics.

Sample: man ls | more

Where to look: Chapter 27, section "Let's Hear It from the man."

mkdir

Purpose: To create a new directory.

Options and arguments:

```
mkdir directory
```

The *directory* argument specifies the name of the new directory. If the name doesn't start with a slash, the new directory is created as a subdirectory of the current working directory. If the name starts with a slash, the name defines the path from the root directory to the new directory.

Sample: mkdir Temp

Where to look: Chapter 6, section "Making directories."

more

Purpose: To display information a screen at a time, so you have time to read it. When the screen is full, more pauses. To tell it to show you more, press the spacebar. To make more stop, press q.

Options and arguments:

```
more [-l] [-r] [-s] [-u] [+linenum] [+/text] [filename]
```

Option or Argument	*Function*
-l	Ignores form-feed characters in the file (that is, Ctrl-Ls, which start a new page). Use this option if the file has a lot of tiny pages of text (System V).
-r	Displays control characters instead of performing their function. For example, the control character Ctrl-H is a backspace; instead of backspacing, this option displays Ctrl-H as ^H (System V).
-s	Squeezes out extra blank lines by displaying only one blank line.
-u	Ignores underscore and backspace characters that can otherwise make text unreadable on the screen.
+*linenum*	Displays the file (or whatever the input to more is) as line *linenum*.
+/*text*	Starts displaying text two lines before the first time *text* appears.
filename	Specifies the file to display.

Sample: more long.memo

Where to look: Chapter 7, section "Gimme just a little at a time."

mv

Purpose: To rename a file or move it from one directory to another.

Options and arguments:

```
mv [-i] oldname newname
```

or

```
mv [-i] filename directory[/newname]
```

Option or Argument	Function
-i	Tells mv to inquire before clobbering an existing file with a moved or renamed file (works only in UNIX System V Release 4).
oldname	Specifies the existing file that you want to rename.
newname	Specifies the new name to use for the file.
filename	Specifies the file that you want to move.
directory	Specifies the directory into which you want to move the file.

Sample: mv old.budget 1995.budget

Where to look: Chapter 5, section "What's in a Name (Reprise)" and Chapter 6, sections "Transplanting files" and "Renaming a directory." Also, "Links, copies, moves, truncation, and other details about file destruction" in Chapter 23 for how mv works with files that have more than one name (link).

nice

Purpose: To run a command with lower priority so that it doesn't hog the computer.

Options and arguments:

```
nice command [arguments] [&]
```

Option or Argument	Function
command	Specifies the command you want to run.
arguments	If you need to provide arguments for the command, type them just as you would if you weren't using the nice command.
&	Runs the command in the background. No one ever uses nice to run programs in the foreground!

Sample: nice long.invoice.rpt &

Where to look: Chapter 16, section "Starting Background Processes."

pack

Purpose: To shrink a file into one "packed" file so that it takes up less space on your disk. This command is obsolete; compress and gzip shrink a lot better.

Options and arguments:

```
pack filenames
```

The *filenames* argument specifies the files to compress.

Sample: `pack chicken.death.patrol`

Where to look: Chapter 14, section "Squashing Your Files."

passwd

Purpose: To change your password.

Options and arguments:

```
passwd [-s]
```

The `-s` option displays status information, including your user name, whether you have a password at all, and when you last changed it (System V Release 4). This option does *not* display your password, though! (Indeed, if you forget your password, there's no way to get it back, although the administrator can change it to something else for you.)

Where to look: Chapter 1, section "Password Smarts," and Chapter 2, " We could tell you the password, but then we'd have to kill you."

pcat

Purpose: To display the contents of a packed file. Packed files have names ending in .z. (That's a small *z*.)

Sample: `pcat sleuth1.doc.z | more`

Where to look: Chapter 14, "Squashing Your Files."

pico

Purpose: To run a simple, screen-oriented text editor.

Where to look: Chapter 13, section "The `pico` the crop."

pine

Purpose: To run a nicely designed e-mail program.

Where to look: Chapter 19, section "Playing Postman Pat with `pine`."

pr

Purpose: To format a text file with page numbers, line numbers, or other options so that it looks nice when you print it.

Options and arguments:

```
pr [-a] [-d] [-f] [-F] [-h text] [-l lines] [-m] [-n] [-o offset] [-t]
   [-w width] [+pagenum] [-columns] filenames
```

Option or Argument	Function
-a	Prints lines across the page. This option is great when you have lots of short lines.
-d	Double-spaces the output.
-f	Uses form-feed characters, not blank lines, to move to the top of a new page.
-F	(Stands for *f*old.) Wraps long lines around to the beginning of the next line, rather than cutting them off (System V).
-h *text*	Prints *text* as the header at the top of each page. If you omit this, pr prints a header consisting of the filename and the date when the file was last changed.
-l *lines*	Sets the page length to *lines* lines. If you omit this, the page length is 66 lines, which is correct when printing at 6 lines per inch on 11-inch paper.
-m	Merge several files together, printing each side-by-side in columns.
-n	Numbers the lines of the file.
-o *offset*	Prints *offset* extra spaces at the beginning of each line, to make a wider left margin. This option is useful if you plan to punch holes in the paper or bind it.
-t	Doesn't print page headers, or blank lines at the end of the file.
-w *width*	Sets the line width to *width* characters. If you leave this out, the line width is 72 characters. Only interesting if you use multiple columns.

Option or Argument	*Function*
+*pagenum*	Starts printing at page *pagenum*.
-*columns*	Prints the file in multiple columns, as in a newspaper or magazine. *Columns* is the number of columns you want.
filenames	Specifies the file(s) you want to format for printing.

Sample: `pr chocolate.story | lpr`

Where to look: Chapter 10, section "Prettying Up Your Printouts."

ps

Purpose: To display information about your processes (jobs).

Options and arguments:

For BSD UNIX:

```
ps [-a] [-l] [-ttty] [-u] [-x]
```

Option or Argument	*Function*
-a	Displays information about all processes. If you omit this option, you see only your processes.
-l	Displays a longer, more detailed version.
-t*tty*	Displays a list of processes that were started by terminal *tty*.
-u	Displays a "user-oriented" report with additional information.
-x	Displays all processes that are running in the background, not using a terminal.

For UNIX System V:

```
ps [-a] [-e] [-f] [-tttys] [-uusernames]
```

Option or Argument	*Function*
-a	Includes information about almost all processes, not just processes you started.
-e	Displays all the processes in the entire system.
-f	Displays a "full," more detailed listing.
-t*ttys*	Displays a list of processes that were started by terminal(s) *ttys*.
-u*usernames*	Displays a list of processes that were started by user name(s) *usernames*.

Where to look: Chapter 16, section "Any Processes in the House?"

pwd

Purpose: To display the name of the current working directory.

Where to look: Chapter 6, section "I've been working in the directory."

r

Purpose: To repeat the last command. It works only in the Korn shell.

Where to look: Chapter 7, "The Korn shell throughout history."

rcp

Purpose: To copy files to or from another computer.

Options and arguments:

```
rcp [-p] [-r] [username@][computer:]filenames
           [computer:]newfilenames
```

Option or Argument	*Function*
-p	Preserves the modification time of mode of the files when you copy them.
-r	If the *filenames* and *newfilenames* are both directory names rather than filenames, copies all the files and subdirectories in the directory.

computer	Specifies the name of the computer you want to copy files to or from. Include it just once, not twice.
username	Specifies your user name on the remote computer, if it is different from the name you use on your usual computer.
filenames	Specifies the file(s) to copy. This argument can be a filename (to copy one file), a filename specification that uses wildcards (to copy a bunch of files), or a directory name (to copy all the files in the directory as well as in its subdirectories).
newfilenames	Specifies the names to give to the copied files. This argument can be a filename (when you are copying one file) or a directory name.

Sample: `rcp accounting:budget.95.draft budget.95`

Where to look: Chapter 21, section "The sweet-and-simple file-transfer program."

rehash

Purpose: To update the table of UNIX commands and the programs they run (used only with the C shell).

Where to look: Chapter 15, section "Take 1."

rlogin

Purpose: To log in to another UNIX computer on a network. See also `telnet`.

Options and arguments:

`rlogin [-l `*`username`*`] `*`computername`*

Option or Argument	***Function***
-l *username*	Specifies your user name on the other computer. If you use the same name on the remote computer as on your own computer, omit this.
computername	Specifies the computer you want to use. The computer must support `rlogin` (most non-UNIX systems don't).

Where to look: Chapter 21, section "The Lazy Man's Remote Login."

rm

Purpose: To delete (remove) a file permanently. If there are other links to the file, the file continues to exist, just not under the name you removed. The rm command deletes just one name (link) to the file.

Options and arguments:

```
rm [-i] [-r] filenames
```

Option or
Argument   *Function*

-i   Asks you to confirm that you want to delete each file.

-r   Deletes an entire directory and all the files it contains. Watch out! You can do a lot of damage with this option! Always use the -i option, too.

filenames   Specifies the file(s) to delete.

Sample: rm budget.95.*

Where to look: Chapter 5, section "Nuking Files Back to the Stone Age" and Chapter 23, section "How You Clobber Files."

rmdir

Purpose: To delete (remove) a directory. Before you delete a directory, delete the files and subdirectories that it contains. The -r option does this for you, but make sure that this is what you really want to do!

Options and arguments:

```
rmdir [-r] directory
```

Option or
Argument   *Function*

-r   Tells rm to delete all the files and subdirectories that this directory contains. Watch out! You can do a lot of damage!

directory   Specifies the directory you want to delete. It must be empty.

Sample: rm Budget/*

Where to look: Chapter 6, section "Amputating unnecessary directories."

rsh

Purpose: To run a command on another UNIX computer. **Note:** Called `remsh` on some systems.

Options and arguments:

```
rsh [-l username] computername command
```

Option or Argument	Function
-l *username*	Specifies your user name on the remote computer. If it is the same as your name on the computer you usually use, skip this.
computername	Specifies the name of the computer on which you want to run the command. The computer must run UNIX (any variety).
command	Specifies the command to run on the other computer.

Sample: `rsh shamu who`

Where to look: Chapter 21, section "One Command at a Time."

set

Purpose: To set a shell variable to the value you specify, or to display the value of the shell variable. In any shell, typing `set` by itself lists the variables that are defined, and their values.

Options and arguments:

For BASH, Bourne, and Korn shells:

```
set
```

or

```
variable=value
```

For the C shell:

```
set [variable=value]
```

Option or Argument	Function
variable	Specifies the variable whose value you want to set.
value	Specifies the value you want to assign to the variable.

Sample (BASH, Bourne, and Korn shells): `workdir=/usr/fred/project/`

Sample (C shell): `set workdir=/usr/fred/project/`

Sample (any shell, to list variables): `set`

Where to look: *MORE UNIX For Dummies,* Chapter 5, "The Shell Game: Using Shell Variables."

sh

Purpose: To run the Bourne shell.

Options and arguments:

```
sh [scriptname]
```

For *scriptname,* type the name of a file containing a Bourne shell script.

Sample: `sh check.all.files`

Where to look: Chapter 2, section "Cracking the Shell."

shutdown

Purpose: To stop UNIX and prepare a workstation to be turned off. This command doesn't work on all workstations — check with a local expert for the correct command. This is the right command for shutting down a Linux system.

Where to look: Chapter 1, "If a train stops at a train station, what happens at a workstation?"

sleep

Purpose: To wait a little while.

Options and arguments:

```
sleep time
```

The *time* argument specifies the number of seconds to wait.

Sample: sleep 5

Where to look: Chapter 14, section "Calendar Games."

sort

Purpose: To sort the lines in a text file.

Options and arguments:

```
sort [-b] [-d] [-f] [-i] [-m] [-M] [-n] [-r] [-u] [-tx]
              [+fields] filename [-o outputfile]
```

Option or Argument	Function
-b	Ignores spaces at the beginning of the line.
-d	Uses dictionary sort order, ignoring punctuation.
-f	Ignores capitalization while sorting.
-i	Ignores nonprinting control characters.
-m	Merges two or more sorted input files into one sorted output.
-M	Treats the first three characters of each line as a three-letter month abbreviation, and sorts by month order, for example, Jan before Feb (System V only).
-n	Sorts based on the number at the beginning of the line. With this option, 99 precedes 100 rather than following it, as it does in usual alphabetical order.
-r	Sorts in reverse order. You can combine this option with any other option.
-u	If the same line occurs in the file more than once, outputs it only once (stands for *u*nique).
-tx	Uses the character *x* to separate fields, rather than white space.

(continued)

Option or Argument	Function
+*fields*	Considers each line to contain a series of fields (fields are separated by white space). When sorting, *fields* specifies the number of fields to skip from the left end of the line. For example, `sort +2` sorts starting at the third field on each line.
filename	Specifies the file containing the text to be sorted.
-o *outputfile*	Specifies that `sort` should send the sorted output to a file, and specifies the name of that file.

Sample: `sort name.list -o sorted.list`

Where to look: Chapter 7, section "Sorting, sort of" and Chapter 14, section "Assorted Files."

spell

Purpose: To look through a text file for words not in the UNIX dictionary.

Options and arguments:

```
spell [-b] [+wordlist] filenames
```

Option or Argument	Function
-b	Uses allegedly British spellings.
+*wordlist*	Adds the contents of the file named *wordlist* to the UNIX dictionary so that words contained in the *wordlist* file are not considered to be misspelled.
filenames	Specifies the file(s) to be spell-checked.

Sample: `spell memo.to.the.boss`

Where to look: This is the only place we tell you about this command. Amaze your friends!

stty

Purpose: To set the options for your terminal.

Options and arguments:

```
stty [charname char] [sane] [[-]tostop] [-a]
```

Option or Argument	*Function*
charname	Specifies the terminal control character that you want to see. (Refer to the table in Chapter 28 for what these characters are.)
char	Specifies the key(s) that you want to use for this terminal control character.
sane	Returns your terminal to a "sane" state, useful if a text editor dies and leaves your terminal in a state where characters don't echo.
-tostop	Turns off terminal stop mode so that output from background jobs can display on your screen.
tostop	Turns on terminal stop mode to prevent output from background jobs from displaying on your screen. (Terminal stop mode is usually on, unless you have turned it off.)
-a	Displays all of the terminal settings.

Sample: `stty erase '^q'`

Where to look: Chapter 28, section "Setting Up the Terminal the Way You Want" and Chapter 16, sidebar "Taming background terminal output."

tail

Purpose: To display the last few lines of a file.

Options and arguments:

```
tail [-r] [-lines] filename
```

Option or Argument	*Function*
-r	Displays the lines in reverse order.
-lines	Specifies the number of lines you want to see (counting from the end of the file).
filename	Specifies the file you want to see the end of.

Sample: `tail memo.to.frank`

Where to look: We don't actually talk about it anywhere, but it's just like the `head` command, stood on its head (or maybe on its tail), in Chapter 5.

talk

Purpose: To talk to another computer user by typing messages to each other on-screen.

Options and arguments:

```
talk user[@computer] [terminal]
```

Option or
Argument **Function**

user   Specifies the user name of the person you want to chat with.

computer Specifies the name of the computer onto which the person is logged.

terminal Specifies the terminal name, if the user is logged on more than once.

Sample: `talk deb@wicca`

Where to look: Chapter 18, section "Can we talk?" See also `finger`, `wall`, and `write` commands.

tar

Purpose: To copy a file to or from an archive file or backup tape or diskette.

Options and arguments:

```
tar [c|r|t|u|x][l][o][v][w][0-9][f tarfile] filenames
```

Option or
Argument **Function**

c   Copies files to a new archive file or tape.

r   Copies files to the end of an existing tape.

t   Displays a list of all the files stored on the tape.

u   Copies files to the tape unless they are already there. If a previous version of a file is on the tape, it copies the new version to the tape (tape only).

x   Copies (extracts) files *from* the archive file or tape.

l   Displays error messages if it can't find the files you want.

Option or Argument	Function
o	When extracting files (copying them from the archive file or tape), changes the ownership of the files to you, instead of their original owners.
v	Displays the names of the files as it copies them, plus a (for *a*rchive, when copying *to* an archive file or tape) or x (for e*x*tract, when copying *from* an archive file or tape).
w	Asks you to confirm copying each file.
0-9	A single digit says which unit to use. If there's only one tape or floppy, it's unit 0. Check with a local guru to find out what value to use.
f *tarfile*	Specifies the name of the archive file. If the archive is on a disk or tape drive, the name will usually be something like /dev/fd096 or /dev/tape.
filenames	Specifies the files you want to copy. If you give directory names, all their files and subdirectories are included as well.

Sample: `tar tvf /dev/tape`

Where to look: Chapter 23, section "Call in the backup squad."

tee

Purpose: To copy text from a pipe into a file. `tee` is most useful for making a log of the output of a slow or long-running program while still seeing its output on-screen. It's also good for debugging scripts so that you can see what's coming out of one program and going into another.

Options and arguments:

```
tee [-a] filenames
```

Option or Argument	Function
-a	Adds material to the end of the files instead of clobbering them.
filenames	Specifies the file(s) to copy material to.

Sample: `find . -atime +30 | tee stale.files`

Where to look: Nowhere, actually, but this is one of John's favorite commands.

telnet

Purpose: To log in to a remote computer, even one that doesn't run UNIX.

Options and arguments:

```
telnet [computername]
```

The *computername* argument specifies the computer that you want to use.

Sample: `telnet wordsworth.com`

Where to look: Chapter 21, section "Logging In, Logging Out." Or *MORE UNIX For Dummies,* Chapter 20, "Telnetting Around the Net."

troff

Purpose: To format text files for output on a high-quality printer or typesetter, using a complex formatting language.

Where to look: If you need to learn how to format text for use with `troff` (or its predecessor, `nroff`), there is a useful overview in *UNIX in a Nutshell* (O'Reilly & Associates, 1986).

uncompress

Purpose: To restore a compressed file to its normal size. A `.Z` at the end of the filename tells you that you've got a compressed file. If a filename ends with `.z` (lowercase) instead, it is packed, and you must use the `unpack` command.

Options and arguments:

```
uncompress [-c] filenames
```

Option or Argument	Function
-c	Displays the uncompressed version of the file, but doesn't save it as a file or delete the compressed file.
filenames	Specifies the compressed files to uncompress.

Sample: `uncompress facts.Z`

Where to look: Chapter 14, section "Squashing Your Files."

unpack

Purpose: To restore a packed file to its original size. A .z at the end of the filename confirms that this is a packed file. If a filename ends with .Z (upper-case) instead, it is compressed, and you must use the uncompress command.

Options and arguments:

```
unpack filenames
```

The *filenames* argument specifies the packed files to unpack.

Sample: unpack user.manual.z

Where to look: Chapter 14, section "Squashing Your Files."

uucp

Purpose: To copy a file to another computer.

Options and arguments:

```
uucp [-m] yourfile computer!newfile
```

Option or Argument	Function
-m	Sends mail to you after the file has been copied.
yourfile	Specifies the name of your file on your own computer.
computer	Specifies the computer to which you want to copy the file.
newfile	Specifies the filename to use on the other computer when creating the file.

Sample: uucp big.news carioca!big.news

Where to look: Chapter 28, section "A Really Gross Old Network."

uudecode

Purpose: To convert a uuencoded file back into its original form.

Options and arguments:

```
uudecode [filename]
```

The *filename* argument specifies the name of the uuencoded file. Reads from standard input if not specified.

Sample: `uudecode uu.incoming`

Where to look: Chapter 15, section "Sneaking Software through the Mail," as well as various sections in Chapter 19.

uuencode

Purpose: To disguise a program as a text file so that you can send it through electronic mail.

Options and arguments:

```
uuencode existingfile decodedname > uufilename
```

Option or Argument	Function
existingfile	Specifies the program (or other file) that you want to disguise as a text file.
decodedname	Specifies the name to be used later for the uudecoded file, after the file is mailed.
uufilename	Specifies the name to use for the uuencoded file.

Sample: `uuencode fish.squish run.me > file.to.send`

Where to look: Chapter 15, section "Sneaking Software through the Mail," as well as various sections in Chapter 19.

vi

Purpose: To run a powerful, but yucky, screen-oriented text editor.

Where to look: Chapter 13, section "Shy vi, the princess of text editors." Also, *MORE UNIX For Dummies,* Chapter 11, "Oy, Vi!"

wall

Purpose: To display a message on-screen to every single user on your entire computer. Use with care!

Where to look: Chapter 18, section "Reading the Writing on the Wall."

wc

Purpose: To count the number of words, lines, and characters in a file.

Options and arguments:

```
wc [-c] [-l] [-w] filename
```

Option or Argument	Function
-c	Displays only the number of characters in the file.
-l	Displays only the number of lines in the file.
-w	Displays only the number of words in the file.
filename	Specifies the name of the text file to count.

Sample: wc chapter.17

Where to look: Right here!

who

Purpose: To tell you who else is using this computer.

Options and arguments:

```
who [-q] [am i]
```

Option or Argument	Function
-q	Displays only user names, not terminal IDs or other information (System V).
am i	Displays your user name, in case you've forgotten, or if you've walked up to a terminal that someone left logged in.

Where to look: Chapter 18, section "Finding Out Who's on Your Computer."

write

Purpose: To display a message on the screen of another user.

Options and arguments:

```
write username [terminal]
```

Option or Argument	Function
username	Specifies the person to whom you want to send a message.
terminal	Specifies the terminal that the person is using. You only need to mention this if the person is using several terminals (or terminal windows) at the same time.

Sample: `write dave`

Where to look: Chapter 18, section "Chatting with People on Your Computer."

zcat

Purpose: To uncompress a compressed file and send the result to standard output (usually the screen). Compressed files have names ending in `.Z`. (That's a capital *Z*.)

Sample: `zcat sleuth1.doc.Z | more`

Where to look: Chapter 14, section "Squashing Your Files."

Glossary

absolute pathname. A pathname that tells you how to find a file by starting at the root directory and working down the directory tree.

address. The name you use to say who is supposed to receive an electronic-mail message. An electronic-mail address consists of the person's user name and, if on a different computer than you are, the name of the computer. See Chapter 19.

Alt key. If your keyboard has an Alt key, it is used as a Shift key; it does nothing on its own. To use the Alt key, hold it down, press and release another key, and release the Alt key. To press Alt-A, for example, hold the Alt key, press and release the A key, and release the Alt key. Simple. Lacking an Alt key, you can usually press Esc, then the letter, to get the same effect.

anonymous ftp. Uses the `ftp` file transfer program and the Internet to copy files from other computers to your own. It is *anonymous* because many computer systems allow anyone to log in and transfer files without having accounts (user names) on the computer. You type `anonymous` as the user name and your electronic-mail address as the password. See Chapter 21.

application. A program that really gets some work done. Some programs just organize the computer, get its parts talking to each other, and do other housekeeping chores. Application programs do real-world work, like word processing or accounting.

argument. Something that appears on a command line after the command. Suppose that you type this line:

```
cp old.file new.file
```

In this command, `cp` is the name of the command or program, `old.file` is the first argument, and `new.file` is the second argument. See Chapter 15 for how to use arguments with shell scripts.

ASCII. American Standard Code for Information Interchange. ASCII defines the codes that the computer uses internally to store letters, numbers, punctuation, and some control codes. Almost all UNIX computers use ASCII (except for some IBM mainframes).

background. UNIX can run many programs at the same time. If a program runs behind the scenes, that is, with no interaction with you, it runs in the background. See Chapter 16.

backslash (\). UNIX uses a backslash to set off otherwise special characters. In the UNIX shell, for example, `\*` is a literal asterisk (a plain `*` matches every file in the current directory); `\\` is an actual backslash, if you want one for some reason. DOS users tend to type backslashes by mistake when UNIX would rather see a regular slash (/).

backup. A spare copy of data to keep on the shelf just in case. If you (or a coworker) delete a file by mistake or if parts of your computer break, you will be inexpressibly happy and smug if you have recently made a backup copy of your important files. Copying files back from your backups is called *restoring*. See Chapter 23.

bang (!). In UNIX-ese, an exclamation point is called a *bang*. The C shell command `!!`, for example, which repeats the last command, is pronounced "Bang! Bang!" Try this with your small children — they will love it.

BASH. The Bourne Again shell, the GNU re-creation of the Bourne shell. Program name is bash.

bin. A directory that contains programs. Your home directory probably has a subdirectory named bin. The system has directories called /bin and /usr/bin. See Chapter 15.

bit. A tiny piece of information that can be either a 1 or a 0. Bits tend to get lumped into groups of eight bits, called *bytes.*

Bourne shell. The Bourne shell is the most widely used UNIX shell. It prompts you with $. Its program name is sh.

Break key. The Break key is used before you log in when you are dialing on a modem to tell UNIX that it has guessed wrong about which kind of modem you're using. You may have to press Break two or three times until you get a proper login: message. Some keyboards have a key labeled Break. If yours doesn't, and you're using a PC with a modem program, try Alt-B or check your modem program's help screen.

BSD UNIX. A version of UNIX developed and distributed by the University of California at Berkeley. BSD stands for Berkeley Software Distribution.

buffer. A small storage area in which information is stored temporarily until it is needed. Lots of things have buffers: printers frequently have buffers to store the next few lines or pages to print; emacs (a text editor) refers to its copies of the files you are editing as buffers.

byte. Eight bits in a row. That is, a series of eight pieces of information, each of which can be either 1 or 0. A little higher math tells you that there are 256 different combinations of eight 1s and 0s. (256 is 2 to the 8th power.) There are, therefore, 256 different values for a byte of information. Most

computers use a system of codes called *ASCII* to determine what each pattern means. One set of 1s and 0s means *A,* another set means *B,* and another set means "end of the line, start a new one."

C. A programming language, invented at the same time as UNIX, in which nearly all UNIX programs are written. C is a great programming language for lots of reasons. C programs look a lot like random punctuation strewn across the page. Luckily, you do *not* have to know C to use UNIX, so we don't talk about it anywhere else in this book.

C shell. The C shell is a UNIX shell written to look like the C programming language, sort of. It prompts you with %. Its program name is csh.

CD-ROM. A computer disk that looks just like a music CD but contains data rather than music.

click-to-type. A system that GUIs (graphical user interfaces) use to control which window you are working in. When you want to move to a different window, move the mouse and click in the new window to tell the GUI that you want to use that window. It's a pain in the neck, actually. See Chapter 11.

clicking. "Clicking a mouse" means moving the mouse until the cursor is on the thing you want to select and then pressing and releasing the mouse button. If your mouse has several buttons, use the leftmost button unless instructed otherwise. See Chapter 11.

client. In X Windows, a program that does real work (as opposed to a program that displays the results on-screen). See Chapter 12.

client-server architecture. A system (used by X) that enables a program (the client) to run on one machine while the program that displays its results (the server) runs on another machine. Confusingly, it is also used in the database world to mean when a presentation or analysis program (the client) runs on one machine and the database engine (the server) runs on another computer. See Chapter 12.

command. What you type to get UNIX to do something. Actually, the *UNIX shell* listens to the commands you type and tries to execute them. Some commands are things the shell knows how to do. Other commands are separate programs, stored in files on the disk. When you type a command, press Enter or Return at the end of the line.

command mode. When you use the ed or vi text editors, you are in either command mode or input mode. In command mode, whatever you type is interpreted as a command. See Chapter 13.

compression. A way to shrink files so that they don't take up so much space. File-compression programs that do this include compress and pack. To uncompress a compressed file, use uncompress, unpack, or zcat. See Chapter 14.

Control key. The key on the keyboard labeled Control or Ctrl. It is used as a Shift key; it does nothing on its own. To use the Ctrl key, hold it down, press and another key, and release the Ctrl key. To press Ctrl-D, for example, hold the Ctrl key, press and release the D key, and release the Ctrl key.

core. An old-fashioned term for "memory." A long time ago (in the '60s and '70s), most memory consisted of thousands of tiny, metal donuts, called *cores,* strung on arrays of teeny, tiny wires. Some UNIX enthusiasts still refer to memory as "core."

.cshrc. The file that the C shell runs automatically when the shell starts. See Chapter 28.

Ctrl key. See *Control key.*

current directory. See *working directory.*

current job. The job most recently started or stopped. When you use the jobs command to list jobs, the current job is marked with a plus sign (+).

cursor. The little indicator on your screen that shows where you are working. Its shape depends on the program you are using. It may be a blinking underscore, a box, an arrow, a little pencil — you name it.

daemon. A process that runs around on its own to see to some housekeeping task. Your computer, or some computer on your network, has a printer daemon whose job is to print things waiting in the print queue.

data. Information, in computer-speak.

directory. A collection of files with a name. A directory can be compared to a file folder that contains one or more files. Directories can also contain other directories. You can think of a directory as a work area because one directory is always the current *working directory.* Directories, particularly directories contained in your home directory, sometimes are called subdirectories, for no good reason.

disk. Also known as DASD (only to IBM types, who pronounce this "daz-dee"), it is a round, flat thing on which information is recorded in much the same way as you record stuff on a cassette tape. See Chapter 9 for descriptions of the various kinds of disks.

diskette. A removable disk, also called a floppy disk. See Chapter 9.

DOS. An operating system patterned in some ways after UNIX. DOS runs on PCs. See Chapter 17 for a comparison of DOS and UNIX commands.

double-clicking. "Double-clicking a mouse" means moving the mouse until the cursor is on the thing you want to use and then quickly pressing and releasing the mouse

button twice. It takes some practice to get the two clicks fast enough but not too fast. If your mouse has several buttons, use the leftmost button unless you are instructed otherwise. See Chapter 11.

dragging. "Dragging with a mouse" means moving the mouse until the cursor is on the thing you want to drag, pressing and holding the mouse button, moving the mouse until the thing is where you want it (with the button still down), and then releasing the mouse button. If your mouse has several buttons, use the leftmost button unless instructed otherwise. See Chapter 11.

dumb terminal. A terminal that has no processing power of its own. It usually doesn't have any nice options either, like mice or screens that can do graphics. See Chapter 1.

editor. See *text editor.*

electronic mail (or e-mail or email). Typed messages sent on a computer network rather than on paper. See Chapter 19.

end of input. Usually the Ctrl-D character.

Enter key. In a UNIX shell, pressing Enter means you have just typed a command and you want UNIX to do it. In a text editor, pressing Enter means you want to begin a new line. The Enter key and the Return key usually do the same thing (your keyboard may have one, the other, or both).

Escape key. The key labeled Escape or Esc. What this key does depends on the program you are using. The vi editor uses it to switch from input mode to command mode.

executable file. A file that UNIX can run like a program. An executable file can contain binary machine instructions the computer knows how to execute, or it can contain a *shell script* (a list of UNIX shell commands)

that UNIX knows how to execute. See Chapter 15.

external command. A command that the shell doesn't actually know how to do. Instead, a program is stored in a file with the same name as the command. If you type the ed command (to run the dreadful ed editor), for example, UNIX runs the program contained by a file named ed.

file. A bunch of information stored together with a name. A file can contain text, programs, or data in any format.

file system. A set of files stored on a disk or on one partition of a disk. A file system has one root directory that contains files and subdirectories. These subdirectories can in turn contain files and other directories. See Chapter 6.

file transfer. Copying files from one computer to another. See Chapter 21.

filter. A small UNIX program used with input or output redirection. The most commonly used filters are the more and sort commands.

fixed disk. A disk that used to be broken but that now works. No, sorry! See *disk.*

flag. See *option.*

floppy disk. A removable disk, also called a *diskette.*

folder. A file that contains electronic-mail messages you have decided to save. See Chapter 19.

foreground. A program currently able to talk to your terminal. See Chapter 16 for information about how to run programs in the foreground or background.

fork. When UNIX starts a new process, it does so by cloning an existing process. The cloning process is known in UNIX-ese as *forking.* Pronounce it carefully to avoid embarrassment.

`ftp.` A file-transfer program that enables you to log in to another computer and transfer files to or from your computer. See Chapter 21.

GUI. A *graphical user interface.* GUIs let you use the computer by pointing at things with a mouse rather than typing commands. The most common UNIX GUI is Motif. GUIs sometimes are called *windowing systems.*

hardware. The physical components of your computer system, that is, the boxes. Your computer hardware may include the computer, terminal, keyboard, screen, modem, printer, mouse, trackball, disk drive, and even a scanner.

header. The first part of an electronic-mail message that contains the address of the sender and recipient, the subject, and lots of other stuff that is less interesting. See Chapter 19.

hidden file. A file with a filename that begins with a period. These files do not appear on regular `ls` directory listings. Use `ls -a` to include hidden files in a directory listing.

home directory. The directory you start in when you log in, usually a subdirectory of `/usr`. You should keep your files in your home directory, or in subdirectories of your home directory.

icon. A cute, little picture used in conjunction with a GUI. A well-designed icon is supposed to be an obvious, unmistakable symbol of whatever it stands for, occupy much less space than do the equivalent words, and be cute. In practice, many icons are peculiar little pictures with no obvious meaning. See Chapter 12.

inbox. See *mailbox.*

incremental backup. A backup copy of only the files that have changed since the last full backup. See Chapter 23.

input mode. When you use the `ed` or `vi` text editors, you are in either command mode or input mode. In input mode, whatever you type is entered into the file. See Chapter 13.

Internet. A large and growing set of interconnected computer networks to which many UNIX systems are directly or indirectly connected.

I/O. Input and output, that is, information going into or coming out of a program, computer, or other computer-type device.

I/O redirection. See *redirection.*

job. A program you started from the shell that can start, stop, and move between the foreground and background. See Chapter 16.

K (also KB or Kilobyte). A measure of memory or disk size that is 1,024 bytes of information. This number happens to be 2 multiplied by itself 10 times, a nice, round number for computers.

kill. To stop a process from running. See Chapter 24.

kludge. Something that works but that the author is embarrassed about. Rhymes with "huge," not with "fudge." Some people spell it *kluge,* and we're sure they too can learn to live productive and useful lives.

Korn shell. An enhanced version of the Bourne shell, written by a guy named Korn. For your purposes, it's mostly like the Bourne shell, and prompts you with a $. Its program name is `ksh`.

line editor. A text editor that deals with text one line at a time. Most modern text editors let you see and work with the file an entire screen at a time. The ed program is a line editor; we recommend that you use something better. See Chapter 13.

link. An additional name for a file. When you create a file, you create its contents, which are stored on the disk, and you give it a name, which is stored in a directory. There is a connection between the filename and its contents. You can create additional filenames and connect them to the same contents by using the ln command. See Chapter 8.

Linux. A free version of UNIX originally written by Linus Torvalds in Finland and now developed by a cast of thousands all over the world, connected by the Internet. See Chapter 3.

local mount. Logically connects several disk drives on the same machine so that they appear as one file system. See Chapter 20.

log in. To identify yourself to the UNIX system and provide your password so that UNIX believes that it's really you and lets you use the computer. You have a login ID, or user ID, or user name, that is, the name by which UNIX knows you. When you finish working, you log out. See Chapter 1.

.login. A hidden file containing a shell script. If you use the C shell, this script runs automatically every time you log in. See Chapter 15.

login directory. See *home directory*.

M, MB, or Megabyte. Measure of memory and disk size that is 1,048,576 bytes, or 1K times 1K, or 2 multiplied by itself 20 times.

mailbox. The directory in which the electronic-mail system puts your incoming mail. See Chapter 19.

man page. A short file of information about a UNIX command. The man command

displays manual pages about all UNIX commands and a few other topics, although they usually are written in a hopelessly technoid style. See Chapter 27.

memory. The storage area where the computer puts information it is working on right now. This is useful for only short-term storage (like until the program stops running or the computer is turned off). For long-term storage, computers put information on disks. Also known as *main memory* or *RAM*.

Meta key. If your keyboard has an Alt key, it is also the Meta key. If not, press the Escape key to achieve the same effect. The effect depends on the program you are running. emacs uses the Meta key for many commands. See Chapter 13.

MIME. (Multipurpose Internet Mail Extensions) A way to attach any kind of file to an e-mail message. See Chapter 19.

modem. A box that connects your computer or terminal to a phone line. It converts information from your computer to little whistling or hissing noises on the phone line and back again.

Motif. A GUI based on X Windows and distributed by the Open Software Foundation. See Chapter 12.

mounting directories. Logically attaching the root directory of one file system to some other directory so that you can treat all the files in the file system as though they were subdirectories. Mounts can be *local* (on the same machine) or *remote* (on a different machine). See Chapter 20.

nerd. A person who spends too much time at the computer. A person, for example, who wanders away from dinner parties to check the computer to see whether any good electronic mail has arrived. (No one we know, of course.)

netiquette. Rules of polite behavior for sending electronic mail. See Chapter 19.

network. A bunch of computers connected by some combination of cables, phone lines, satellites, or whatever. A network enables computers (and their users) to share information and peripherals. They are especially good for sharing printers (so that you can all share one good but expensive laser printer) and for passing around electronic mail.

NeXTstep. An extremely cool GUI that runs on NeXT machines. See Chapter 11.

NFS. Network File System. A network system that lets you treat files on another computer in more or less the same way you treat files on your own computer. See Chapter 20.

NIS. Network Information System. A database containing the user names, machine names, and directory names that an NFS uses to give consistent names on all machines on a network. See Chapter 20.

Novell NetWare. A network system that works on PCs and UNIX. See Chapter 20.

OPEN LOOK. A GUI based on X Windows and developed by AT&T. Most people use Motif instead. See Chapter 12.

operating system. A special program that controls the way the computer, keyboard, screen, and disks work together. UNIX is an operating system, as is DOS.

option. Known also as a *flag* or *switch.* An option is something that tells UNIX how to do a command. You type an option on the command line after the name of the command, separated from the command by a space. All options begin with a dash (-). The ls command used with the -l option, for example, produces a file listing with more information about each file.

parent directory. The directory that contains the current working directory. That is, the current working directory is a subdirectory of the parent directory.

password. A secret blend of herbs and spices . . . no! A secret series of characters known only to you. You type your password when you log in. See Chapter 1 for tips on choosing a password.

pathname. Instructions for how to get to a file. An *absolute pathname* tells you how to find a file beginning at the root directory and working down the directory tree. A *relative pathname* tells you how to find the file starting where you are now.

PC. A personal computer, usually one running DOS. As a UNIX user, you now can sneer at PCs as "just toys." Now you have a "real computer." Ha! A PC can be used to act as a terminal so that you can use a computer running UNIX. (One of the authors is doing that at this very moment.) A big-enough PC can run UNIX on its own (that's what the other author is using.) See Chapter 1.

peripheral. Something that lets the computer communicate with the outside world — mainly with you. The keyboard, screen, mouse, printer, and modem all are peripherals.

permissions. Whoever has permission to look at, change, and execute stuff in a file or directory. See Chapter 5.

pipe. The | character, used to redirect the output of one command so that it becomes the input of another command. See Chapter 7.

policy independence. A characteristic of X Windows in which windows can look and act any way the software developers want. This idea is the converse of the idea that, if all the windows on your screen look and act in a similar way, they will be easier for you to use. See Chapter 11.

portable software. Software (programs) that can be run on a number of different kinds of computers. UNIX is portable because it runs on an amazing number of different types of computers.

PostScript. A computer language spoken by printers and the programs that communicate with these printers. PostScript enables printers to print a wonderful array of characters in all kinds of sizes and shapes, as well as pictures. When a program wants to print something on a PostScript printer, rather than just send the characters to print, it has to send a PostScript program that tells the printer how to print the stuff. See Chapter 10 for more than you want to know.

process. A running program. See Chapter 24.

.profile. A hidden file that contains shell commands. If you use the Bourne or Korn shell, this file runs automatically every time you log in.

program. See *software*.

prompt. The character or characters displayed whenever UNIX (or some other program) is waiting for you to type something. The two common UNIX prompts are $ (if you use the Bourne or Korn shell) or % (if you use the C shell).

queue. A waiting line, just as in real life. The most common queue is the print queue, in which the output of lp or lpr commands waits in line to get printed. See Chapter 10.

RAM. *R*andom-*a*ccess *m*emory. See *memory*.

read-only. A file that can be read (copied, and so on) but not written (changed). UNIX has a system of permissions that enables the owner of the file, the owner's group, or all users to have or not have permission to read, write, or execute the file. See Chapter 5.

real-time. Right now, as opposed to whenever the computer gets around to it.

redirection. To hijack the output of a command, which is usually on-screen, and put it somewhere else (this process is called *output redirection*). Alternatively, you can use information from somewhere else as the input for a command (called *input redirection*) rather than take the input from the keyboard. To redirect the output of a command to a file, use the > character. To redirect the input of a command from a file, use the < character. To redirect the output of one command to become the input to another command, use the pipe (|) character. See Chapter 7.

remote login. Logging in to another computer from your own computer. This process requires that your computer be on a network or have a phone connection. See Chapter 21.

remote mount. Using NFS to connect directories from disk drives on other machines so that they appear as part of your file system. See Chapter 20.

request ID. The ID number of a print job as it waits in the print queue for the printer daemon to get around to printing it. You need to know the request ID if you want to cancel printing when, for example, the output is horribly fouled up and wasting lots of paper. See Chapter 10.

Return key. When you use a UNIX shell, pressing Return means that you have just typed a command and you want UNIX to do it. When you use a text editor, pressing Return means that you want to begin a new line. The Enter key and the Return key usually do the same thing (your keyboard may have one, the other, or both).

RFS. Remote File System. Like NFS, a program that lets you treat files on another computer in more or less the same way as you treat files on your own computer. See Chapter 20.

root. See *superuser.*

root directory. The main, top-level directory on a disk. All the files on the disk are in either the root directory or a subdirectory of the root directory (or a sub-subdirectory, and so on).

rotating backups. Not using the same tapes or diskettes every time you make a backup. By rotating among two, three, or more backup sets, you have a longer history and a more reliable system. See Chapter 23.

screen editor. A text editor that deals with text an entire screen at a time. The `vi` and `emacs` programs are screen editors. See Chapter 13.

script. See *shell script.*

SCSI. Small Computer Systems Interface. A way to connect a disk drive to a computer. A SCSI disk (pronounced "scuzzy," except in some parts of California, where they say "sexy" — typical) can connect to any SCSI-compatible connector used by workstations, PCs, and Macs.

search path. A list of directories in which UNIX looks for programs. See Chapter 15.

server. See *X server.*

shar message. An electronic-mail message that contains a shell script that re-creates one or more files when you run it. A clever way to send nontext files through electronic mail. See Chapter 15.

shell. A UNIX program that listens for commands you type and tries to execute them. There are several UNIX shells, including the Bourne shell, Korn shell, BASH, and the C shell. See Chapter 2.

shell script. A file that contains a list of UNIX shell commands. You can *run* a shell script, thereby telling UNIX to execute every command in the list. See Chapter 15.

slash. The / character UNIX uses in pathnames. A / by itself, or at the beginning of a pathname, means the root directory of the file system. Slashes are used also between one directory name and the next, and between the directory name and the filename in long pathnames. See Chapter 6.

snail-mail. A mail system in which you print the message you want to send to another person, address a paper envelope of the correct size to fit the paper, insert the paper in the envelope, close the envelope, find a postage stamp, and place the entire thing in a U.S. mailbox. Many UNIX users find electronic mail simpler, faster, and more convenient. See Chapter 19.

soft link. A link that contains the name of another file, which may be on another file system. A soft link makes it look as though the file from the other file system is in a directory on your own file system. Also called a *symbolic link.* See Chapter 8. See also *link.*

software. A set of instructions (also called programs) that tell a computer to do something. In contrast to hardware, which includes the physical components of your computer, software is composed of information on a disk (or tape, or whatever).

Solaris. A version of UNIX, based initially on BSD UNIX and later on System V Release 4, distributed by Sun for use on Sun workstations.

subdirectory. See *directory.*

superuser. The user name with which you can do all sorts of dangerous things to the system, including creating new user names and installing new hardware and software.

Also known as *root.* With luck, you don't know the password for the superuser. If you do, *use it carefully.* The system administrator really should be the only person who logs in as the superuser.

SVR4. Release 4 (the final version) of UNIX System V from AT&T. Contains more features than any six people would ever want to use.

switch. See *option.*

symbolic link. See *soft link.*

system administrator. The person whose job it is to keep the computer, and possibly the network, running.

System V. A version of UNIX developed and distributed originally by AT&T, later by UNIX System Labs, and now by Novell.

tape. A computer tape stores vast amounts of information but is not convenient to use. Tapes are used primarily for making backup copies of information, for which they are terrific. With luck, your system administrator backs up your files to tape regularly. See Chapter 9.

telnet. A program that enables you to log in to another computer from your computer. See Chapter 21.

terminal. A screen and keyboard connected to a computer somewhere else. The terminal doesn't run UNIX and all those neat programs itself, it just lets you use the computer that does.

terminal emulator. A program that enables a big, powerful computer to act like a dumb, cheap terminal. Commonly, a PC can run a terminal emulator so you can use another computer running UNIX (see Chapter 1). UNIX includes a simple terminal emulator called cu. See Chapter 21.

terminal output stop mode. A terminal setting in which a background job stops if it tries to send anything to your screen.

text editor. A program that lets you create files of text and edit (or change) them. The most common UNIX text editors are ed, vi, and emacs. See Chapter 13.

text file. A file that contains lines of text. All the stuff in a text file must be ASCII characters — no bizarre control codes, data, programs, or the like. You can use the cat command to look at a text file on-screen. If a file looks like it was written by Martians when you use the cat command to view it, it's not a text file.

text formatter. A program that reads text files and creates nice-looking formatted output. The most common UNIX text formatters are troff, nroff, and TeX. See Chapter 13.

trackball. A pointing device, equivalent to a mouse lying on its back, that lets you move the cursor on the screen. See Chapter 11.

UNIX. An operating system written by a couple of people at Bell Laboratories in 1972. They also wrote the C programming language. Since then, several variants of UNIX have appeared, including BSD UNIX, System V UNIX, and Linux.

UNIXWare. Novell's version of UNIX. Descended from SVR4.

usenet. A very large, very informal, very disorganized network through which many megabytes of news, rumor, and gossip are distributed every day. See Chapter 28.

user name. The name by which UNIX knows you. You enter this name when you log in. Also known as your *user ID* or *login ID.* See Chapter 1.

utility. A small, useful program. UNIX comes with some utilities like `diff` and `sort`.

uucp. The UNIX-to-UNIX copy program. One of the ways that mail, `usenet` news, and random files can be sent between computers. See Chapter 28.

uuencoded file. An electronic-mail message that contains a shell script that, when you run it, re-creates one or more binary files. This is a clever way to send binary files through electronic mail. See Chapters 15 and 19.

virtual memory. A sneaky trick by which UNIX pretends to have more memory than it really does. When you are not looking, UNIX copies information from memory to the disk to free up space in memory. When you need the information on disk, UNIX copies it from the disk back into memory. Virtual memory is generally invisible, except when a program uses it too enthusiastically; then the computer spends all its time copying stuff back and forth to the disk and no time doing useful work, a condition called *thrashing*.

wildcard. A special character that acts like a joker when used in filenames or pathnames. UNIX has two: * and ?. See Chapter 7.

WIMP. *W*indows, *i*cons, and *m*ouse *p*ointing. See Chapter 11. See also *GUI*.

window. A rectangular area of the screen in which a program displays something. If you use a GUI, you can have several windows on-screen at a time, each displaying a different program. See Chapter 11.

window manager. A program (Motif comes with one) that gives the screen the overall look of a GUI. See Chapter 12.

Wizard. A person who knows more about UNIX than is really healthy. Encourage wizards to get outside once in a while.

word processor. A program that lets you create documents — files that contain text, pictures, and formatting codes. UNIX word processors include WordPerfect and Microsoft Word. See Chapter 13.

working directory. The directory you are working in. The `pwd` command tells you your working directory.

workstation. A computer with a big screen, a keyboard, and a mouse. If it runs UNIX, it's called a workstation; if it runs DOS, it's called a PC. And if it runs Macintosh Finder (or whatever that system is called), it's called a Mac.

X server. A program that draws the pictures and displays the text on-screen if you use X Windows or a GUI based on X Windows. See Chapter 12.

X terminal. A terminal that can run X so that you can use X Windows or Motif. It has a little computer in it to do the X stuff. See Chapters 1 and 11.

X window system, or just X. A GUI designed at MIT. Motif is based on X. See Chapter 11.

XENIX. A version of UNIX developed by Microsoft, of all people, and now maintained and distributed by SCO (Santa Cruz Organization).

Yellow Pages. See *NIS*.

Index

(continued)

(continued)

Title	Author	ISBN	Price
			12/20/94
INTERNET / COMMUNICATIONS / NETWORKING			
CompuServe For Dummies™	by Wallace Wang	1-56884-181-7	$19.95 USA/$26.95 Canada
Modems For Dummies™, 2nd Edition	by Tina Rathbone	1-56884-223-6	$19.99 USA/$26.99 Canada
Modems For Dummies™	by Tina Rathbone	1-56884-001-2	$19.95 USA/$26.95 Canada
MORE Internet For Dummies™	by John R. Levine & Margaret Levine Young	1-56884-164-7	$19.95 USA/$26.95 Canada
NetWare For Dummies™	by Ed Tittel & Deni Connor	1-56884-003-9	$19.95 USA/$26.95 Canada
Networking For Dummies™	by Doug Lowe	1-56884-079-9	$19.95 USA/$26.95 Canada
ProComm Plus 2 For Windows For Dummies™	by Wallace Wang	1-56884-219-8	$19.99 USA/$26.99 Canada
The Internet For Dummies™, 2nd Edition	by John R. Levine & Carol Baroudi	1-56884-222-8	$19.99 USA/$26.99 Canada
The Internet For Macs For Dummies™	by Charles Seiter	1-56884-184-1	$19.95 USA/$26.95 Canada
MACINTOSH			
Macs For Dummies®	by David Pogue	1-56884-173-6	$19.95 USA/$26.95 Canada
Macintosh System 7.5 For Dummies™	by Bob LeVitus	1-56884-197-3	$19.95 USA/$26.95 Canada
MORE Macs For Dummies™	by David Pogue	1-56884-087-X	$19.95 USA/$26.95 Canada
PageMaker 5 For Macs For Dummies™	by Galen Gruman	1-56884-178-7	$19.95 USA/$26.95 Canada
QuarkXPress 3.3 For Dummies™	by Galen Gruman & Barbara Assadi	1-56884-217-1	$19.99 USA/$26.99 Canada
Upgrading and Fixing Macs For Dummies™	by Kearney Rietmann & Frank Higgins	1-56884-189-2	$19.95 USA/$26.95 Canada
MULTIMEDIA			
Multimedia & CD-ROMs For Dummies™, Interactive Multimedia Value Pack	by Andy Rathbone	1-56884-225-2	$29.95 USA/$39.95 Canada
Multimedia & CD-ROMs For Dummies™	by Andy Rathbone	1-56884-089-6	$19.95 USA/$26.95 Canada
OPERATING SYSTEMS / DOS			
MORE DOS For Dummies™	by Dan Gookin	1-56884-046-2	$19.95 USA/$26.95 Canada
S.O.S. For DOS™	by Katherine Murray	1-56884-043-8	$12.95 USA/$16.95 Canada
OS/2 For Dummies™	by Andy Rathbone	1-878058-76-2	$19.95 USA/$26.95 Canada
UNIX			
UNIX For Dummies™	by John R. Levine & Margaret Levine Young	1-878058-58-4	$19.95 USA/$26.95 Canada
WINDOWS			
S.O.S. For Windows™	by Katherine Murray	1-56884-045-4	$12.95 USA/$16.95 Canada
MORE Windows 3.1 For Dummies™, 3rd Edition	by Andy Rathbone	1-56884-240-6	$19.99 USA/$26.99 Canada
PCs / HARDWARE			
Illustrated Computer Dictionary For Dummies™	by Dan Gookin, Wally Wang, & Chris Van Buren	1-56884-004-7	$12.95 USA/$16.95 Canada
Upgrading and Fixing PCs For Dummies™	by Andy Rathbone	1-56884-002-0	$19.95 USA/$26.95 Canada
PRESENTATION / AUTOCAD			
AutoCAD For Dummies™	by Bud Smith	1-56884-191-4	$19.95 USA/$26.95 Canada
PowerPoint 4 For Windows For Dummies™	by Doug Lowe	1-56884-161-2	$16.95 USA/$22.95 Canada
PROGRAMMING			
Borland C++ For Dummies™	by Michael Hyman	1-56884-162-0	$19.95 USA/$26.95 Canada
"Borland's New Language Product" For Dummies™	by Neil Rubenking	1-56884-200-7	$19.95 USA/$26.95 Canada
C For Dummies™	by Dan Gookin	1-878058-78-9	$19.95 USA/$26.95 Canada
C++ For Dummies™	by Stephen R. Davis	1-56884-163-9	$19.95 USA/$26.95 Canada
Mac Programming For Dummies™	by Dan Parks Sydow	1-56884-173-6	$19.95 USA/$26.95 Canada
QBasic Programming For Dummies™	by Douglas Hergert	1-56884-093-4	$19.95 USA/$26.95 Canada
Visual Basic "X" For Dummies™, 2nd Edition	by Wallace Wang	1-56884-230-9	$19.99 USA/$26.99 Canada
Visual Basic 3 For Dummies™	by Wallace Wang	1-56884-076-4	$19.95 USA/$26.95 Canada
SPREADSHEET			
1-2-3 For Dummies™	by Greg Harvey	1-878058-60-6	$16.95 USA/$21.95 Canada
1-2-3 For Windows 5 For Dummies™, 2nd Edition	by John Walkenbach	1-56884-216-3	$16.95 USA/$21.95 Canada
1-2-3 For Windows For Dummies™	by John Walkenbach	1-56884-052-7	$16.95 USA/$21.95 Canada
Excel 5 For Macs For Dummies™	by Greg Harvey	1-56884-186-8	$19.95 USA/$26.95 Canada
Excel For Dummies™, 2nd Edition	by Greg Harvey	1-56884-050-0	$16.95 USA/$21.95 Canada
MORE Excel 5 For Windows For Dummies™	by Greg Harvey	1-56884-207-4	$19.95 USA/$26.95 Canada
Quattro Pro 6 For Windows For Dummies™	by John Walkenbach	1-56884-174-4	$19.95 USA/$26.95 Canada
Quattro Pro For DOS For Dummies™	by John Walkenbach	1-56884-023-3	$16.95 USA/$21.95 Canada
UTILITIES / VCRs & CAMCORDERS			
Norton Utilities 8 For Dummies™	by Beth Slick	1-56884-166-3	$19.95 USA/$26.95 Canada
VCRs & Camcorders For Dummies™	by Andy Rathbone & Gordon McComb	1-56884-229-5	$14.99 USA/$20.99 Canada
WORD PROCESSING			
Ami Pro For Dummies™	by Jim Meade	1-56884-049-7	$19.95 USA/$26.95 Canada
MORE Word For Windows 6 For Dummies™	by Doug Lowe	1-56884-165-5	$19.95 USA/$26.95 Canada
MORE WordPerfect 6 For Windows For Dummies™	by Margaret Levine Young & David C. Kay	1-56884-206-6	$19.95 USA/$26.95 Canada
MORE WordPerfect 6 For DOS For Dummies™	by Wallace Wang, edited by Dan Gookin	1-56884-047-0	$19.95 USA/$26.95 Canada
S.O.S. For WordPerfect™	by Katherine Murray	1-56884-053-5	$12.95 USA/$16.95 Canada
Word 6 For Macs For Dummies™	by Dan Gookin	1-56884-190-6	$19.95 USA/$26.95 Canada
Word For Windows 6 For Dummies™	by Dan Gookin	1-56884-075-6	$16.95 USA/$21.95 Canada
Word For Windows For Dummies™	by Dan Gookin	1-878058-86-X	$16.95 USA/$21.95 Canada
WordPerfect 6 For Dummies™	by Dan Gookin	1-878058-77-0	$16.95 USA/$21.95 Canada
WordPerfect For Dummies™	by Dan Gookin	1-878058-52-5	$16.95 USA/$21.95 Canada
WordPerfect For Windows For Dummies™	by Margaret Levine Young & David C. Kay	1-56884-032-2	$16.95 USA/$21.95 Canada

Fun, Fast, & Cheap!

CorelDRAW! 5 For Dummies™ Quick Reference
by Raymond E. Werner

ISBN: 1-56884-952-4
$9.99 USA/$12.99 Canada

Windows "X" For Dummies™ Quick Reference, 3rd Edition
by Greg Harvey

ISBN: 1-56884-964-8
$9.99 USA/$12.99 Canada

Word For Windows 6 For Dummies™ Quick Reference
by George Lynch

ISBN: 1-56884-095-0
$8.95 USA/$12.95 Canada

WordPerfect For DOS For Dummies™ Quick Reference
by Greg Harvey

ISBN: 1-56884-009-8
$8.95 USA/$11.95 Canada

Title	Author	ISBN	Price
DATABASE			
Access 2 For Dummies™ Quick Reference	by Stuart A. Stuple	1-56884-167-1	$8.95 USA/$11.95 Canada
dBASE 5 For DOS For Dummies™ Quick Reference	by Barry Sosinsky	1-56884-954-0	$9.99 USA/$12.99 Canada
dBASE 5 For Windows For Dummies™ Quick Reference	by Stuart J. Stuple	1-56884-953-2	$9.99 USA/$12.99 Canada
Paradox 5 For Windows For Dummies™ Quick Reference	by Scott Palmer	1-56884-960-5	$9.99 USA/$12.99 Canada
DESKTOP PUBLISHING / ILLUSTRATION/GRAPHICS			
Harvard Graphics 3 For Windows For Dummies™ Quick Reference	by Raymond E. Werner	1-56884-962-1	$9.99 USA/$12.99 Canada
FINANCE / PERSONAL FINANCE			
Quicken 4 For Windows For Dummies™ Quick Reference	by Stephen L. Nelson	1-56884-950-8	$9.95 USA/$12.95 Canada
GROUPWARE / INTEGRATED			
Microsoft Office 4 For Windows For Dummies™ Quick Reference	by Doug Lowe	1-56884-958-3	$9.99 USA/$12.99 Canada
Microsoft Works For Windows 3 For Dummies™ Quick Reference	by Michael Partington	1-56884-959-1	$9.99 USA/$12.99 Canada
INTERNET / COMMUNICATIONS / NETWORKING			
The Internet For Dummies™ Quick Reference	by John R. Levine	1-56884-168-X	$8.95 USA/$11.95 Canada
MACINTOSH			
Macintosh System 7.5 For Dummies™ Quick Reference	by Stuart J. Stuple	1-56884-956-7	$9.99 USA/$12.99 Canada
OPERATING SYSTEMS / DOS			
DOS For Dummies® Quick Reference	by Greg Harvey	1-56884-007-1	$8.95 USA/$11.95 Canada
UNIX			
UNIX For Dummies™ Quick Reference	by Margaret Levine Young & John R. Levine	1-56884-094-2	$8.95 USA/$11.95 Canada
WINDOWS			
Windows 3.1 For Dummies™ Quick Reference, 2nd Edition	by Greg Harvey	1-56884-951-6	$8.95 USA/$11.95 Canada
PRESENTATION / AUTOCAD			
AutoCAD For Dummies™ Quick Reference	by Ellen Finkelstein	1-56884-198-1	$9.95 USA/$12.95 Canada
SPREADSHEET			
1-2-3 For Dummies™ Quick Reference	by John Walkenbach	1-56884-027-6	$8.95 USA/$11.95 Canada
1-2-3 For Windows 5 For Dummies™ Quick Reference	by John Walkenbach	1-56884-957-5	$9.95 USA/$12.95 Canada
Excel For Windows For Dummies™ Quick Reference, 2nd Edition	by John Walkenbach	1-56884-096-9	$8.95 USA/$11.95 Canada
Quattro Pro 6 For Windows For Dummies™ Quick Reference	by Stuart A. Stuple	1-56884-172-8	$9.95 USA/$12.95 Canada
WORD PROCESSING			
Word For Windows 6 For Dummies™ Quick Reference	by George Lynch	1-56884-095-0	$8.95 USA/$11.95 Canada
WordPerfect For Windows For Dummies™ Quick Reference	by Greg Harvey	1-56884-039-X	$8.95 USA/$11.95 Canada

FOR MORE INFORMATION OR TO ORDER, PLEASE CALL ▶ 800. 762. 2974

For volume discounts & special orders please call Tony Real, Special Sales, at 415. 655. 3048

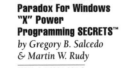

12/20/94

"A lot easier to use than the book Excel gives you!"

Lisa Schmeckpeper, New Berlin, WI, on PC World Excel 5 For Windows Handbook

**Official Hayes Modem
Communications
Companion**

by Caroline M. Halliday

ISBN: 1-56884-072-1
$29.95 USA/$39.95 Canada

Includes software.

**PC World Excel 5
For Windows Handbook,
2nd Edition**

*by John Walkenbach
& Dave Maguiness*

ISBN: 1-56884-056-X
$34.95 USA/$44.95 Canada

Includes software.

**PC World DOS 6
Handbook, 2nd Edition**

*by John Socha, Clint
Hicks, & Devra Hall*

ISBN: 1-878058-79-7
$34.95 USA/$44.95 Canada

Includes software.

**PC World Word
For Windows 6
Handbook**

*by Brent Heslop
& David Angell*

ISBN: 1-56884-054-3
$34.95 USA/$44.95 Canada

**PC World Microsoft
Access 2 Bible,
2nd Edition**

*by Cary N. Prague
& Michael R. Irwin*

ISBN: 1-56884-086-1
$39.95 USA/$52.95 Canada

Includes software.

**"Easy and enjoy-
able to read, well
structured and so
detailed you cannot
fail to learn! It's the
best computer book
I have ever used."**

*John Wildsmith, Gateshead,
England, on PC World
Microsoft Access 2 Bible,
2nd Edition*

**PC World WordPerfect 6
Handbook**

by Greg Harvey

ISBN: 1-878058-80-0
$34.95 USA/$44.95 Canada

Includes software.

**QuarkXPress
For Windows Designer
Handbook**

*by Barbara Assadi
& Galen Gruman*

ISBN: 1-878058-45-2
$29.95 USA/$39.95 Canada

**Official XTree
Companion, 3rd Edition**

by Beth Slick

ISBN: 1-878058-57-6
$19.95 USA/$26.95 Canada

**PC World DOS 6
Command Reference
and Problem Solver**

*by John Socha
& Devra Hall*

ISBN: 1-56884-055-1
$24.95 USA/$32.95 Canada

**Client/Server
Strategies: A Survival
Guide for Corporate
Reengineers**

by David Vaskevitch

ISBN: 1-56884-064-0
$29.95 USA/$39.95 Canada

**"PC World Word
For Windows 6
Handbook is very
easy to follow with
lots of 'hands on'
examples. The
'Task at a Glance'
is very helpful!"**

Jacqueline Martens, Tacoma, WA

**"Thanks for publish-
ing this book! It's
the best money I've
spent this year!"**

*Robert D. Templeton, Ft. Worth,
TX, on MORE Windows 3.1
SECRETS*

FOR MORE INFORMATION OR TO ORDER, PLEASE CALL ▶ 800 762 2974   For volume discounts & special orders please call
Tony Real, Special Sales, at 415. 655. 3048

IDG BOOKS

Order Center: **(800) 762-2974** *(8 a.m.–6 p.m., EST, weekdays)*

12/20/94

Quantity	ISBN	Title	Price	Total

Shipping & Handling Charges

	Description	First book	Each additional book	Total
Domestic	Normal	$4.50	$1.50	$
	Two Day Air	$8.50	$2.50	$
	Overnight	$18.00	$3.00	$
International	Surface	$8.00	$8.00	$
	Airmail	$16.00	$16.00	$
	DHL Air	$17.00	$17.00	$

*For large quantities call for shipping & handling charges.
**Prices are subject to change without notice.

Ship to:

Name _____

Company _____

Address _____

City/State/Zip _____

Daytime Phone _____

Payment: ☐ Check to IDG Books (US Funds Only)

☐ VISA   ☐ MasterCard   ☐ American Express

Card # _____ Expires _____

Signature _____

Subtotal _____

CA residents add
applicable sales tax _____

IN, MA, and MD
residents add
5% sales tax _____

IL residents add
6.25% sales tax _____

RI residents add
7% sales tax _____

TX residents add
8.25% sales tax _____

Shipping _____

Total _____

Please send this order form to:

IDG Books Worldwide
7260 Shadeland Station, Suite 100
Indianapolis, IN 46256

*Allow up to 3 weeks for delivery.
Thank you!*

IDG BOOKS WORLDWIDE REGISTRATION CARD

Title of this book: UNIX For Dummies, 2E

My overall rating of this book: ❏ Very good [1]   ❏ Good [2]   ❏ Satisfactory [3]   ❏ Fair [4]   ❏ Poor [5]

How I first heard about this book:

❏ Found in bookstore; name: [6]

❏ Advertisement: [8]

❏ Word of mouth; heard about book from friend, co-worker, etc.: [10]

❏ Book review: [7]

❏ Catalog: [9]

❏ Other: [11]

What I liked most about this book:

What I would change, add, delete, etc., in future editions of this book:

Other comments:

Number of computer books I purchase in a year: ❏ 1 [12]   ❏ 2-5 [13]   ❏ 6-10 [14]   ❏ More than 10 [15]

I would characterize my computer skills as: ❏ Beginner [16]   ❏ Intermediate [17]   ❏ Advanced [18]   ❏ Professional [19]

I use ❏ DOS [20]   ❏ Windows [21]   ❏ OS/2 [22]   ❏ Unix [23]   ❏ Macintosh [24]   ❏ Other: [25]_____
(please specify)

I would be interested in new books on the following subjects:
(please check all that apply, and use the spaces provided to identify specific software)

❏ Word processing: [26]

❏ Data bases: [28]

❏ File Utilities: [30]

❏ Networking: [32]

❏ Other: [34]

❏ Spreadsheets: [27]

❏ Desktop publishing: [29]

❏ Money management: [31]

❏ Programming languages: [33]

I use a PC at (please check all that apply): ❏ home [35]   ❏ work [36]   ❏ school [37]   ❏ other: [38] _____

The disks I prefer to use are ❏ 5.25 [39]   ❏ 3.5 [40]   ❏ other: [41]_____

I have a CD ROM: ❏ yes [42]   ❏ no [43]

I plan to buy or upgrade computer hardware this year: ❏ yes [44]   ❏ no [45]

I plan to buy or upgrade computer software this year: ❏ yes [46]   ❏ no [47]

Name: _____ Business title: [48] _____ Type of Business: [49] _____

Address (❏ home [50] ❏ work [51]/Company name: _____)

Street/Suite# _____

City [52]/State [53]/Zipcode [54]: _____ Country [55] _____

❏ **I liked this book!** You may quote me by name in future
IDG Books Worldwide promotional materials.

My daytime phone number is _____

IDG BOOKS

THE WORLD OF COMPUTER KNOWLEDGE

❏ YES!

Please keep me informed about IDG's World of Computer Knowledge.
Send me the latest IDG Books catalog.